CARVER COUNTY LIBRARY

SIBERIA

Landscapes of the Imagination

SIBERIA

A CULTURAL HISTORY

A. J. Haywood

2010

OXFORD
UNIVERSITY PRESS

Oxford University Press, Inc., publishes works that further
Oxford University's objective of excellence
in research, scholarship, and education.

Oxford New York
Auckland Cape Town Dar es Salaam Hong Kong Karachi
Kuala Lumpur Madrid Melbourne Mexico City Nairobi
New Delhi Shanghai Taipei Toronto

With offices in
Argentina Austria Brazil Chile Czech Republic France Greece
Guatemala Hungary Italy Japan Poland Portugal Singapore
South Korea Switzerland Thailand Turkey Ukraine Vietnam

Published by Oxford University Press, Inc.
198 Madison Avenue, New York, New York 10016

www.oup.com

Oxford is a registered trademark of Oxford University Press

Co-published in Great Britain by Signal Books

Library of Congress Cataloging-in-Publication Data
Haywood, A. J.
    Siberia : a cultural history / A.J. Haywood.
       p. cm.—(Landscapes of the imagination)
    "Co-published in Great Britain by Signal Books"—T.p. verso.
    Includes bibliographical references and indexes.
    ISBN 978-0-19-975417-5; 978-0-19-975418-2 (pbk.)
1. Siberia (Russia)—Civilization.   2. Siberia (Russia)—History.   3. Siberia (Russia)—
History, Local.   I. Title.
    DK757.3.H39 2010
    957—dc22   2010013867

Illustrations: A. J. Haywood: 259; altair.co.uk: 104; dreamstime.com: xi, xix, 120, 125, 154,
161, 168, 184, 189, 202, 221; erpmusic.com: 192; istockphoto.com: 101, 243; © Nigel Young/
Foster & Partners: 97; shutterstock.com: 1, 13, 39, 53, 61, 112, 194, 235, 256, 262;
wikipedia commons: 17, 22, 31, 43, 70, 75, 81, 85, 98, 101, 116, 129, 141, 145, 153, 176,
227, 277, 279; World History Archive/Alamy: 266

9 8 7 6 5 4 3 2 1

Printed in the United States of America
on acid-free paper

Contents

Preface & Acknowledgements

Before setting foot in Siberia, like most people, I imagined it mostly as a distant but somehow exotic place of extreme cold, and a region of vast forests and steppe filled with exiles. It seemed like Australia—my place of birth—in an ice-box. When I happened to come across someone who had travelled through Soviet-era Siberia with a guitar and collected Russian folk songs, my fascination grew. Several years would pass, however, before I crossed the Urals myself. In January 1992, at a time when the Soviet Union had ceased to exist but Russia was caught in colliding worlds of the past and present, I travelled to Moscow and stayed with a family to round off a Russian language course I was doing at Melbourne University. The Moscow I found in early 1992 was a chaos of systems—some things worked by the old rules, others by the new, and the whole economy had moved out of the shops and onto Moscow's bustling streets. Visits to St. Petersburg followed, and in 1998 I finally had the opportunity to travel to Siberia for a couple of months spent working on chapters of a guidebook for an international publisher.

The Siberia I found in 1998 was, as in Moscow six years earlier, a twilight zone between the old and the new way of doing things. Each visit to a region is different in its own way, however, and this was also true for the Siberia I visited most recently to research this book. I was surprised to find that some streets in cities had become unrecognizable because of traffic and advertising hoardings. By and large, the hotels had been partially or fully renovated. Extreme poverty had, if not disappeared, become less of a problem. (The villages nevertheless remain Siberia's problem zone.) Restoration of buildings had moved ahead, even if much still needed to be done. A mood of neglect had given way to an upbeat optimism and functioning everyday life. Although the financial crisis of 2008-9 halted some projects, this trend will undoubtedly continue. Beyond the towns, the beauty of Siberia's physical landscape remained a stabilizing constant. Crossing large parts of this landscape in trains, communal taxis, buses and in boats to research this book was as enjoyable as the distances were exhausting.

Despite enormous progress, the task of "restoring Siberia" is as monumentally large as Siberia itself. Its historic churches, for example, condemned to neglect for so much of the Soviet period, are in poor shape and their beauty is often found within decaying baroque forms rather than in restored detail. Another of the large tasks facing Siberia, moreover, is the lack of a cultural context in books or in digital sources with which to interpret and understand these cultural landmarks. This book is hopefully a step towards overcoming the deficit—for the armchair reader with a fascination for foreign places, for the traveller on an organized tour—who can use it as a complement to the tour and engage in a dialogue with Siberia—and finally for the independent traveller who can use it as a resource for breaking out on his or her own.

❧

I am indebted to many people for their help while researching and writing this book. In particular, I would like to thank Svetlana Cherkashina from Grand-Tour in Tyumen (www.gt-russia.com) for organizing a tour of the town at such short notice. Many thanks in Krasnoyarsk to Maria Khramova of Planeta-Tour (incoming@planeta-tours.ru; www.planeta-tours.ru), who provided invaluable assistance by arranging accommodation in Krasnoyarsk and in Irkutsk. Both provided highly professional support.

Special thanks to Dr. Holger Finken from the German Academic Exchange Service (DAAD), who helped in pre-planning. In Novosibirk, Anja Hess, Tatjana Molodzowa and colleagues from the Informationszentrum (IC) Novosibirsk des Deutschen Akademischen Austauschdienstes offered invaluable support and insight into the region. In Irkutsk, many thanks to staff at the Baikal Hostel (www.baikalhostels.ru) for practical assistance and language support. Thanks also to Lina Tagirova in Listvyanka/Irkutsk, and to staff at the Gostinitsa Mayak (Listvyanka) and the Gostinitsa Angara (Irkutsk) for advice, assistance and good conversation. Thanks also to Nick Brody in Yekaterinburg, Neil and Joanna in Irkutsk, Elena Pikorovskaya in Frankfurt am Main, and in Göttingen Gert Schröder and Ina Schröder. Thanks especially to my wife Sylvia Möhle for support and encouragement. The opinions expressed in this book nevertheless reflect personal interpretations and views, and any errors of fact are my own.

Introduction

Heaven and Hell

It would be odd to talk about the meaning of Siberia for the world. It is known to every schoolchild. Strangers looking at the map only ask: "Are the dimensions correct?"

Nikolay Rerikh (1874-1947)

For today's traveller, a journey to Siberia begins amid bustling scenes of departure on the crowded platform of Moscow's Yaroslavl Station or adjacent Kazan Station. Passengers mill at the head of the platform, waiting in expectation with luggage strewn at their feet. The electronic information boards announce train numbers and their distant destinations: Khabarovsk, Ulan-Ude, Vladivostok, Novokuznetsk—far-flung and exotic-sounding corners of Russia. The kiosks do a busy trade in last-minute supplies such as biscuits, nuts, bars of chocolate, pastries, water and the ubiquitous Chinese instant noodles. Brakes wheeze and emit exhausted sighs. In the distance railway workers tap wheel hubs on the carriages, making a *puk-puk* sound with long-handled hammers while listening for loose parts. One by one, the travellers collect their belongings and move off towards their waiting trains. You join them, struggling with your luggage. You fumble inside your pocket for your passport and ticket to show the conductor stationed at the carriage door and strictly controlling access. You board. Then, punctually, the doors close and the carriage fittings begin to creak. You feel the motion of the train and the platform gradually recedes, giving way to ranging yards and the Moscow suburbs. Perhaps a Russian fellow passenger will add finality to departure by announcing *poekhali* ("we're off").

The first time I made the journey by train into Siberia, in 1998, was in a first class compartment from Moscow on the Yekaterinburg flagship, the Urals Express. I was to be the only passenger in my carriage for the entire journey. Early on, one of the two conductresses began a long monologue over the PA system, greeting me with an effusive "Esteemed passengers!" She explained that "we" would be crossing some of Russia's great rivers and passing through very many important towns on our way to Asia. She listed them one by one. About five hours later we reached Yaroslavl and crossed the Volga river.

For much of the journey after that, the conductresses polished the carriage. Outside the window, the flat, green landscape slipped by, and no one who turned or raised a head to gaze at us as we passed could have imagined from our dusty exterior how brightly our stainless steel fittings inside glistened as the locomotive hauled us eastwards.

The next time I travelled to Siberia, my train by-passed Yaroslavl altogether, taking a more southerly route to the Urals via Kazan. Either way, at a certain stage in the journey the wide plains of European Russia break up into a dense patchwork of fields. The train slows, climbs, winds through a landscape of rolling hills and fields with bundles of hay, then slips across a geographical border: the beginning of Asia.

Landscape of Extremes

If Asia begins once the train starts to descend the Urals, Siberia begins where the Urals cease. It ends where the Pacific Ocean begins. The distances are immense. It takes about a day and a night to reach the Urals from Moscow by train. After that, the traveller needs about another five and a half days to cross Siberia. If you board a plane in the east in Vladivostok and fly west for seven hours, you can arrive in Moscow fifteen minutes before you departed.

The Siberian land mass stretches for about 2,800 miles from the Urals to the Pacific coast, giving it approximately the width of the United States near the Canadian border, or making about 300 miles wider than Australia at its broadest point. If you include the Kamchatka Peninsula and Chukotka, which juts out into the northern Pacific fifty miles west of Alaska, it is about 3,700 miles wide.

In the north Siberia is washed by the Arctic Ocean and its three Siberian seas: the Kara Sea, the Laptev Sea and the Eastern Siberian Sea. The passage across them, known as the northern sea route, is usually only navigable by icebreaker during the brief summer. In the far north, the Urals protrude into the Kara Sea to form an archipelago of islands known as Novaya Zemlya. Once a ship passes through the narrow Yugra Strait between one of these islands and the mainland, it enters Siberian waters.

Even Siberia's smaller rivers are giants in comparison with those of other regions. Most wind northwards to spill into the Arctic Ocean. In winter, they freeze over and once the ice becomes thick enough, some, like the Ob in western Siberia, are opened up to vehicles and used as "ice roads" between towns and settlements. In the spring the ice begins to break up and flow towards the Arctic Ocean. It is a powerful display of nature that sees water mounting behind still frozen sections of the river in the northern latitudes, finally bursting its banks and creating enormous *taiga* swamplands.

The fact that most of Siberia's rivers flow blindly into the ocean did not escape pre-Soviet and Soviet planners, who thought they could be put to better use. In the 1980s the Ob and Irtysh became the focus of grand schemes to reverse rivers back into Central Asia for irrigation. Fortunately for Siberia's ecosystem, these have so far come to nothing, although projects in Kazakhstan would cause the Aral Sea to recede dramatically.

Historically, rivers provided the way into Siberia and were the highways of Russian colonization. As well as the Ob and Irtysh, major ones included the Yenisey, which has long been the focus of efforts to transport goods into and out of central Siberia via the northern sea route; the Lena, which drains the upland of central Siberia; the Yana, Indigirka and Kolyma rivers in the north-east; and the Amur and Ussuri, which merge to flow into the Pacific. Lake Baikal, the world's largest body of fresh water, is fed by some 336 large rivers, but only one—the Angara—flows out of it.

Broadly speaking, a band of Arctic tundra in the far north forms a

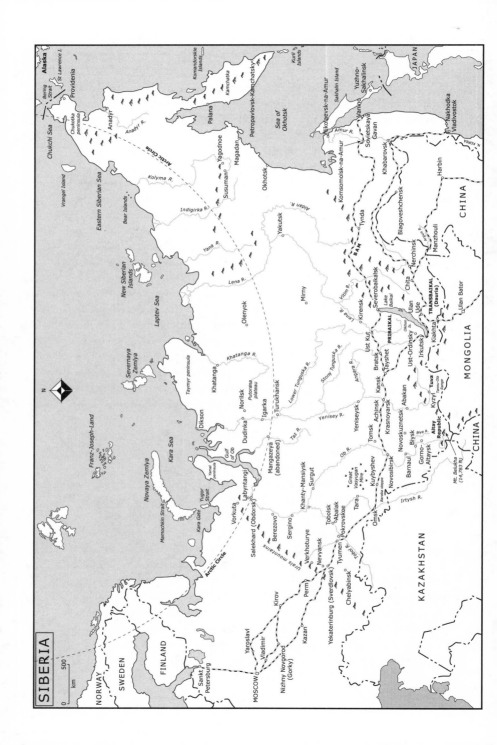

200-mile arc across the subcontinent, growing wider than this in some parts. Conditions, understandably, are harsh here, but lichen and mosses grow and provide nourishment for reindeer, and shrubs and herbs blossom during a brief summer growing season. South of this frozen ribbon, the landscape changes to taiga (pronounced in Russian with the stress on the final syllable). This Turkic word describes the famous coniferous cedar, larch, spruce and pine forest that spreads in a broad belt across Siberia. In upland regions of central Siberia it can be dense with larch. Whereas the tundra is inhabited by reindeer, fox, smaller species of rodents and various aquatic birds or birds of prey, the taiga provides a home to larger mammals such as wolves, bears and reindeer. Indirectly, it was the taiga—or rather its inhabitants such as the ermine, squirrel, wolverine and, the most prized of all taiga-dwellers, the sable—that first attracted the attention of European Russians to Siberia.

In the south, Siberia borders on Kazakhstan, China in the north-western region of Dzungaria, Mongolia, and a longer stretch of border with China again in the far east—much of it following the Amur river. This southern border of steppe, mountains and rivers cuts a swathe through the culturally rich regions of Central Asia, Inner Asia and the far east. The south offered a way into Siberia for various groups of settlers, whether ancient nomads of the Bronze Age or thirteenth-century Mongols who arrived in campaigns of conquest begun by Ghengis Khan. The fertile steppe regions of Siberia were the cradle of new civilizations that rose and declined over the millennia.

Siberia's climate is legendary for cold, harsh winters during which the mercury can plunge as low as - 71°C in the inland north-east, yet in summer temperatures reach 34°C. Under permafrost conditions water accumulates on the surface above the frozen soil, causing swamps to form and creating perfect breeding conditions for mosquitoes and other insects. Siberia's mosquitoes are so plentiful that they are said to be able to kill an unprotected human being within a few hours. Reindeer (caribou) move or are herded to the tundra coasts in summer where the cooler conditions and winds minimize insect harassment. In the northern forested regions of western Siberia, the local Khanty indigenes build large, smoking fires of green logs in August to protect their herds.

Although temperatures on the southern steppe regions are milder, these are extreme by western European standards. Nevertheless, in steppe regions south of Krasnoyarsk it is still possible to find orchards as well as irrigation systems surviving from ancient times. Nadezhda Krupskaya, who followed Lenin into Siberian exile in 1898 and married the revolutionary, mentions how she and Lenin planted an orchard in the yard of their house in the town of Shushenskoe. Today, with a large shift of population into the cities, the orchards are being abandoned and in some cases destroyed by fire in misguided attempts to kill off ticks (a problem throughout Siberia).

The Humdrum and the Bizarre

While in Novosibirsk researching this book, I fell into conversation with a group of Russians at the next table in a restaurant. Elena, the most outgoing of them, thought it was a good idea to write about Siberia. She was attractive, probably in her late thirties, and neatly dressed in jeans and a light floral blouse against the sticky heat.

Why did she think it a good idea, I asked her.

"Because Siberia is *usual*, just like any other place," she said.

The next day, I was taken around Novosibirsk and proudly shown its sights by Elena and her husband. Like most Siberians I met, they were helpful. Sometimes help came in unusual forms. One man I met on a train—in tracksuit trousers and sporting three-day beard growth—thought the best way he could help was by citing the famous lines from the poet Fyodor Tyutchev. "You cannot understand Russia with the mind," Tyutchev wrote, "you can only believe in it." My travelling companion, exposing the widening crevice of his backside as he hauled himself into upper berth, thought this especially summed up Siberia.

I thought Elena was probably right in most regards about Siberia's *usualness*. A walk around a large city like Novosibirsk on the Ob, Omsk on the Irtysh or Krasnoyarsk on the Yenisey offers scenes of the familiar and everyday urban world. The traffic in Siberia's cities is choking and loud, as in all metropolises. It can get uncomfortably hot. Ribbons of dark bitumen shimmer in the surprisingly intense heat of day. Siberians go shopping, pause for a break at a café, sit on benches on wide grassy strips beneath lime trees, or watch their children play in parks. None of this normalcy should surprise us, but it does surprise us because of what is often a one-dimensional view of Siberia.

Over the centuries—from the writing of the seventeenth-century breakaway Orthodox priest Avvakum to the gulag writings of the twenti-eth century—Siberia has come to be portrayed as anything but normal. Indeed, it has often been synonymous with a sort of hell.

Siberia has also often conjured up images of the bizarre. The earliest perceptions of the region east of the Urals, say Yuri Slezkine and Galya Diment in *Between Heaven and Hell*, were of a place where people slaugh-tered their children, ate their dead or had been enclosed by God within high mountains (the Urals) and gates made of copper. In the sixteenth century wild rumours circulated in European Russia about human beings in Siberia who died each winter after water trickled out of their noses and caused them to freeze to the ground. Trees suddenly exploded in this strange land. Here people ate by putting food under their hats and shrug-ging their shoulders. Some Siberians were believed to lack heads altogether and had eyes on their chests and mouths between their shoulders.

Siberia was an unknown land, and today it retains some of its fasci-nation as a large landscape that is impossible to know or understand in its entirety. Put another way, Siberia is simply too big and too complex to grasp completely.

Although gulags, the Soviet prison camps, were a fact of life all over Russia in the twentieth century, Siberia is particularly associated with a prison system that saw the innocent and the guilty lumped together and transported into a frightening other world. For those who experienced this world, there was good reason to believe it was nothing less than hell on earth.

The tradition of using Siberia as a prison and place of exile in fact began centuries before Stalin filled gulags from the 1930s with the victims of his purges. After the death of Stalin in 1953 the gulags were gradually disbanded and replaced by a contemporary prison system. But in this system, too, Siberia played its special role. I heard that right up until Boris Yeltsin's time, narcotics offenders from all over Russia were dispatched to a prison "colony" outside Omsk and housed inside a compound with four towers and guards armed with automatic weapons. After serving the bulk of their terms, offenders were allowed to live just outside the compound on probation. Hard labour had become occupational therapy in Siberia. They dedicated themselves to carving traditional wooden boxes and other handicrafts, while authorities tried to wean them off their drug habits.

The gulags today are cold, windswept sites of rusting barbed wire, roads seemingly leading nowhere and decaying buildings slowly being reclaimed by the taiga. Some of the worst ones were situated in the north-east near Magadan, a town founded on forced gulag toil and built expressly to manage the system of convict labour in the gold and uranium mines of the north-east. Other clusters of gulags were situated in the dense taiga and in the tundra north of Krasnoyarsk. Several years ago a small boom in "dark tourism" saw a trickle of visitors being ferried up there on river cruises to former nickel mining gulags in Norilsk and, in the case of one tour agency that sells itself under the motto "Siberia, it's hot!", to abandoned Gulag 503 near Ermakovo. Gulag 503 was a place where inmates slaved in freezing conditions on a section of Stalin's grandiose railway intended to run across the extreme north of Siberia. Some of its inmates also harvested timber in the taiga or built the harbour at the remote town of Igarka.

Alexander Solzhenitsyn's *A Day in the Life of Ivan Denisovich* graphically captures the nightmare conditions in such camps, even if he was imprisoned in Kazakhstan and not Siberia. Life was unimaginably brutal. During the mass repression period of the 1930s it was not uncommon for 300 prisoners to be squashed into cells built to hold twenty. Survivors told of being packed in so tightly that even turning in their sleep had to be performed as a writhing, collective mass. It is difficult to grasp such horror. Nevertheless, to this day only one memorial site actually exists on the site of a former gulag. This gulag memorial is in European Russia near the Urals town of Perm, known as Perm 36.

Whereas cities like Novosibirsk, Krasnoyarsk and Omsk give an insight into everyday metropolitan life in Siberia, Tobolsk offers another perspective. It embodies the early history of the region and has been formally declared the tourism capital of Western Siberia. The historical core remains very much intact, and approaching it by rail from the south gives a splendid view of the town's early eighteenth-century stone *kremlin* (fortress) perched upon a bluff over the Irtysh. The lower town below the kremlin has retained a sleepy character, and in summer it echoes with birdsong. Whitewashed stone buildings are crumbling into the floodplain, but boarding around some suggests that restoration will one day begin. Ramshackle wooden buildings, paint peeling off their cracked boards, bend and sway in the midday heat. Some of these, too, are earmarked for restoration.

Tobolsk Kremlin

I also walked through some unflattering suburbs in the upper town. Siberia is not just comprised of beautiful wilderness; it also has some monumentally ugly housing estates. Sometimes its unexpected juxtapositions lend it an almost poetic dimension. I found the sprawling "micro-region" district of Tobolsk offered startling surprises. While walking around the busy streets I encountered a funeral procession and suddenly found myself staring into the bleached face of a corpse lying on the back of a passing truck. Around the deceased, men in dark suits and women with bright blouses and kerchiefs looked on with expressions of mourning.

❧

There is much to discover in Siberia and not all of it can be covered in one book or on one visit. This book begins in the Urals with Yekaterinburg and continues across western Siberia via Tyumen and selected regions and towns to the shores of Lake Baikal in eastern Siberia. A chapter takes the reader north along the Irtysh and Ob rivers to Salekhard in the tundra, and a final chapter covers Magadan and the gulags in the far north-east. With a few obvious exceptions, the order of chapters is practical and can be easily followed by the traveller on a journey. However, trips north along the rivers or, for the very adventurous, across the Arctic Ocean, are almost journeys in themselves. Similarly, the route along the Yenisey from Kyzyl to Krasnoyarsk is presented in a way intended to illustrate the change of landscape and culture between steppe, taiga and tundra. Apart from short cruises south of Krasnoyarsk and services leading upriver from Kyzyl, however, passenger shipping on the Yenisey is mostly confined to the stretch north of Krasnoyarsk.

Finally, as with any book on a region so large, this one is selective and a starting point. From this starting point, however, I hope that others will be encouraged to explore further in writing or in travel this fascinating part of the world.

SIBERIA

Chapter One
CRADLE OF CIVILIZATIONS

Siberia is part of Asia and has been the home for millennia of a variety of peoples and cultures. The lives of early Siberians were shaped by the landscape and became diverse because of it. The southern steppe produced a semi-nomadic, pastoral way of life. The forests lent themselves to the lifestyle of the hunter, some of whom migrated with reindeer between the tundra of the north and the *taiga* farther south. On the coasts and around the rivers Siberians fished and hunted in a landscape of abundance. We rarely think of this remarkable region as a cradle of civilizations, but Siberia is known to be the origin of the native North Americans, whose ancestors probably migrated across a land bridge to present-day Alaska before moving south through the Americas. At the same time, Siberia is Russia's sixteenth-century "North Asian colony". It was distant enough from Russia and sufficiently foreign to qualify as a part of the New World. But Siberia is also contiguous to Russia, which simply extended its borders outwards to embrace this new land and draw it into the Old World. Some might say that this paradox of Siberia—of being a New World within the Old—is at the heart of understanding not only its past and present, but also its future.

The origins of the name Siberia are Tartar and probably came from thirteenth-century Mongol usage. The Russians began calling the area "Siberian Land", then simply Siberia. For our purposes, the story of Siberia begins in the Pleistocene era, a period that started some 600,000 years ago and lasted until about 10,000 years ago, during which large regions of

Siberia lay under glacial ice. From around 100,000 years ago the first Siberians began migrating onto the subcontinent from Eastern Europe and Central Asia. It was a gradual process that occurred throughout the Stone Age, during a time when giant mammoths and woolly rhinoceroses lumbered across Eurasia and North America. Not surprisingly given the prevalence of ice and a hostile climate, these Stone-Age settlers lived predominantly in the south and engaged in a semi-nomadic way of life based on hunting and gathering. They preyed on the giant animals and in the absence of forests for timber they often depended on mammals for skin, bones and tusks to build their dwellings. They also used bones, tusk or stone for weapons and to craft rudimentary tools.

About 25,000 years ago a new phase of the Ice Age caused the large rivers of western Siberia to dam, creating the vast Great Siberian Lake, which washed across much of today's Western Siberian Plain. This inland sea covered a distance of over nine hundred miles from north to south and is believed to have existed in one form or another until approximately 13,000 years ago.

Partly because of the Great Siberian Lake, western Siberia is not particularly well-endowed with Stone-Age remains. Some of the earliest preserved signs of human habitation are carved stone and bone figurines unearthed further east in a 30,000-year-old Upper Palaeolithic settlement on the Kova river, a tributary of the Angara, which flows from Lake Baikal. Many of these finds are today housed in the Hermitage Museum in St. Petersburg, which has a section dedicated to the Palaeolithic (early Stone-Age) period. Stone discs, ivory and bone objects found near Krasnoyarsk— the so-called Afontova Gora finds—also form part of the collection and date from around 20,000 years ago.

Two other important sites from the Stone Age are located on and around the Angara near Lake Baikal and today are known as the Malta and Buret sites. The Malta site is about fifty miles north-west of Irkutsk and probably dates back about 20,000 years. The early Siberians lived in houses built in hollows they dug in the ground and covered with bones, wood and earth, but they also kept moveable summer dwellings, probably hunted mammoth, hairy rhinoceros, reindeer and bison, and are known to have used fire for cooking and keeping warm.

Finds include some thirty Venus figurines made from mammoth ivory. Many of these are slender, clothed figurines with extraordinarily re-

An Evenk *chum*, nomadic dwelling

alistic facial features. The most remarkable of the Malta finds is a tapered three-inch naked Venus with long curling hair and hands resting in her lap. The Buret objects, unearthed directly on the Angara, are from the same epoch and include five figurines, one of these carved from serpentine and others crafted in ivory.

A little over 10,000 years ago, during the late Palaeolithic and early Mesolithic era, the climate grew warmer, the forest regions of the south spread northwards and early Siberians gradually dispersed and populated all of Siberia. By 8,000 years ago (the Neolithic era) Siberia's landscape had taken the form we find today and its giant mammals had died out. This period was also one in which the fairly uniform existence of Siberians gave way to diverse lifestyles shaped by the resources and the features of regional landscapes. While conditions were still far too severe to allow crop cultivation or the raising of livestock, early Siberians developed new tools to support hunting in forests or fishing in Arctic waters or along the rivers. The Siberians of eight millennia ago were also now starting to keep domesticated dogs and use basic utensils for cooking, such as ceramic pots. The disappearance of the giant mammals in Siberia coincided with a change in the type of dwellings they used. The pit dwellings of Palaeolithic Siberians, no longer suitable to the nomadic lifestyle that evolved as the giant mammals were replaced by smaller species of the forests, gave way to the *chum*—wigwam-like collapsible structures used by indigenous Evenk Siberians today.

BRONZE-AGE CULTURES

During the Bronze Age, which began about 4,500 years ago, a rich variety of cultures established themselves on the southern steppes of Siberia, overlapped, succeeded each other and spread out over large parts of the subcontinent. These cultures marked the gradual beginning of pastoralism in Siberia. The first of them was the Afanasevo Culture from 2500 BCE, based in a region stretching west of Minusinsk (south of Krasnoyarsk) between the Altai Mountains and the Sayan Mountains. The Afanasevo were a Europoid people who built dwellings semi-submerged in the ground and covered with a wooden-framed roof. From about 1700 BCE they gave way to a vast constellation of cultures that took root in Central Asia, often referred to as the Andronovo. This extended northwards from Central Asia into western Siberia and brought new techniques in forging metals such as the use of furnaces for creating tools, weapons and works of art. The Andronovo people lived in scattered settlements—up to a dozen sunken rectangular huts of wood that were often about fifty yards in length. They were also migratory, and would travel by foot across the steppe between summer and winter pastures, taking with them cattle and sheep, their two most important breeds of livestock.

Eventually, they were supplanted by the so-called Karasuk Culture, which formed in the Yenisey Basin from about 1300 BCE and survived until 700 BCE. The Karasuk people were highly skilled at metal casting and metalwork, and archaeological finds suggest that they had mastered the art of horse riding, which gave them greater mobility. Their primary occupation was cattle breeding, however, and their lifestyle was still semi-settled rather than one of nomadic pastoralism in that—like their predecessors—they lived for the most part in large rectangular dwellings sunk into the earth. These were large structures of about 1,600 square feet that stood alone or occasionally in pairs on the steppe. The ability of the Karasuk people to ride horses stood them in good stead to develop trade contacts with societies farther west and north of the Yenisey Basin, and it is believed that they ranged widely over a region as far west as the Urals and north to Yakutia. Small settlements around the Ob river appear to have ground grain and developed a greater dependence upon crop agriculture.

Another Bronze-Age people, the Glazkov Culture, flourished from about 1800 to 1300 BCE east of the Karasuk people in a wedge-shaped region that took in Lake Baikal and a swathe extending north to the Lower Tunguska river.

A feature of all these Bronze-Age cultures was the movement away from matriarchal-type societies—best illustrated by the female figurine idols—to more patriarchal forms that saw widows forcibly buried with their deceased husbands. There are also suggestions that shaman religious practices arose in Siberia during the period of the Glazkov Culture.

THE SCYTHS

As the first millennium BCE progressed, a new pattern of equestrian cultures unfolded across Siberia and the steppes of Eurasia—the Scyths. One of these, the Tagar Culture, thrived from about 800-200 BCE in the Minusinsk Basin around the Yenisey river. The Tagars were excellent horseriders who combined a settled lifestyle of livestock breeding and husbandry with phases of migratory herding across the steppe, and they buried their dead in *kurgany*, huge mounds or tumuli constructed above a burial chamber. With the Iron Age now in full swing in Siberia, the Tagars not only used ferrous metal to craft daggers and arrow heads, but also forged mouth bits and harnesses for their horses. The Salbyk kurgan (near Abakan) from about 400 BCE is one of the most celebrated reminders of this period. Another is the Arzhan complex of grave mounds in Tuva, a necropolis situated in the grassy foothills of the Western Sayan Mountains, on an ancient trade route that linked the Minusinsk Basin with northern China and Mongolia.

Closely related to that of the Tagars was the Pazyryk Culture, which took shape in the Altai from about 1000 to 200 BCE and reached its peak in the period 450-250 BCE. In contrast to the semi-nomadic Tagar people, the Pazyryks were mounted nomadic pastoralists who used saddles on their horses and rode between pastures carrying lightweight, collapsible yurts— the round, felt-covered dwellings with wooden frames used by the semi-nomadic people of the steppe. In the Hermitage Museum collection today is one of the world's oldest carpets, found in a Pazyryk grave known as the Great Pazyryk Mound, excavated in 1949. Another Scythian culture, the Slab Grave Culture, co-existed from about 1300 to 300 BCE in a large region covering the Pribaikal (just west of Lake Baikal), the Transbaikal (east of Lake Baikal in Buryatia) and south going into Mongolia; it was so named for the vertical stone slabs that typify the grave sites.

The arrival of the Huns before the turn of the millennium marked a new stage in Siberia's rich cultural development. Probably originating in today's Mongolia, the Huns—like the Pazyryks—lived in yurts, which they carried with them to their pastoral grounds. It is believed that from around 200 BCE some 24 different groups of Huns united and set out across Eurasia, reaching the Lake Baikal region and occupying a sixty-mile-wide swathe of land beginning on the eastern shore in the Transbaikal, as well as the region around Tuva, Khakassia and the Altai. The Turkic-speaking Huns brought with them new methods of working iron and, being equestrian nomads, were responsible for a more widespread use of saddles in Siberia. A highly effective Hun bow was introduced to Siberia and used for hunting and fighting, and new impetus was given to a Siberian style of art based on the figurative depiction of animals that had been common among the Scyths.

Turkic and Mongol States

By the beginning of the first century AD, the Mongol-based empire of the Huns had disappeared from Siberia and fresh waves of Mongols moved into the southern steppe regions. One of these, the Tu-Gyu, arrived from Central Asia and settled in the Altai. Their arrival was a significant step for Siberia, as in the mid-sixth century it culminated in the creation of a Turkic-speaking feudal dominion, known as the Turkic Khaganate. The cultural epicentre of the Turkic Khaganate was the Altai, but over several decades its centre drifted eastwards into the Orkhon river valley of Mongolia, and in the late sixth century the Khaganate ruptured into separate western and eastern empires. The southern regions of Siberia formed part of the Eastern Turkic Khaganate, which came under attack from Uyghur tribes, a Turkic people of Central Asia, and was finally destroyed in 745, becoming integrated into a large Central Asian Uyghur Empire.

When the Turkic Khaganate disintegrated it created an opportunity for another Turkic group, the Yenisey Kirghiz, to establish their own khanate in Siberia. This heralded an important new phase as the khanate is seen as being the first Siberian state and was accompanied by flourishing trade relations between Siberian peoples and Central Asia. The origins of the Turkic-speaking Yenisey Kirghiz can be traced back to nomadic tribes who fled Mongolia during the rule of the Huns and merged with an ancient Europoid group of cattle breeders known as Dinlin (or Dingling), who had earlier settled in the upper valley of the Yenisey river.

The influence of the khanate was enormous, and this empire rose to the height of its power in the ninth century when the Yenisey Kirghiz crushed the Uyghurs and took control of present-day Mongolia. Their state survived in one form or another until the thirteenth century.

Shamanism, a nature-based, animistic religion centred around a spiritual relationship between the inner life of human beings and a physical world imbued with its own spirits, had long been practised in a variety of forms by the peoples of Siberia, and the Yenisey Kirghiz were no exception. They also intensified the use of agriculture in southern Siberia, built irrigation systems in the Minusinsk Basin south of Krasnoyarsk and were reputed to have excellent cultivation skills. Similarly, their metal forging skills were highly developed, allowing them to take full advantage of the deposits of gold, copper and iron in the Altai.

The existence of this first Siberian "state" was a crucial turn of events, but Siberia would be visited by another invading force from Central Asia before the Russians arrived to create their own Asian colony out of this vast and rich cultural tapestry. The man at the head of this force was Genghis Khan. By the time he had finished he had created the world's largest contiguous empire in its day—a multi-ethnic colossus that encompassed most of Asia, Central Asia, Eurasia and parts of Europe and the Middle East.

In the thirteenth century Genghis Khan united diverse Mongol tribes and founded the Mongol state. Thenceforth the Mongols set their sights upon Siberia and made the subcontinent their first possession. The Yenisey Kirghiz were unable to withstand the Mongol onslaught and around 1270 they finally succumbed and their empire collapsed. Within three years from 1207 Genghis Khan's son, Jochi, subjugated the people of Siberia whom the Mongols knew as the "forest people" (the forest-dwelling indigenous tribes) and all but the most far flung peoples of the north were now vassals of the Mongols. The groundwork was gradually laid for the political form of Siberia that the Russians would find when their campaigns of conquest began.

In 1224, just three years before Genghis Khan died (most likely from disease, an attack or a fall from a horse), he divided his empire into four provinces. Various parts of Siberia fell to three of his sons, roughly split geographically into one region west of the Ob river, another from the Ob to the Sayan Mountains, and a third region taking in the Pribaikal lands just west of Lake Baikal, extending south-west into Central Asia and east into the Mongol heartland.

The Mongol rulers introduced a system of collecting tribute from their subjects, demanding animal pelt from those who inhabited the dense coniferous forests (the true taiga), and seeking livestock or crafted goods from the peoples of the steppe. The region west of the Ob taken by Jochi, Genghis Khan's eldest son, fell into the hands of his own son (the grandson of Genghis Khan), Batu, who forged a Golden Horde that galloped from the Urals into Eastern Europe, conquered one European region after the other and was finally halted in 1241 on the Neustadt meadows outside Vienna. His Golden Horde effectively made vassals of all Russia except the Novgorod Republic in the north-west, and Russia's princes came to terms with the situation by collecting and paying tribute to the Mongols, formally becoming subservient to them but running their own feudal administrations.

The influence of these Mongols on Siberia was enormous. They are said to have been the first to carry the news outside that Siberia was a land rich in animals providing valuable pelts, and the region around Lake Baikal was settled by a large number of Mongol-speaking tribes. Many Mongolian words also found their way into the languages of other indigenes or ancient people.

This unwieldy territory controlled by the Golden Horde disintegrated from the fourteenth century. Wracked by political strife and destabilized by invasion and by a Moscow whose star was on the rise and which was about to supplant Novgorod as the most powerful dominion in Russia, the Mongol Empire disintegrated into separate khanates. Four of these existed on Russian territory from the fifteenth century, each ruled by its own khan: the Khanate of Crimea, Khanate of Kazan, Khanate of Astrakhan and the Khanate of Sibir (Siberia).

THE KHANATE OF SIBIR

The first capital of the Khanate of Sibir was in present-day Tyumen (Chimgi-Tura), today a city of some 600,000 inhabitants on the plains of western Siberia. Later, the centre shifted to Isker (also called Qasliq or Sibir), located just outside the present-day city of Tobolsk. The territory of this Khanate of Sibir took in a large part of western Siberia, extending from the Urals to the forest steppe of the Baraba Plain (west of modern-day Novosibirsk). It was dominated by a couple of families and their heads who squabbled and intrigued to gain the upper hand. The last of the Siberian khans was a leader by the name of Khan Kuchum.

Khan Kuchum ruled over an ethnically diverse group of subjects who included Siberian indigenous Khanty and Mansi populations, indigenous Selkups, Tartars and Bashkirs, and Bukharan traders who regularly visited from Central Asia or had settled in the khanate. Like the other khans of Central Asia, he exacted tribute from the indigenous people inhabiting the forests of the north. This tribute was known by its Turkic name *yasak*, and was adopted both as a word and as a practice by the Russians. The Bukharans acted as a religious elite in this khanate, and it was during the reign of Kuchum in the sixteenth century that efforts were made to convert his Tartar subjects to Islam.

The designation Tartar has been used loosely and often incorrectly over the centuries to describe a wide variety of Siberians or, indeed, anyone with Mongolian features. The Tartars of the Khanate of Sibir had their origins in the Turkic-speaking Kipchak tribes who lived on the Eurasian steppe in a region north of the Aral Sea to the Black Sea. After being defeated by Mongols in 1245, some moved north, and with this gradual migration they assimilated other groups or influenced them, developing into a culturally independent people who spoke a variety of Turkic dialects but especially one closely related to Kipchak. Today, about 500,000 Tartars live in Siberia, and about 180,000 of these are descendants of the western Siberian Tartars who inhabited the Tyumen-Tobolsk region, the Baraba Steppe between the Irtysh river and Novosibirsk (mostly around present-day Barabinsk), and the Tom river around Tomsk. The remaining 300,000 or more are descendants of Tartars who moved there from the Volga river and the western Urals region from the late nineteenth century until the 1920s. The majority of Siberia's Tartars today practise Islam, which especially on the Baraba Steppe is heavily influenced by shamanism and infused with deities and spirits of nature, such as those of water, the forest or fire.

In terms of political organization, the Khanate of Sibir was very much a Central Asian feudal state with an elite class of rulers based around the khan, his sons, Tartar princes and a variety of local nobles. Most of the ordinary Tartars paid yasak to their rulers, and so too did indigenous groups who had been subjugated by the khans, including the Khanty and Mansi around the Irtysh and Ob rivers.

INDIGENES BEFORE RUSSIAN COLONIZATION

It is convenient for nations to imagine a land on the eve of conquest as being empty, especially if it is an unknown land—*terra incognita*. When the Russians arrived in Siberia, however, some 250,000 indigenes inhabited the region between the Urals and the Pacific. Encounters with the indigenes ranged from the cautious to the brutal. The eighteenth-century German historian Gerhard Friedrich Müller captures one aspect of this encounter when he describes the advance of seventeenth-century Russians eastwards from Yakutia.

> From 1636 attempts were made from Yakutsk to sail the Arctic Ocean. The rivers Jana, Indigirka, Wasea, Kolyma were named one after the other. No sooner was the latter reached than they [the Russians] wanted to know what lay on the other side in order to force the people who lived there to pay tribute as well as to take advantage of sable hunting that they hoped to find there. The first journey from the Kolyma in an eastern direction was undertaken in 1646 by a group of volunteers called Promyshlennye (hunter-traders)... They found the ocean covered in ice, but also an ice-free channel between the pack ice and the mainland... On discovering a bay between the cliffs on the banks they sailed into it. There they encountered Chukchi natives... The goods were laid out on the shore, the Chukchis took what they wanted and put in their place walrus tooth or objects made of walrus tooth. No one wanted to venture on land to the Chukchis. Furthermore, there was no interpreter experienced in the Chukchi language. They were content to have made this first discovery and returned along the Kolyma.

The scene described by Müller was "silent trade", a method of exchanging goods prevalent among the indigenes even before the arrival of the Russians. Not all contact with indigenes, however, was as circumspect as this. The Yakuts, writes historian Yuri Slezkine in his *Arctic Mirrors* (1994), tell a story of Russians arriving, building towers, dropping sweets and biscuits onto the ground and, when the women and children tried to retrieve them, crushing the Yakuts with logs that they threw down, after which the Russians opened fire.

The indigenes living in Siberia on the eve of the Russian colonization were scattered in some two dozen ethnic groups whose lifestyle depended on fishing, hunting and trapping, and the herding of reindeer. During the 1920s, when Soviet ethnologists set about classifying native Siberians, these became known as the "indigenous small peoples of the north". "Small numbered" or "small minority" perhaps better captures the Russian meaning (*malochislenny*).

Those who came in contact with Russians earliest were the Khanty (Ostyak) and Mansi (Vogel), who had paid tribute to the khans of Sibir but also traded fish and walrus tusk (ivory) with European Russians even before the era of colonization. They lived mostly in the forested river valleys and taiga swamps of western Siberia, speaking a language related to Finnish and Hungarian. Although the bear is worshipped or enjoys a high status among many groups of indigenous Siberians, the Khanty and Mansi have a highly developed form of bear cult. According to James Forsyth in his *A History of the Peoples of Siberia*, traditional bear rites survived well into the twentieth century:

> The dead animal was welcomed by the villagers, who performed a ritual dance around it. Inside the successful hunter's house the bear's skin was spread out on the table with its head, decorated with a red cloth, lying between its paws, and food and drink set before it. The bear was the "guest" during a feast at which the village people, wearing masks of birch-bark, pantomimed the bear hunt, touched the bear while making vows, told tales and sang songs.

In the north and straddling the Urals live Nenets, who along with other fishing, hunting and reindeer peoples in the tundra across much of the circumpolar region—Enets, Nganasans and Selkups—are often called Samoyeds. The language of Samoyeds probably branched off from the Finno-Ugric family of the Khanty and Mansi around 6,000 years ago. Better known to the outside world, however, is the breed of dog named after them, which they used to herd reindeer or pull sleds—also popularly known as the Samoyed.

Traditional reindeer herding followed a similar pattern right across the tundra region of Siberia, and where reindeer herding survives this continues today: the herds spent the winter in the edge of the forest zone or in the protection of valleys, but moved to the coast of the Arctic Ocean in summer to escape the mosquitoes and other insects. The reindeer people, whose number includes non-Samoyed indigenes of the north-east such as tundra Chukchis and Koryaks, migrated with their reindeer or captured herds at river crossings. Full-time herding is thought to have become more prevalent from the eighteenth century, following a decline in the number of wild reindeer.

At the time of the Russian annexation, groups of Kets (earlier called Yenisey Ostyaks) lived on the middle reaches of the Yenisey river, and in the extreme north-east the Russians encountered Kereks, Koryaks, Chukchi and Yukaghirs. The latter were often used by Russians as guides during expeditions to Kamchatka, where Koryaks and Itelmens lived. Along with Ainus from the Kuril Islands and Nivkhi (often called Gilyaks) from the Amur region, and Eskimos and Aleuts from the extreme north-east, all of these communities are usually brought together in a larger grouping of "Paleo-Asiatic" peoples.

The largest group of indigenous people, known collectively as Tungus and today usually called Evenks, inhabited a vast area that began as far west as the Ob river in western Siberia and ended at the Pacific seaboard. Most, however, lived east of the Yenisey in the forests of eastern Siberia and in the traditional Tungus heartland around Lake Baikal. This reindeer people hunted wild reindeer and other forest mammals, but also used domesticated reindeer as pack animals or rode them using saddles. Close relatives of the Evenks, the Evens inhabited a north-eastern region in Yakutia and on the Pacific seaboard around Magadan. Related groups of Nanais, Negidals, Oroks, Orochis and Udeghes lived in the southern Far East region around Khabarovsk, Sakhalin Island and the Amur river.

When defining who was indigenous or not, Soviet ethnographers of the 1920s relied very much on the mores of imperial times. They took into account political expediency, indigenous traditions, the hunting and gathering lifestyle, and ethnological and linguistic knowledge of the day. The Turkic-speaking people with roots reaching back into Central and Inner Asia were, according to their criteria, not viewed as indigenous, although some are descendants of those arriving in ancient times. The Turkic peoples include the Tartars of Siberia, as well as diverse groups inhabiting the southern regions around the Altai, Tuva and Khakassia. Another group

Siberian brown bears

not considered indigenous by Soviet ethnographers was the Turkic-speaking Sakha (Yakuts), whose origins go back to mixing between Tungus and Turkic-Mongol peoples such as Uyghurs, Buryats and Khakass. It was not until about the seventeenth century that the present-day ethnic make-up of the Sakha completely took shape.

Siberia's natural abundance traditionally played a central role not only in the hunting or herding livelihoods of the indigenous peoples, but also in their myths and spiritual world. The natural world (including "inanimate" objects) was believed to be inhabited by spirits. The bear is the most important of all creatures and throughout the whole of Siberia bear cults of one type or another predominate. At the heart of these cults is the belief that the bear is the ancestor of human beings, a world view also found outside Siberia in Korea and in North America among indigenes. Two types of brown bear are found in Siberia: the Siberian brown bear (*Ursus arctos collaris*) and the Kamchatka brown bear (*Ursus arctos beringianus*). They are usually attributed with supernatural or godly qualities, as well as powers over the other creatures, making them the focal point for order within the natural world.

Among the birds the eagle, and particularly the golden eagle (*Aquila chrysaetos*), has a special place in shamanism. In Buryat culture, for instance, an eagle is considered to have had sexual union with a woman and created the first shamans. Kets see the eagle as the shaman's most important helping spirit in rituals. In their rituals the Koryak shamans of the north-east frequently work with wolves and eagles as well as bears. A shaman in Tuva will imitate the cry of a wolf if he or she wishes to frighten people.

Although they play a lesser role in rituals, dogs have also played a crucial role in the lifestyle of the indigenous peoples, mainly in the north. The Siberian husky is believed to have been first bred by Chukchis from the north-east of Siberia some four millennia ago in order to hunt reindeer and draw sleds, whereas the Samoyed (Bjelkier) dog originates from the north-west and—like the Siberian husky—is one of the world's most ancient breeds. This too is traditionally used for herding reindeer or for sleds. The highly endangered Siberian tiger (*Panthera tigris altaica*), the so-called king of the taiga, features less prominently largely because it is found only in the far east Amur-Ussuri region and around Khabarovsk. Only about 400 are believed to survive today.

Yermak's Conquest

The person credited with opening up the floodgates of Russian colonization is the sixteenth-century Cossack Yermak Timofeyevich, portrayed in the nineteenth century as a Russian version of the Spanish conquistador Hernán Cortés.

The Cossacks were at the forefront of Siberia's annexation, and they continued to play an important role in developments there right up to the civil war of the early 1920s. Their origins are found in Turkic (Tartar) and later Slavic horsemen who formed military groups on Russia's southern steppe. From the fifteenth century their numbers were boosted by Ukrainian and Russian peasants who fled serfdom and sought freedom on the steppe. From the sixteenth century two groups or "hosts"came to prominence. Those on the middle Dneiper river helped protect the borders of Muscovy Russia. The others, the Zaporozhian Cossacks, were mostly brigands and occasional farmers with their centre on Sich, an island in the Dneiper, deep in the southern Ukraine. Virtually all other Cossack hosts, such as those on the Don river, descended from the Zaporozhian Cossacks. Led by elected *atamans* (military heads), the Cossacks lived from booty. After failing in attempts to create their own Cossack state in 1648, however, they gradually lost all autonomy, became integrated into Russia's military and were often used by the tsar to quash uprisings. Today, they are better known for their choirs.

Not a lot is known about Yermak, and what we do know largely comes from a collection of epic tales compiled between the sixteenth and eighteenth centuries: the *Siberian Chronicles*. These are the work of scholars and religious men who wrote, rewrote and adapted oral accounts, documents and folklore over the centuries. Some important ones are the *Yesipov Chronicle* (1636) and the *Kungur Chronicle*, forming part of the *Remezov Chronicle* written by the Siberian historian and cartographer Semyon Remezov (c.1642-c.1720) in the late seventeenth century. Another from the seventeenth century, the *Stroganov Chronicle*, was partly based on the archives of the Stroganov merchant family.

Most writers of the region's early history relied on the *Siberian Chronicles* as a significant source. They include the German historian Gerhard Friedrich Müller, whose moniker was the Father of Siberian History. In his *Conquest of Siberia*, he takes an eighteenth-century view of events by describing Yermak as "nothing more than a fugitive Cossack of the Don, and chief of a troop of banditti who infested the shores of the Caspian Sea."

The other leading protagonist in the Russian expansion into Siberia was the powerful family that sponsored Yermak, the Stroganovs. The Stroganovs were wealthy peasants who settled in the Pomore region of north-east Russia and earned fortune, power and nobility as merchants and industrialists from the sixteenth century. Once Russia had eradicated the Khanate of Kazan in the 1550s, the way was open for Russians to move into the Urals region around Perm. The Stroganovs received a charter from Ivan the Terrible (Ivan IV, 1530-84) to colonize the Kama river region. This virtually made them rulers over the lands and it was only a matter of time, therefore, before their attention would shift to the vast region on the other side of the Urals, long known for its fur.

From around the 1450s, Renaissance Europe had been particularly fond of luxury fur goods that reflected the pomp and status of its nobility, and Russia was perfectly placed to fulfil a demand for the most prized of pelts: sable and marten. Sables (*Martes zibellina*), relatives of the marten, were not found in North America, but the taiga forests of Siberia had them in abundance, and prices on the European markets for their fur were high.

In 1555 the Khan of Sibir, Yediger, rattled by the sudden collapse of the Khanate of Kazan, sent emissaries to Moscow, declared himself Ivan's vassal and promised to pay tribute. His successor, Kuchum, stopped the payments, however, murdered the Russians' ambassador in Sibir in 1573 and then launched attacks west of the Urals. Tied down with the Livonian War, Ivan agreed to a proposal from the Stroganovs that he allow them to move into Siberia.

Yermak Timofeyevich, through an unusual set of circumstances, became the person for the job. Events around the Don and Volga rivers played an important role. After the Russians had captured the khanates of Kazan and Astrakhan in the mid-sixteenth century, trade with Persia and Central Asia flourished. But so too did the number of Cossack bandits who attacked the tsar's boats and caravans, forcing the tsar to dispatch troops to protect merchants and launch campaigns against the bandits of the Don and Volga. Most gangs were defeated, but Müller says one group of about 6,000 under the command of Yermak escaped and made its way to Oryol (Orel), about 200 miles south-west of Moscow. As fate would have it, members of the Stroganov family were based there. They gave Yermak supplies in exchange for being left in peace, and watched as Yermak set out in 1581 to attack Kuchum, who Yermak had heard was unpopular among his people. The Cossack and his men were stopped by the onset of winter, however, spent the rest of the winter reorganizing, and the following season set out again. This time, according to Müller's history, the Stroganovs gave them provisions, firearms (according to Müller, Yermak had none until then), and even military colours to give the bandits the appearance of being well-drilled troops.

In the year 1582 Yermak and perhaps as many as 5,000 men launched their attack on the khanate. Their number, says Müller, soon fell to about 1,500 through disease, fatigue and casualties inflicted by Tartars, but eventually Yermak and about 500 men advanced towards the capital of the Khanate of Sibir, Isker (Qasliq or Sibir) outside Tobolsk in western Siberia, won a decisive battle near the capital and arrived in Isker itself to find that Kuchum had escaped and the town was deserted. The bandit duly placed himself on the khan's throne and began collecting tribute from the indigenous peoples and Tartars of the region. Müller writes: "Thus this en-

Yermak Timofeyevich

terprising Cossack was suddenly exalted from the station of a chief of banditti to the rank of a sovereign prince. It does not appear from history whether it were at first his design to conquer Siberia, or solely to amass a considerable booty."

Khan Kuchum had survived the battle for Isker but he and his troops were forced to abandon the capital and retreat beyond reach of Yermak, who found himself facing ambushes in the taiga. He may have had the Khanty, Mansi and rank-and-file Tartars lining up to pledge him temporary loyalty (which they did not always do), but Yermak also "felt the precariousness of his present grandeur". The attacks robbed him of his ability to completely control the region and as a result many of his troops died of hunger.

According to Müller's version, the precariousness of Yermak's situation was the reason why the Cossack decided to dispatch an emissary to Ivan the Terrible and declare the acquisitions to be Russia's. He also sent 5,000 pelts to whet Ivan's appetite for more. Ivan the Terrible, needless to say, responded with unbridled enthusiasm and is said to have sent Yermak a coat of chain mail. He also sent him reinforcements of 500 men.

The gift of chain mail, if this is true, would be the Cossack's downfall. There are various versions of the story of Yermak's demise, but the most common one is that in 1585 Kuchum lured Yermak into an ambush by letting it be known that a group of Bukharan merchants from Central Asia would be travelling through with food. Another version, in the *Yesipov Chronicle*, merely recounts that Kuchum was preventing Bukharan traders getting through. Müller gives an account of the last hours:

> The Russians to the number of about 300 lay negligently posted on a small island, formed by two branches of the Irtysh [river]. The night was obscure and rainy; and the troops, who were fatigued with a long march, reposed themselves without suspicion of danger. Kutchum Chan [Khan Kuchum] apprised of their situation, silently advanced at midnight with a select body of troops, and having forded the river, came with such rapidity upon the Russians, as to preclude the use of their arms. In the darkness and confusion of the night, the latter were cut to pieces almost without opposition; and fell a restless prey to those adversaries, whom they had been accustomed to conquer and despise. The massacre was so universal that only one man is recorded to have

escaped, and to have brought the news of this catastrophe to his countrymen at Sibir. Yermak himself perished in the rout, though he did not fall by the sword of the enemy... After many desperate acts of heroism, he cut his way through the troops who surrounded him, and made his way to the banks of the Irtysh. Being closely pursued by a detachment of the enemy, he endeavoured to throw himself into a boat which lay near the shore; but stepping short, he fell into the water, and being encumbered with the weight of his armour, sank instantly to the bottom.

Historians today question Müller's version of events (Yermak may even have served the tsar in the Livonian War before returning to the Volga in 1582 and launching an attack with 840 men later that year). Yet the years after Yermak's death saw his stature grow. When Siberia's first archbishop, Cyprian, arrived in 1621, he collected oral records from surviving Cossacks and commissioned early versions of the *Chronicles* that lent Yermak a religious character. Superstition surrounded the body of Yermak, and touching it was said to cure illness.

After the one survivor carried the news of Yermak's death back to the remaining men in Isker, the party apparently fled back across the Urals. By that time, hunger and attacks had diminished the original group and its reinforcements to a mere 150 men. They later chanced upon a group of Russian Cossacks arriving under the command of a military governor by the name of Ivan Mansurov, and together the men returned to Siberia and wintered in a stockade they built at the confluence of the Ob and Irtysh rivers (near today's Khanty-Mansiysk). Although this shelter was eventually abandoned, it was the first of many stockades that would soon spring up across Siberia.

The annexation of Siberia occurred at a breathtaking pace, all the more remarkable for the harsh climate and—for European Russians—it being an unknown land inhabited by people they knew just as little about. Russians returned to found the first town, Tyumen, in 1586. By 1619 the fort of Yeniseysk had been established just north of Krasnoyarsk on the Yenisey. In 1632 Yakutsk was founded, and by 1639 the Russians had reached the Sea of Okhotsk on the Pacific coast. In 1648 Semyon Dezhnev made a first attempt to sail around the north-east cape and through the Bering Strait to the Pacific. In 1697 the Russians penetrated into the Kamchatka

Peninsula, and by 1733 they had jumped the Pacific and arrived in Alaska on a new continent.

The first wave of colonists in Siberia consisted of military governors known as *voevody*, who established fortresses (*kreposti*) and stockades (*ostrogy*) in western Siberia on or near the sites of existing settlements in the Khanate of Sibir. These were assisted by fully-fledged military Cossacks, but also by ordinary soldiers and servicemen. As James Forsyth explains, all were expected to supplement wages with plunder. At the same time, he says, a system whereby the military governors demanded gifts or levied their own taxes established itself in Siberia, as these received no salary. This system had been abolished in European Russia in the mid-sixteenth century, but in Siberia it became a feature of its landscape of colonization.

The Russians continued the practice long established by other conquerors of demanding yasak from the indigenes and Turkic peoples they subdued. Furthermore, it was not uncommon for hunters with an appetite for valuable pelts to rush in ahead of these state functionaries. Accounts even suggest that the indigenes would sometimes naively laugh at what they considered to be a preposterously unequal trade: pots, pans, axe-heads and so forth in exchange for vast quantities of sable pelts that—unbeknown to them—were worth a fortune on the European market. Notwithstanding, resistance among indigenes to the newly arrived Russians was inevitable, considerable and a significant feature of Russia's annexation of Siberia.

The collapse of Sibir had removed a major political obstacle to colonization. But another barrier—less a physical or political barrier than a psychological one—persisted long after the campaign of Yermak, and crossing it had been akin to leaping over one's own shadow. Although Ivan the Terrible—Russia's ruler who in a rage had struck and accidentally killed his own son with a staff—added "Tsar of Sibir" to his list of titles and Siberia was now part of Russia, Siberia continued to occupy an ambivalent place in the imagination. This barrier, this shadow, had its own name—it was called "the rock" or "the belt"—but it is better known to us today as the Ural Mountains.

Chapter Two
A Frontier Beyond
The Urals and Yekaterinburg

"The procession stretched out in a long line along the broad Sibirsky Trakt... And so we approached the place where a stone pillar with a coat of arms stood on the border. On one side was Perm Province, on the other side was Tobolsk Province. This was where Siberia began. Here our long cortege stopped. Someone seized a 'small handful of native soil'. Generally everyone seemed a little moved."
Vladimir Korolenko (1853-1921), deported to Siberia in 1879

The early European travellers crossing into Siberia from the west arrived from the Novgorod Republic, which dominated Russia between the eleventh and fifteenth centuries and at its height stretched from the Baltic Sea to the Urals. The Novgorod region occupies a unique place in Russian history as it is seen as the cradle of modern Russia. It was in this region that Rurik, a Varangian (Viking) chieftain, established his dynasty in 862. Two decades later, Rurik's successor Oleg united this and other conquests into the powerful Ukraine-based republic of the Kiev Rus, and from the early twelfth century a Novgorod Republic established itself and thrived in part because of its ties with the German-dominated Hanseatic League of traders.

The Novgorod traders used two routes, both of which involved sailing up the rivers and hauling their boats between rivers on a couple of short portages. Both of the routes they took were in the north, leading into Siberia either near the town of Salekhard where the Gulf of Ob widens and runs to the Arctic Ocean, or near Berezovo, several hundred miles south of the Gulf of Ob. There were good reasons for using such a northerly route. One was that few Tartars lived there, so traders met less resistance. Another was that the valuable fur-bearing animals sought by the Russians lived in the forests of the Siberian *taiga* of the north.

By the early sixteenth century Russians were trading along the northern coast from the Kara Sea to the mouth of the Ob, and some adventurous traders were possibly sailing to the Yenisey river. The vessels they used were small coastal boats known as *kochi* (kochas), capable of carrying between six and seven tonnes, and if we can believe legends told by indigenes, lighter boats even reached the mouth of the Indigirka river in eastern Siberia.

In 1601 a customs house was built in the town of Verkhoturye, some 200 miles north of Yekaterinburg. A new road route was created north-east from Yaroslavl to the town of Solikamsk, the last major settlement in European Russia. From there travellers passed through the customs house before following the road's extension to Tyumen and the town of Tobolsk. The Verkhoturye crossing became the only legal way in and the only way out of Siberia, and here the tsar's officers maintained a rigid customs regime on the "border" to collect taxes from those entering or leaving Siberia and to catch corrupt administrators returning with Siberian fur or other goods they knew would earn them a small fortune back in European Russia. Verkhoturye developed into a bustling "port" leading into and out of Siberia, and goods bound for Siberia were hauled on sledges

Verkhoturye, c.1910

across European Russia and the Urals throughout winter and stored there for transportation deeper into the subcontinent during the season. In spring, once the ice had broken up on the Tura, Tobol, Irtysh and Ob, the goods were loaded onto vessels and carried north towards Berezovo and then eastwards across the taiga to Mangazeya (situated on the Taz river inside the Arctic Circle) and beyond. Another early route from Verkhoturye allowed the Russians to move their goods (much of this gunpowder, salt and flour) eastwards along the rivers from the town of Surgut (founded in 1594) towards Tomsk, which would be founded in 1604 on the Tom river.

One traveller who crossed at Verkhoturye was the Scottish physician, John Bell (1691-1780). Bell was born in Antermony in Scotland, studied medicine in Glasgow and after arriving in St. Petersburg in 1714 was attached to Russia's newly appointed ambassador to Persia as a medical assistant. From that time on he became something of a wandering physician for the nobility, crossing Siberia to China in 1719 with an embassy and later accompanying Peter the Great to Derbent and the Caspian Gates. Accounts of his journeys appeared in 1762 as *Travels from St. Petersburg in Russia to Diverse Parts of Asia*; a classic of travel literature and widely read and influential in its day, it still makes for some of the most interesting early reading about Siberia.

> About midnight we came to a village called Martinsky; here having changed horses, we soon reached the mountains named Verchatorsky-Gory [the Urals], where we found the snow very deep, and a strong frost still continued. We kept on our journey, ascending and descending these high and steep mountains for the space of fifteen hours. In such of the valleys as are fit for culture, are found Russian villages well peopled. And, where the woods are cut down, there appeared a beautiful landskip [landscape], even at this bleak season. These mountains divide Russia from Siberia. They run in a ridge from north to south, inclining a little to the east and west of these points. They are quite covered in woods, consisting of tall firs... and other trees natural to the climate; and abound with game and various kinds of wild beasts. Their length, from north to south, I cannot ascertain; but compute their breadth, where we passed, to be about forty English miles. But they are not so high as the mountains I have seen in Persia, and other parts of the world.

Having passed these mountains, we descended, on the 11th [of December, 1719], into a country finely varied with plains and rising grounds, interspersed with woods, villages, corn-fields, and pasturage; and, in the evening, reached the town called Verchaturia [Verkhoturye], from Verch which signifies high, and Tura the name of the river on which the town stands.

Verchaturia is pleasantly situated upon a rising ground, and fortified with a ditch and palisades. It is governed by a commandant, who has under him a garrison, consisting of some regular troops and Cossacks. What makes Verchaturia considerable, is its being a frontier town, and commanding the only entry from Russia into Siberia. Here is a custom-house, where all merchants are obliged to make entry of what sums of money or merchandise they carry into Siberia, or from Siberia into Russia; on all which is charged a duty of ten per cent to his majesty.

The route Bell followed was long known as Babinov's Road, a path hacked out of the forests by a man named Artemy Babinov who is thought to have based it on an existing trail used by Khanty and Mansi indigenes of the region. It began near the cathedral in Solikamsk and by no coincidence—for it soon developed a religious flavour as the way into Siberia for missionaries—was extended to run directly alongside the Holy Trinity Monastery (Svyato-Troytsky Monastir) in Tyumen, inside western Siberia.

In the late seventeenth century a tsarist decree foresaw construction of a new road that began in Moscow and petered out in present-day Mongolia. Construction started in earnest from 1730 and continued well into the nineteenth century. In its many incarnations this was the main road across Siberia for postal coaches and travellers. It was known variously as the Sibirsky Trakt (Siberian Trakt), the Moskovsky Trakt (Moscow Trakt), the Great Siberian Post Road, or simply as the Great Post Road. Everyone travelling in Siberia used this road.

TRAVEL ON THE SIBIRSKY TRAKT

By 1753 internal customs had been abolished, the Verkhoturye crossing became obsolete and Verkhoturye declined into a sleepy backwater. Now, shorter and more direct routes could be sought across Siberia. Thus began a gradual shift southwards, bringing Yekaterinburg onto the road into Siberia, but by-passing historically significant but inconveniently situated towns such as Tobolsk or Yeniseysk. Both of these would later be by-passed again by the main Trans-Siberian Railway line.

Travel on the Great Siberian Post Road was an arduous and often hazardous venture. In winter the traveller had to contend with blizzards. In summer the Baraba Steppe between Omsk and Novosibirsk metamorphosed into a breeding ground for voracious gnats and mosquitoes, and at any time of year the Baraba was notorious for bandits who rode up from the southern steppe to demand tribute or take hostages. This dangerous situation continued right into the nineteenth century.

John Bell mentions the bandits in his record of travels from the early eighteenth century, and a century later an unusual British traveller, James Holman (1786-1857), briefly notes scurrying across the Baraba Steppe, observing that he had just left its most "unwholesome part" and that he was "indebted to the heavy rains that had been falling, and which prevented the usual rapid decomposition of animal and vegetable matters."

Holman, like others before and after him, obviously had not relished the idea of travelling along this section of the Sibirsky Trakt. Unlike others, however, he did this as a blind man. His book, *Travels through Russia, Siberia, Poland, Austria, Saxony, Prussia, Hanover etc. Undertaken during the Years 1822, 1823, and 1824, while Suffering from Total Blindness* (1825), is an interesting account of a journey that took him as far east as Irkutsk.

On his expedition Holman bounced across Siberia in a relatively comfortable buggy. Generally the choices of vehicles on the Great Siberian Post Road were a rudimentary horse-drawn cart without springs known as a *telega*, a *kibitka*, a covered cart or in winter a sledge, or the more comfortable buggy known as a *tarantass*. A tarantass was a three- or four-horse wagon with a long chassis that reduced the jolting travellers suffered on a telega or kibitka. In 1840 the Russian writer Vladimir Sollogub (1813-62) likened a tarantass (also the title of one of his stories) to a cross between a dragonfly and a kibitka, while Alexandre Dumas *père* (1802-70) in his *Impressions de voyage en Russie* described it as a huge engine boiler on four wheels with a window at the front to survey the countryside and an entrance on the side. It had no steps, no seating and was filled with straw inside, he said. But sometimes families would remove the straw and place several mattresses on the floor so they could travel through the night and save on inn costs.

Travellers usually had to purchase their own tarantass, and the chances were high that the driver would have a predilection for vodka. The telega, in contrast, was standard equipment for the post road. It was commonly used until the late nineteenth century. In his *The New Siberia*, a book published on the eve of the twentieth century, the traveller Harry de Windt (1856-1933) writes:

> I could not wish my worst enemy a protracted journey in one of these torture boxes. There can, however, be little damage done in a "telega", for the occupant sits with his feet dangling only a few inches from the ground. An upset is therefore of little consequence, but the continual strain of clinging on, to say nothing of the violent oscillations, alternating with jolts that seem to drive the brain through the skull, exhaust the strongest man... I found it impossible to keep a cigarette between my teeth, and my hands were soon sore and blistered from holding on to the rough sides.

In 1890 the Russian writer and playwright Anton Chekhov (1860-1904) travelled to Sakhalin Island and spent several months investigating conditions in the prison settlement there. On reaching Irkutsk he wrote a lively letter in which he describes the hardships of travelling the Great Siberian Post Road. He uses the old Russian measurement of a *verst*, which is just over a kilometre:

> All my experiences in Siberia I divide into three periods. (1) From Tyumen to Tomsk, fifteen hundred versts, terrible cold, day and night, sheepskin, felt boots, cold rains, winds and a desperate life-and-death struggle with the flooded rivers. The rivers had flooded the meadows and roads, and I was constantly exchanging my trap for a boat and floating like a Venetian on a gondola; the boats, the waiting on the bank for them, the rowing across, etc., all that took up so much time that during the last two days before reaching Tomsk, in spite of all my efforts, I only did seventy versts instead of four or five hundred. There were, moreover, some very uneasy and unpleasant moments, especially when the wind rose and began to buffet the boat. (2) From Tomsk to Krasnoyarsk, five hundred versts, impassable mud, my chaise and I stuck in the mud like flies in thick jam. How many times I broke my chaise (it's my own property!) how many versts I walked! How bespattered my coun-

tenance and my clothes were! It was not driving but wading through mud. How I swore at it all! My brain would not work, I could do nothing but swear. I was utterly exhausted, and was very glad to reach the posting station at Krasnoyarsk. (3) From Krasnoyarsk to Irkutsk, fifteen hundred and sixty-six versts, heat, smoke from the burning woods, and dust—dust in one's mouth, in one's nose, in one's pockets; when you look at yourself in the glass, you think your face has been painted. When, on reaching Irkutsk, I washed at the baths, the soap-suds off my head were not white but of an ashen brown colour, as though I were washing a horse.

BEYOND THE WATERSHED OF IMAGINATION

Bell described the customs post. De Windt and Chekhov paint a vivid picture of the physical hardship of travel on the roads inside Siberia. But what about the crossing of the Urals themselves, this psychological threshold?

Inspired by the descriptions of Central Asia by Alexander von Humboldt, a writer and artist by the name of Thomas Witlam Atkinson (1799-1861) made his first crossing of the Urals in 1844 and began what would be a decade of travels in Siberia and Central Asia. Atkinson sketched whatever he saw and he also wrote a book about his journeys entitled *Oriental and Western Siberia; a Narrative of Seven Years' Exploration and Adventures in Siberia, Mongolia, the Kirghis Steppes, Chinese Tartary, and a Part of Central Asia.* In it he describes how he is accompanied along the road for a few miles from one town by some locals before they leave him and he begins the climb into the Urals alone. The group stops in a forest grove so "that we might take our leave in the true Siberian fashion," eating and drinking, then they shake hands in farewell. He ascends the Urals. These have, he says, "no striking features. There are no rugged mountain summits to break the monotony of the well-rounded hills covered with pine and larch. Some of the valleys are cultivated, and the new-grown rye was now looking fresh and green." He reaches the highest point, notes that it is neither high nor spectacular, mentions some pretty pines again and remarks that "the descent into Asia is somewhat more abrupt than would be the descent to the European side."

This is the view of a free man. In the winter of 1849-50, the writer Fyodor Dostoevsky (1821-81) crossed the Urals at exactly the same point as Atkinson to begin what would amount to four years of imprisonment in Siberia and another five years in exile serving in a regiment. He was held briefly in Tobolsk and later taken to Omsk, where he saw out the prison term. Dostoevsky writes:

> They were insignificant towns [in European Russia] and seldom, but we left on a public holiday and everywhere there was enough to eat and drink. We froze horribly. Our clothes were warm, but we sat, for instance, 10 hours on the sledge and stopped at only five or six stations. The cold froze my heart and I was barely able to get warm in the rooms. But strangely, I was able to completely recover on the journey. In the Perm district we spent one night in 40 degrees below zero. I wouldn't recommend it to you. Totally unpleasant. The moment of crossing the Urals was sad. The horses and sledges sank in snow. A snowstorm raged. We got out of the sledges—it was night time—and stood waiting while they were pulled out again. Snow was everywhere. A raging snowstorm. The frontier of Europe. Ahead was Siberia, and in her the secret of our fate. Behind us, everything that had happened—it was sad and tears came to my eyes. All along the way the peasants ran out to look at us, and although we were in shackles, at the stations they took from us three times the price...

That same year Dostoevsky described being fleeced by peasants at European stations, the harsh winter conditions and his tears on crossing the mental divide, a highly opinionated traveller published a book in London under the harmless title of *Travels in Siberia*. He illustrates another nineteenth-century approach to the Urals, this time that of the self-aggrandizing bigot. Our hero's name was S. S. Hill Esq. Initially he was filled with lofty "visions of new scenes and new modes of life" ahead, pontificating that "the passage of mountains is always among the remarkable events in a traveller's progress, and more especially, whatever may be their character, physically considered, when they divide great empires or portions of empires inhabited by people of dissimilar habits and manners." He continues:

> After thus dismissing the past, we now fixed our thoughts more fully upon the countries before us. We were about to enter a new region, in

another quarter of the globe, inhabited in some parts, by nations and tribes not yet subdued to admit more exact laws and government than are necessary to raise them from the sad state of man in his original barbarism to the first degrees of civilisation, and, in other parts by tribes not even physically overcome, or in a condition to take the first step in the common progress of man from the condition of the savage to that of refined life. We were about to enter that country, rather known to the world in its character of a penal colony, than as the nurse of new races of men doomed to multiply indefinitely, and reserved to unite in the general efforts of man to raise and ameliorate his condition.

STROGANOVS, DEMIDOVS AND THE INDUSTRIAL HERITAGE OF NEVYANSK

Two families did particularly well out the Urals in the early days of Russian expansion into Siberia. One of these was the wealthy Stroganov family of merchants and industrialists. The founding father of the dynasty was Fyodor Lukich Stroganov, whose son Anikey Fyodorivich (1497-1570) established a string of salt works in 1515 at the tender age of eighteen. In 1558 Ivan the Terrible gave the family its big break in the Urals when he granted the Stroganovs large holdings of land in the Perm district, and the family opened up salt mines. Anikey's sons Semyon, Yakov and Grigory built on the family empire by founding iron works in the Urals and trading in fur and other goods. Soon the family was establishing its own towns in the Urals and their estates swelled with serfs (bonded peasants), salt workers, tradesmen, guards and translators—anyone, in fact, who might add to the family's fortune. But their activities did not stop there. The Stroganovs were involved in hunting walrus for its tusks (walrus ivory), and they caught and processed seals for blubber in the Arctic waters. Money lending was another of their branches of business.

When Yakov and Grigory died in 1577-78, this commercial empire fell to Semyon and his nephews, who financed the expedition of the brigand Cossack Yermak into the feudal Khanate of Sibir. During the so-called Time of Trouble, a period of interregnum between the death of the last Rurik ruler in 1598 and the ascension of the Romanov dynasty to the throne in 1613, the family helped prop up Russia's government financially, and when they offered a helping a hand in the defence of the Pomore region in north-east European Russia during the Great Northern War, the

Stroganovs were rewarded with hereditary titles. Peter the Great accorded the only surviving line of Stroganovs in the eighteenth century—that of Semyon—the title of baron.

When John Bell passed through Solikamsk, situated 230 miles north of Perm, he was already acquainted with members of the family:

> Solikamsky [Solikamsk] is famous for having many salt-pits in its neighbourhood, the property of my worthy friend Baron Stroganof, by virtue of a grant from his majesty. The Baron has brought these works to such perfection, that he is able to serve all Russia with salt; and could besides furnish a considerable quantity for exportation, were there any demand.

The second of the powerful dynasties that left its mark on the Urals is that of the Demidovs, whose name is associated with numerous towns in western Siberia, but especially Barnaul, today capital of the Altai Region.

The first of the Demidov towns was Nevyansk, today a sleepy Urals outpost of some 25,000 inhabitants about 55 miles north of Yekaterinburg. Thomas Witlam Atkinson visited it in the mid-nineteenth century. "I arrived at two o'clock in the morning," he writes, "and was taken to the castle. This is one of the oldest Zavods [factories] in the Oural [Urals]; it was built on the small river Neva under the direction of Nikite Demidoff [Nikita Demidov]. Sent from Tula by Peter the Great, about the year 1701 or 1702, to examine the mines in these regions, near which he soon after established himself, Demidoff may truly be considered the founder of the iron and other works in the Oural."

Nevyansk was famous not just for its iron works. In the eighteenth century it became home to a large population of Old Believers, descendants of the religious dissenters who had broken away from the Russian Orthodox Church in the seventeenth century after the patriarch Nikon (1605-81) introduced Church reforms. Religious icons are their legacy, and many of these can be found in Yekaterinburg.

In Nevyansk itself a statue of Nikita Demidov and Peter the Great celebrates the two men who paved the way for the town's foundation. Other attractions of this early Urals town are its Historical-Local Studies Museum (Istoriko-Kraevedchesky Muzey) situated in a former Gostiny Dvor, a late nineteenth-century merchants' yard that, as elsewhere in Russia, was composed of a series of buildings and yards offering a place to

Nevyansk and its leaning tower

trade goods and often a place to stay for local and out of town merchants. The museum was founded in 1913 and has exhibits on the cultural history of Nevyansk, its industrial heritage and the natural history of the region. Understandably, it has a strong focus on minerals.

Another of the attractions of this modest but historic Urals town is its neoclassical revivalist cathedral dating from the late nineteenth century. This was reconstructed in 2003 after being almost completely destroyed in Stalin's antireligious campaigns of the 1930s. The town's most unusual building today, however, is the so-called Nevyansk Leaning Tower (Naklonnaya Bashnya), apparently used by the Demidovs as a mint and mentioned by Atkinson in 1844: "About two hundred paces from the castle stands a very fine brick tower, much out of the perpendicular; there is a subterraneous passage to it, now closed up. In this building the silver brought from the Altai was refined... It is also said that the first Demid-offs concealed here the fugitives who escaped from Tobolsk and other regions of Siberia, employing them in the mines and iron-works..."

The tower probably dates from the late 1720s and is remarkable because, unlike the Leaning Tower of Pisa, only sections of Nevyansk's equivalent are out of square. Builders, it seems, tried to compensate for subsidence during construction by trimming the stone blocks. The top of the tower, which affords spectacular views over the countryside if one can gain entry, is near-vertical. Other explanations for the lean are more imaginative and florid. According to one, a tilt was deliberately created towards Tula—the original stamping ground of the Demidovs. Another claims that Akinfy Demidov tossed the architect off the tower so no better work could be created. The building wept for its creator, which explains why water tends to drip down just one side of the tower after rainfall.

YEKATERINBURG: MINERALS AND MINING

> "I drove out of Tyumen on the third of May after spending in Ekaterinburg two or three days, which I devoted to the repair of my coughing and haemorrhoidal person. Besides the public posting service, one can get private drivers that take one across Siberia. I chose the latter: it is just the same. They put me, the servant of God, into a basketwork chaise and drove me with two horses; one sits in the basket like a goldfinch, looking at God's world and thinking of nothing... The plain of Siberia begins, I think, from Ekaterinburg, and ends goodness knows where; I should say it is very like our South Russian Steppe, except for the little birch copses here and there and the cold wind that stings one's cheeks."
>
> Anton Chekhov, *Letters*, 1915

In 1720 Peter the Great (1672-1725) gave orders for the Russian engineer, geographer and historian Vasily Tatishchev to found a large industrial town in the Urals for exploitation of the region's mineral wealth. Tatishchev (1686-1750), who is also credited with founding the Urals towns of Perm and Orenburg, travelled to the small village of Shatash, situated on a tributary of the Iset, but soon realized that for his large factory he would need more water than it could provide. He chose a location on the Iset itself and called the new town Yekaterinburg, after Catharine I, the wife of Peter the Great (not to be confused with Catherine II, or "Catherine the Great").

Yekaterinburg was formally established in 1723 around a metallurgical factory on the banks of the Iset and took shape over the ensuing decades with the help of its co-founder, Georg Wilhelm de Gennin (1676-1750), a German officer from Lower Saxony and of Dutch descent. The town began minting coins in 1725 and supplied the Russian empire with copper coins for the next 150 years. In 1726 another factory was opened up to process precious stones from the Urals, which soon found favour in St. Petersburg and abroad in the salons of Europe.

The two men responsible for the development of the new town complemented each other well, according to the Urals writer Dmitry Mamin Sibiryak (1852-1912). De Gennin brought his excellent understanding of mining, while Tatishchev contributed with his universal knowledge and vision. Like St. Petersburg, Yekaterinburg was the planned product of a draughtsman's drawing board, and in 1781 it briefly became the capital of a region that included Perm—a status that it relinquished to Perm in 1796. A large number of foreigners, especially Germans, moved to the city, which became known as Siberia's "window to Europe", and the social texture of the city was very much influenced by the peasants and trades people who settled.

The nineteenth century saw Yekaterinburg grow into a centre for gold and precious stones and it gradually become a hub of intellectual and cultural life in the Urals. It also acquired importance as a headquarters of regional administration in the mid-century, but its heritage and its backbone remained rooted in mining, and because of this it received the special status accorded to some Russian towns as "centres of mining", bringing with it certain formal privileges. One such privilege was the right to possess its own military contingent to defend the mines and works. By 1819 its significance was such that Tsar Alexander I travelled here to inspect his factories.

By this time Yekaterinburg was a long-standing stop on the Sibirsky Trakt and therefore a hub for travellers heading east into Siberia. With the development of railways it received another boost. The first line, which connected it with Perm in European Russia, was finished in 1885, and a year later track was laid to Tyumen, the first major town in Siberia.

From the 1820s neoclassical buildings rose up along wide, tree-flanked avenues in Yekaterinburg. Neoclassicism, with its high columns and austere embellishment, had surfaced in Siberia late in the eighteenth century and gradually gained momentum in the course of the next few decades. One of the main protagonists of the movement working in Yekaterinburg at the time was Mikhail Malakhov (1781-1842).

When Thomas Witlam Atkinson visited Yekaterinburg in the 1840s he found an attractive city dominated by its city pond and factories, built around what today is known as Historical Square (Istorichesky Skver). He was also impressed by the number and magnificence of its large mansions. These, he said, were

> equal to any found in the best European towns; the rooms are spacious, lofty, and beautifully finished; their decorations executed with excellent taste; they are also splendidly furnished indeed, supplied with almost every luxury as well as comfort. With many of these fortunate persons, their mode of living equals the splendour of their habitations. Attached to most of their dwellings are large conservatories, in some of which are very choice collections of tropical plants and flowers, such as few would expect to find in so severe a climate.

On the eve of the Russian Revolution Yekaterinburg had become a bustling city with about 100,000 inhabitants and almost fifty factories that churned out metallurgical and industrial goods for tsarist Russia.

While Yekaterinburg played a significant role in Urals mining and industry, and to this day is one of Russia's industrial powerhouses, events in the early twentieth century have tended to have a greater influence on our perception of it today. The Bolsheviks, who later formed the basis of the Communist Party of the Soviet Union, had a strong following in the Urals. Between October 1917, when the October Revolution took place, and the end here of the civil war in 1923, the Bolsheviks controlled Yekaterinburg for all but a one-year period (from July 1918). For that one year Yekaterinburg found itself in the hands of anti-Bolshevik White forces under the command of Admiral Alexander Kolchak. In 1923, after Kolchak's forces had fled, the Bolsheviks created a Urals region that stretched from the northern Arctic coast to the steppes and Kazakh border of the south. One year later, in 1924, the city was renamed Sverdlovsk after the leading Bolshevik in the Urals, Yakov Sverdlovsk (1885-1919). The name stuck and was only changed back to Yekaterinburg in 1991.

One event in particular during the civil war would have a profound effect on Yekaterinburg. In mid-1918, while war raged and legions of Czech-Slovak prisoners of war who supported the White forces fought westwards towards Yekaterinburg, Tsar Nicholas II and members of the royal family were executed here in the basement of a house owned by a local engineer and builder by the name of Nikolay Ipatiev.

Throughout the twentieth century, Yekaterinburg continued to grow in significance, becoming a vital industrial centre for tanks and munitions during the Second World War. Because of its military-industrial complex—about one-third of the workforce was employed in military industries towards the end of the Soviet era—Sverdlovsk was a closed city for much of the communist period and foreigners were kept at arm's length. More important than the Romanovs during this period was another man whose nickname of "Tsar Boris" reflected his style of government (but not the chaos of the period, which also had a parallel with the last days of tsarist rule). This man was Boris Yeltsin (1931-2007), who rose in the echelons of the Communist Party and headed it here between 1976 and 1985.

A couple of unusual events happened during Yeltsin's time in Sverdlovsk. One was an outbreak of anthrax from a biological weapons plant situated on the outskirts of the city in 1979. The other preceded the outbreak by two years; apparently under orders from the Politburo in Moscow, Yeltsin gave instructions for the engineer's house, Dom Ipatiev, to be razed one night, removing the physical reminder of the Romanov killings. Today, a memorial church stands on the site.

Yekaterinburg is a vibrant city, and much has changed here in recent years. One of the changes is to be found in the Romanov memorial itself. When I first visited in 1998, the Romanov death site was a sorrowful and vacant lot surrounded by crumbling buildings just east of the City Pond. A small chapel had been erected on the site to the Grand Princess Elisabeth Fyodorovna, elder sister of Russia's last tsarina Alexandra and also murdered by the Bolsheviks, and plans did exist for a church but not the money to build it. The impression I gained was that no one quite knew what to do with the site; nor did everyone agree with the proposal to build a church. For several years, only a small cross pointed to the tragic events. It was only in 2000 that construction finally went ahead on a church. It was finished within an impressive time-span of three years.

Another change is in the mood and texture of the city. The Yekaterinburg of the late 1990s retained some of its character as a closed city. Though interesting, it also had a seedy edge and a reputation for crime, especially organized crime. I met two Mormons by chance and one of them had not spoken for two weeks since knocking on the door of an apartment one day only to have a gun held to his head by the occupant. Yet this was a period of relative boom, before the banking crisis of 1998 erased the savings of ordinary Russians. Less than two years after the crisis Yekaterinburg was being compared to Birmingham (in Britain), which had reinvented itself after the decline of heavy industry. While heavy industry still plays an important role in Yekaterinburg today, it is now also a financial and service centre; it has a large tourist sector, and a—by Russian standards—sizeable middle class can be found these days walking along its broad avenues.

A Walk through Yekaterinburg

A good place to begin exploring Yekaterinburg is ploshchad 1905 Goda, a square situated in the heart of town near an upmarket shopping street and street artists' zone-in-the-making called ulitsa Veynera, Yekaterinburg's mini-equivalent to Moscow's Arbat. The square is crowned by a statue of Lenin, inscribed with the quotation: "Everything that we have achieved shows that we rely on the most wonderful thing in the world: strength—the strength of the workers and peasants."

This was once the site of the Epiphany Cathedral (Bogoyavlensky Sobor), a market and a monument to Alexander II (1818-81), whose most important legacy to Russia was the overdue reforms that abolished peasant serfdom. Ploshchad 1905 Goda is traditionally the place where crowds gather to celebrate or demonstrate, and the most important of these demonstrations took place during the 1905 revolution, which saw Russians rising up against the autocratic rule of Tsar Nicholas II and demanding democratic reforms. The square received its current name from the Bolsheviks in 1919. By that time the memorial to Alexander II had been removed, and in the 1930s the church itself was completely demolished.

Across the road, where once the market was held, a new city Soviet was erected between 1947 and 1954, built for the most part by German prisoners of war held in Siberia, and since 1991 this has been the home of the city duma (council). During the Moscow coup of 1991, when the old guard attempted to wind back the clock on Mikhail Gorbachev's glasnost reforms, plans are said to have been hatched for Boris Yeltsin to run Russia from a bunker in Yekaterinburg. As we know, the coup failed, and Yeltsin continued his rise from being responsible for local city housing to heading the Sverdlovsk region Communist Party, finally becoming Russia's first post-Soviet president.

From here it is only a short walk east along prospekt Lenina to reach the Gorodskoy Prud (City Pond), along the way passing one of the more interesting stone buildings on this part of prospekt Lenina, the Urals Mining School (Uralskoe Gornoe Uchilishche) at no. 33, a school for children of local factory employees but whose main purpose was as an academy to educate boys between the age of fourteen and seventeen in mining theory and practice. The first of the Urals mining schools were founded at two factories near Yekaterinburg by Tatishchev in 1721, but in 1723 both of these were transferred to Yekaterinburg by de Gennin. This building was completed in 1853 and almost a decade later began operating as a mining school. During the Second World War it was turned into a hospital to treat wounded soldiers and today is a local high school.

Istorichesky Skver (Historical Square) is set around the innovative mid-eighteenth-century dam constructed from Urals larch, which generated energy for the factories around it, including the mint which opened in 1725. The square took on its current appearance as a result of landscaping in the 1970s.

Turning right without crossing the bridge and following the western embankment of the Iset through a small geological park filled with local rocks from the Ural Mountains, you reach the Museum of Fine Arts (Muzey Izobrazitelnikh Iskusskv) at ulitsa Voevodina 5. The museum is spread over two floors in an unprepossessing but reworked eighteenth-century building on the banks of the river. Downstairs is its pride and joy: the cast-iron Kaslin Pavilion, a joint effort between tradesmen in Paris (some of the work was done there) and local metal workers. Cast-iron work is a strong feature of the museum's collection, which also includes icon paintings in the style of craftspeople in Nizhny Tagil, some 100 miles north of Yekaterinburg, and works by Italian, Dutch, and French painters. The icons are situated upstairs on the second floor (based on the Russian system, where the ground floor is considered the first floor) to the left, where over 700 exhibits, large and small, date from the fifteenth to the nineteenth centuries.

The Urals have a rich tradition of icon painting, and this is largely thanks to wealthy merchants and industrialists such as the Stroganovs and the Demidovs, who commissioned new works, and to the Old Believers of Nevyansk who continued the art of icon painting. (A second museum building at ulitsa Vaynera 11 houses contemporary Russian art.) From here it is a short walk across to ulitsa Malysheva 46, to the Sverdlovsk Region Local Studies Museum (Sverdlovsky Oblastnoy Kraevedchesky Muzey), housing crafts and arts from the Sverdlovsk region. Nearby is a small stone bridge dating from 1840 leading to the eastern side of the Iset and the Museum of the History of Architecture and Industrial Technology in the Urals (Muzey Istorii Arkhitektury i Promyshlennoy Tekhniki Urala), standing where the production of iron began in the 1720s. One section of the museum covers the history of the architecture in Yekaterinburg. In the museum yard a small bust of Peter the Great commemorates his decision to industrialize the Urals, leading to the foundation of Yekaterinburg.

Further north, the theme shifts to the natural world at the Nature Museum (Muzey Prirody), which contains some interesting Stone-Age fossils. Here, too, a map shows the extent in the Urals region of the Great Siberian Lake that covered much of western Siberia about 25,000 years ago. (This explains some strange eel-like fossils in the collection.)

Just east of the wooden water tower near prospekt Lenina is the monument to the two founders: Vasily Tatishchev and Georg Wilhelm de Gennin, and behind it a memorial to a city cathedral that stood here from the eighteenth century and was razed in the 1930s.

Tatishchev was not just a founder of Yekaterinburg; he also played a crucial role in shaping our perception today of what constitutes Europe and Asia. Until the reforms of Peter the Great and the new focus on making Russia a European nation, Russians did not devote much energy to trying to define where Europe ended and Asia began as it meant little to them. It is said that the ancient Greeks considered the divide between Europe and Asia to be the Don, which they thought flowed from the Arctic Ocean. From the fifteenth century it dawned on most geographers that the Greeks had been wrong about the Don. Because no waterway separated the two continents, however, the unease outside Russia (in Europe) was great. How could a contiguous land mass also contain a border between Europe and Asia? Then, once Russia started to invent itself as European under Peter the Great, it became important inside Russia to create a boundary that defined the limits of the continents. In stepped Tatishchev, wearing his geographer's hat. Despite being uncomfortably ill-defined in the south, the Urals did run to the ocean. And so the Urals were declared the boundary between familiar Europe and the "foreign" continent of Asia. (Today an obelisk about 25 miles out of town marks a section of the

Yekaterinburg: nineteenth-century architecture

boundary between Europe and Asia, although there is talk of erecting a new one at a different location in the Urals.)

An imposing cream-coloured building directly across the road at prospekt Lenina 35 dates from the 1860s and was home to mining officials before being reconfigured into the regional courthouse. A few doors along at ulitsa Lenina 37 stands the neoclassical former Mining Repository Building dating from 1821, which today houses a small collection of jewellery and precious stones in the Museum of the History of Stone-Cutting and Jewellery Art (Muzey Istorii Kamnereznovo i Yuvelirnovo Iskussstva).

Walking east (away from the pond) along prospekt Lenina you eventually reach a small monument to Alexander Popov (1859-1905) alongside the main post office. Popov was born in the Urals region not far from Verkhoturey, studied physics, electrical engineering and later theology, and went on to become a pioneer in wireless technology. He is said to have invented the wireless in the late 1890s, but fell into the shadow of Guglielmo Marconi, who filed his own wireless patent in 1896 apparently based on Popov's wireless. This prompted Popov to go public with a series of articles in the press.

From here, following ulitsa Pushkina north past the memorial, the visitor enters the Literary Quarter of Yekaterinburg. Take the first street to the right (pereulok Pochtovy) to the building on the corner at ulitsa Tomacheva 21. Even if your interest in icons is only passing, the collection inside the private Nevyansk Icon Museum (Muzey-Nevyanskaya Ikona) is worth visiting for the quality and range of its icons—some 250 dating from the sixteenth to the twentieth centuries. Backtracking, the building on the corner of pereulok Pochtovy and ulitsa Pushkina (pereulok Pochtovy 19) dates from the 1840s and is another of the mansions once occupied high-ranking mining officials and thought so ostentatious by Atkinson on his travels.

While many important writers have blown through the Urals on their way to Siberia, two authors in particular stand out for being intricately involved in the people and culture of the region. One of these is Pavel Bazhov (1879-1950), who is well-known for his collections of fairy tales based on traditional folklore of the Urals. The most famous of these tales is *The Malachite Casket*, a series of 52 narratives told to a young boy by a watchman living in the Urals. Bazhov was born into a working-class family, and he saw the Russian Revolution of 1917 as a way out of the very real social inequalities of his day. He worked as a journalist and wrote about the history of the Urals region while gathering the tales that he would publish in 1939. All his works were written in the house at ulitsa Chapaeva 11, now also the House and Museum of P. P. Bazhov (Dom-Muzey P. P. Bazhova).

The second of the major Urals writers is Mamim-Sibiryak (1852-1912), whose house at ulitsa Pushkina 27 (Literature-Memorial House-Museum Mamim-Sibiryak; Literaturno-Memorialny Dom-Muzey D.N. Mamima-Sibiryaka) is today a museum dedicated to his life and work.

Mamin-Sibiryak was born in Visim, near Verkhoturke, the son of a priest, and after attending school there moved to Yekaterinburg, where he enrolled in a seminary for two years in the mid-1860s. He later moved to Perm and then to St. Petersburg, where he studied at the Medical Academy. He gave up his veterinary studies to study law, but ill health forced him to return to Yekaterinburg in 1877, and he bought the house that is now the museum and wrote some of his early works from here. The majority of his works are based around Urals life and the beauty of the area. He was 25 when he returned, and it was in Yekaterinburg that he met his first wife, Maria Alekseeva. His early novel, *Mountain Nest*, was partly inspired by her and satirized Urals factory owners. The marriage ended, however, and he moved back to St. Petersburg with his second wife, Maria Abramova, who died in 1891 while giving birth. He would later marry the governess of his daughter, and *Tales for Alyonushka* was based on bedtime stories he told his ailing daughter while caring for her. His best-known works include *The Privalov Fortune* (1883) and *Mountain Nest* (1884), and his short story collections *Ural Stories* (1895) and *Siberian Stories* (1889).

In one memorable passage of *The Primalov Fortune*, Mamin-Sibiryak describes his beloved Urals through the eyes of his central character:

> Privalov took a deep breath when they walked out onto the balcony, which commanded an excellent view across all of Uzel, its surroundings and the line of the Ural Mountains stretching out from north to south as a dark silhouette. True, the mountains were not very high in this part and formed a small elbow through which bubbled the Uzlovka, a mountain stream... Altogether, the view of town was very good and pleasing to the eye, a patchwork of colours formed by gardens and brightly painted churches. It was a lively Siberian town with little in common with its brethren in Russia. Clearly, life brimmed here at every step. Within the thick belt of pine forest embracing the town on all sides were up to a dozen large, smoking factories and settlements, and strung along the banks of the Uzlobva were the summer dachas of the local wealthy. Privalov stared to the south-east to Mt. Mokhlatenkaya—there the undulating plain was flooded in haze to the horizon, gradually falling towards the blessed steppes of Bashkiriya.

The Literary Quarter is a quiet and—in summer—leafy part of town. Further along, where ulitsa Pushkina doglegs into ulitsa Proletarskaya, is a statue of the Russian poet Alexander Pushkin (1799-1837), backed by small gardens and flanked by museums dedicated to literary history. Walking along ulitsa Proletarskaya, you find the Literature-Memorial House & Museum of F.M. Reshetnikov (Literaturno-Memorialny Dom-Muzey F.M. Reshetnikova) at No. 6. Reshetnikov was born the son of a postal officer and part of this stone, two-storey house is dedicated to his life and work, complemented by other exhibits on the theme of postal and coach workers.

The next museum in the group on ulitsa Proletarskaya is the Museum of Urals Literary Life in the Twentieth Century (Literaturnaya Zhizn Urala XX Veka), located at no. 10. Further on is the Museum of Dolls and Children's Books (Muzey Kukol i Detskoy Knigi) at no. 16, inside the building where Mamim-Sibiryak lived when he first moved to Yekaterinburg. In addition to this cluster of museums, a Museum of Urals Literary Life in the Nineteenth Century (Literaturnaya Zhizn Urals XIX Veka) is situated at ulitsa Tolmacheva 41, reached by taking the side street towards the church and walking back along ultisa Tolmacheva. Two other interesting museums are also within easy walking distance of the Literary Quarter: the Museum of Photography (Muzey Fotografii) at ulitsa Karla Libknekhta 36; and south of here and the complex of memorials to the Romanovs, situated at ulitsa Karla Libknekhta 26, is the Yekaterinburg History Museum (Muzey Istorii Yekaterinburga). Before reaching these, however, you pass the Romanov memorial.

THE ROMANOV MURDERS AND CHURCH-ON-BLOOD

Turning right at the theatre building on ulitsa Proletarsky, you emerge behind one of Yekaterinburg's most visited attractions—the place where the last tsar and members of his family were held and executed in 1918. A small set of stone stairs winds around a large cross and stone figures depicting the members of the murdered royal family. Behind this is the Church-on-Blood (Khram na Krove), completed in 2003 on the site of the engineer Dom Ipatiev's house, where the executions took place. An extremely impressive church that covers 29,700 square feet, it doubles as a memorial to the Romanovs and the members of their entourage who were also executed.

After the February 1917 revolution broke in Russia, Nicholas II was forced to abdicate and the family—Nicholas, Alexandra, their children Olga and Tatyana (both in their early twenties) and the teenage children Maria, Anastasia and thirteen-year-old Alexei—were placed under house arrest in Tsarskoe Selo, the imperial palace situated sixteen miles outside Petrograd. Life in Tsarskoe Selo had been a quiet routine of rising early, walking with the dog in the parkland, lunch and working the garden, followed by dinner and sleep. The children came down with measles just after

Church-on-Blood: Romanov memorial

the imperial family's arrest.

In early August it became clear that the Bolsheviks had a good chance of controlling the workers' councils (Soviets) in Moscow and St. Petersburg and successfully overthrowing the provisional government (it ruled Russia between February and October 1917). The Romanovs and their entourage of about fifty were transferred to Tobolsk—possibly due to fears of their becoming the focus of counter-revolution or fear for their safety should the capital sink into chaos—arriving on 6 August and were placed in the former governor's residence there.

Later, once the Bolsheviks had overthrown the provisional government, they sent a new commissioner, Vasily Yakovlev, described by Charles Sydney Gibbes, Alexei's English tutor, as a man who looked like a "clever sailor" rather than one of culture, whose job it was to escort the Romanovs out of Tobolsk. In the spring of 1918 preparations were apparently made to transfer the family to Moscow, possibly to put them on trial, but intervention by Urals Bolsheviks caused a change of plan, and the family was brought to Yekaterinburg. In anticipation of their arrival, a house dating from the 1870s and owned by the local engineer Nikolay Ipatiev was taken over. Because the tsarevich Alexei had fallen ill in Tobolsk the family was transported in two stages, with Nicholas, Alexandra and Maria arriving in Yekaterinburg on 30 April. The remainder of the family joined them about three weeks later. The day Nicholas' group arrived in Yekaterinburg a large crowd turned out at the main railway station and shouted abuse, resulting in the tsar and his group being forced to disembark at one of the minor city stations.

The imperial family had been subject to varying degrees of insult or offensive behaviour from their captors since the time of their arrest in Tsarskoe Selo, and this is said to have continued in Yekaterinburg. According to Pierre Gilliard, the children's French tutor, the grand duchesses slept on the floor in Dom Ipatiev.

Gibbes, along with Gilliard and the servants, was released and later returned to Yekaterinburg after it fell to the White forces. He describes in *The Last Days of the Romanovs* the different personalities of the children as he saw them. Olga, he says, had the lightest hair in the family, was easily irritated, harsh but extremely religious and had a talent for playing and composing music. "It seems to me that she loved her father more than anybody else." Tatyana is portrayed as being very thin and darker than the others.

"Her eyes made her look different from all of her sisters who showed their souls through their eyes. She was reserved, haughty, and not open hearted, but she was the most positive... She was always preoccupied and pensive and it was impossible to guess her thoughts... She was her mother's favourite..." Maria, Gibbes says, "was a young woman of broad build. She was very strong; for example, she could lift me up from the ground," while Anastasia "was short, stout and was, in my opinion, the only one in the family that appeared to be ungraceful... If she had grown and got slim she would have been the prettiest in the family. She was refined and very witty." Alexei, the tsarevich, is described as having "a kind heart and was very fond of animals. He could be influenced only by his feelings, and would not yield to authority. He submitted only to the emperor. He was a clever boy but was not fond of books. His mother loved him passionately."

Around midnight on 17 July 1918, the family was awoken, told that the White Army had surrounded the house and were led into the cellar. Along with Nicholas, Alexandra, Olga, Tatyana, Maria, Anastasia, and Alexei were the family physician Eugene Botkin, Alexandra's lady-in-waiting Anna Demidova, their cook Ivan Kharitinov and Nicholas' footman Alexei Trupp. A contingent of about ten Red Guards entered the cellar, which had been prepared with wooden partitioning to prevent bullets ricocheting. Yakov Yurovsky, the Bolshevik charged with looking after the family in Yekaterinburg, shot Nicholas in the heart, giving the signal for others to execute their targets. Alexandra is also believed to have died immediately, but most of the children are thought to have survived the executioners' shots, including the daughters whose diamond-lined corsets prevented the bullets penetrating.

According to an interesting book by Wendy Slater, *The Many Deaths of Tsar Nicholas II*, which looks into the Romanov executions and focuses on what the Romanovs mean to Russia, none of the bullets came from Latvian riflemen who were part of the execution party. The survivors, however, appear to have been finished off with the bayonets mounted on their weapons. The victims were loaded onto a truck and taken to a disused mine outside town where they were thrown into a flooded ditch and covered with branches.

It was a poor attempt to dispose of the bodies. The mine was inadequate, so the following night, after the Bolsheviks had tried to burn some of the corpses, the victims were loaded onto a truck and driven towards a deeper one nearby. But the truck became bogged down on the way and it was decided to bury the family temporarily under the road. The White forces took Yekaterinburg a short time later and the Romanovs remained where they had been buried. The Whites also sealed off Dom Ipatiev in order to investigate the events, and later set up headquarters there. Ipatiev himself was allowed to return and live in part of the house.

In the 1920s, after the Bolsheviks had regained control of Yekaterinburg, the house was turned into a museum dedicated to the revolution (with some displays about the Romanovs). Later it was variously a museum on atheism and an archive. It remained common knowledge, however, that this was where the Romanovs had been murdered, and each year on the anniversary of their death flowers turned up in front of the house. In 1977 Boris Yeltsin apparently received the order from Moscow to destroy the house (purportedly to ease traffic flow in the area), an action which duly took place on 28 July that year.

That, as far as the Soviet authorities were concerned, should have been the end of the story, but it was not to be. New details about the Romanovs' sojourn in Dom Ipatiev and the execution became public when an article written by the man who led the execution, Yakov Yurovsky, was found in Paris. It was because of this new information that the bodies were eventually traced and, in 1991, exhumed. Yet mystery continued to surround the find, partly due to lingering doubts about the real identity of the people buried, even after DNA testing suggested that the nine bodies found were members of the royal family. Two bodies were missing, however. In 2008 the remains of Alexei and either Anastasia or Maria were found about 200 feet from the others. DNA testing has now proved all identities beyond doubt.

In 1998 during a state funeral the nine bodies were interred in the SS Peter & Paul Cathedral in St. Petersburg. Meanwhile, the pit in which the Romanovs were first buried, known as Ganina Yama (situated about ten miles outside Yekaterinburg) is now the site of a monastery with seven wooden churches, each dedicated to a member of the family.

The family, along with some of their servants, were canonized in 1981 in a highly controversial act that made them saints of the Orthodox Church Abroad, whereas inside Russia they were canonized as passion bearers, a status below martyrdom but meaning that they faced their death in a Christian fashion.

The dispute over the Romanovs' political rehabilitation dragged on for several years after Maria Vladimirovna Romanova, who is believed by many (including herself) to be the surviving titular head of the Romanov dynasty, went to court in Moscow over the issue. The General Office of Public Prosecution in Moscow rejected rehabilitation, but in 2008 a high court decision ruled that the Romanovs were indeed victims of political repression ("Red Terror").

Alongside the church is a small chapel dedicated to Alexandra's sister, the Grand Princess Elisabeth Fyodorovna, who was murdered near the Urals town of Alpaevsk and declared a martyr by the Orthodox Church (inside Russia) in 1992.

The building behind the chapel is the Urals Patriarchal Church (Uralskoe Patriarshee Podvorye), the main residence of the patriarch for the region, with its own church. It dates from 2003 and includes exhibitions of Urals icons.

From Voznesenskaya Gorka to the Opera

Across the road from the Church-on-Blood stands the Ascension Church (Voznesenskaya Tserkov), the oldest of the churches surviving in Yekaterinburg, and alongside this gardens attached to the historic Rastorguev-Kharitonov House.

Thomas Witlam Atkinson described this area in the mid-nineteenth century, leaving us with a feel for the former character of the neighbourhood. The first church he mentions is the Ascension Church, and the mansion and gardens he mentions are today known as Rastorguev-Kharitonov House on the hill directly opposite the Church-on-Blood.

> Ekaterineburg is the capital of the Oural, and on entering the town from the north a church and some large mansions are seen on a high hill to the left overlooking the lake, a beautiful sheet of water, which extends several versts in a westerly direction, until hid behind the woods of Issetzskoi. One of these mansions, built by a very rich man who accumulated his immense wealth from gold mines, is of enormous dimensions, and from its elevated situation has a most imposing effect, commanding views of the Oural far to the north and west, until lost in distant haze. The Zavod of Verkne Issetzskoi [the factories located around Historical Square], with its churches and public buildings, stands

out beautifully in the centre of the view, while in the foreground and beneath is the lake, with several public and private edifices on its shores. The gardens belonging to this mansion, with the green-houses and hot-houses, are extensive and well laid out: they are open to the public in summer, and form a pleasant promenade. Formerly there was a splendid and choice collection of plants in the green-houses, but for many years past they have been neglected.

Because of the walled bluff and traffic it is necessary to walk back a short distance along ulitsa Karla Libknekhta in order to reach the area known as Voznesenskaya Gorka. The bluff was where Yekaterinburg's military commander once resided, offering a view of his town. By the late eighteenth century the ruins of this house were cleared to make way for the baroque-inspired Ascension Church, whose main body was finished in 1818; work on it continued until the turn of the twentieth century. During the Soviet period the Ascension Church housed various museums before reverting to use as a church in 1991. It is being restored.

Alongside the church are the gardens, probably those mentioned by Atkinson, and a mansion dating from the 1790s. The neoclassical mansion and gardens take their name from the owners, the related Rastorguev and Kharitonov merchant families. Both were Old Believers and are rumoured to have created a network of underground tunnels beneath the park and mansion in order to hide their gold and to flee should they ever be persecuted. The park itself (Kharitonovsky Sad) dates from the 1820s and has an attractive artificial lake and small gazebo.

From the rear of the church or gardens, walking east one block and turning right (south) into ulitsa Lunacharskovo and continuing to the corner of ulitsa Pervomayskaya, you find the War History Museum (Voenno-Istorichesky Muzey) at ulitsa Pervomayskaya 27. This is difficult to miss because of the tanks and rocket launchers parked outside. The museum has photographs of the spy plane flown by US pilot Francis Gary Powers (1929-77) that was shot down over the Urals in May 1960, triggering a crisis in relations between the Soviet Union and the United States during the Cold War. Here, too, is a small surviving scrap of Powers' U2 spy plane.

At the time, Powers was on a mission for the CIA and flew a high-altitude aircraft built by Lockheed. After taking off from a base at Peshawar in Pakistan at 6.26 a.m. on 1 May 1960, he flew into Soviet airspace and over Siberia to the Urals, where the Russian military launched a surface-to-air missile that struck its target. Powers managed to parachute safely from the plane but fell into Soviet hands, and although his aircraft had a destructor unit, Powers had apparently been unable to activate it in time. For Nikita Khrushchev, the US misadventure had a positive side, allowing him to cement his power by bringing some new and friendlier faces into his Politburo, but by not taking a harder line (which would have sunk his policy of peaceful co-existence) he was also seen by some as being too soft. Powers, sitting in a Russian cell for several months, was put on trial in August 1960 for photographing secret military installations and taping Soviet radar signals while crossing Siberia; he was sentenced to ten years imprisonment. In February 1962 the Soviet Union pardoned Powers after the pilot's parents petitioned the Soviet government, and he was exchanged for a Soviet spy held captive by the Americans.

From here this walk continues south to prospekt Lenina, the wide, tree-lined boulevard from where you can walk west (turn right) to the monumental Opera Theatre (Operny Theatr) at prospekt Lenina 46a. The theatre is home to opera and ballet and is the work of the St. Petersburg architect V. H. Semenov, who started work after winning a national competition. It opened in 1912 and was renovated and embellished in the 1980s with some luxurious touches such as chandeliers.

Across from the theatre, perched on a stone and addressing the dense traffic that today is a feature of urban life in Yekaterinburg, is the man who gave the city its name after the Soviet government changed it in the 1920s—the leading Bolshevik Yakov Sverdlov. He was once tipped to be Lenin's successor. Today only the region—Sverdlovk Oblast—bears his name.

While Yekaterinburg is the administrative centre of the Urals Federal District which, along with the Far East and Siberia federal districts, is one of three on the Siberian subcontinent, Siberia proper begins down the road towards the first city founded after the Yermak campaign: Siberia's "Dallas", the oil metropolis of Tyumen.

Chapter Three
TYUMEN: DALLAS IN SIBERIA

"Siberia is a cold and long country. I drive on and on and see no end to it. I see little that is new or of interest, but I feel and experience a great deal. I have contended with flooded rivers, with cold, with impassable mud, hunger and sleepiness: such sensations as you could not get for a million in Moscow! You ought to come to Siberia. Ask the authorities to exile you."

Anton Chekhov, 1890, writing to his brother Alexander

The conductress on the trolley bus was hard to spot at first, but I eventually found her, disguised in a black mesh blouse and violet-coloured plastic sandals. She took my money and promised to tell me when I reached my stop, one of the large hotels dating from the Soviet era; it loomed grimly above a busy boulevard, close to the business heart of the capital of resource-rich Tyumen Region. She was not the only well-camouflaged conductress on public transport in Tyumen. Another I later saw was wearing a fake leopard-skin polyester top and tight black trousers, and if not for the telltale black purse slung around her waist, I probably would not have noticed her either at first glance.

I was finding Tyumen an unusual town. It is the kind of place where the extravagant, the unusual and the mundane seemed to find roles in the same play. Later that day I also caught sight of a woman walking past a bus stop with mud-splattered high, leather boots and miniskirt. No one else seemed to pay much attention to her as she picked her way around the large puddles that had formed on the pavement after an afternoon shower, and she probably would not even have stood out at all if not for her mud-splattered boots and one unusual detail: she carried a kitchen sink under one arm.

The women with the kitchen sink on one of Tyumen's busiest streets struck me as a surreal vision in this town of almost 600,000 inhabitants. Much about Siberia, however, can suddenly appear surreal, even in a moment of boredom waiting for a bus. In this sense, Chekhov was right—it can be boredom infused with intense experiences.

Siberia is notorious for the cold Chekhov writes about to his brother, but few people talk about its heat. The sticky mid-summer blaze can be dizzying at times; it is compounded by the fumes of traffic in cities, by the ever-present white noise of Siberian radio blaring hits from the *marshrutki*—collective line taxis—or kiosk loud speakers, and by the kaleidoscope of billboards along the streets. Mobile phones; white goods; real estate; building marts; more building marts—Siberians are urged to consume. There are wide boulevards and uneven pavements, high heels and tight t-shirts that swell around large male biceps, dogs trotting along the pavement in pairs or gangs of three. Distance unfolds or stands still in a Siberian traffic jam that would do London proud. And then a woman with a sink walks by.

Tyumen is situated on the banks of the Tura river, a minor artery in Siberian terms, but significant in historical terms as an early transport link between Verkhoturye, the oldest settlement on the eastern flank of the Urals, and the Tobol river, into which the Tura flows about forty miles to the east. Several hundred miles north of this confluence as the crow flies, the Tobol reaches the town of Tobolsk and merges with the Irtysh; this river in turn joins the Ob near Khanty-Mansiysk, and empties into the Kara Sea. Appearances, therefore, are deceptive: an inconspicuous Tyumen river at the foot of high banks of crumbling sand provides a historic link with a great river to the north and beyond that with the ocean.

This is the oldest town in Siberia and thanks to the oil, gas and mineral resources in the region's far north (most of these in two autonomous regions) it is also one of Siberia's most prosperous and dynamic.

There were many early signs of the vast quantities of resources lying in the north of Tyumen Region. A Croatian theologian and writer by the name of Juraj Križanić (1618-83), banished to Siberia presumably for his activities as a Catholic missionary, is said to have noted the presence of bituminous shale in the Ob river basin, and one member of Daniel Gottlieb Messerschmidt's expedition into Siberia in the 1720s also remarked on combustible bitumen on his travels. Exploration began in earnest in the 1930s but it was not until the late 1950s and early 1960s that the oil and gas reserves were exploited on a large scale. By the late 1960s Tyumen, a provincial town with a strong merchant tradition and many villages in its midst, was catapulted into the centre of development of Siberia's far north fossil fuel reserves. From that time on it became the administrative capital for Russia's energy and oil export needs, and home to large state-owned re-

Tyumen oilfield

source companies. In the early 1960s the Tyumen State Oil and Gas University was established, and today this funnels its expertise into large gas or oil conglomerates such as Gazprom and Rosneft.

The year 1965 was an important one for the region. Although many new oil-field discoveries had already been made in the north, it was the Samotlor field that marked the turning point. This was the largest discovery in the Soviet Union and one of the world's ten largest deposits of oil. It turned the small outpost of Nizhnevartovsk, situated on the Ob east of Surgut, into a bustling oil centre.

One of the most serious problems faced by Soviet developers was not the harsh climate—though this did not make exploitation easier—nor the geological nature of the oil deposits (most reservoirs of oil here are not deep), but the shortage of workers in remote regions. Initially they were flown up to camps and spent several weeks there on exhausting shifts, but between the 1960s and the 1980s a number of "company" towns were established to complement historic ones like Berezovo (the first place where commercial quantities of oil were extracted), Surgut, Khanty-Mansiysk and Salekhard (Obdorsk), all founded centuries earlier during the Russian annexation. Some of the new towns, like Nefteyugansk, had a "neft" (oil) prefix in their name, while the purpose of others like Noyabrsk or Urengoy could only be guessed at by their location deep in the remote *taiga*. Most are located not in Tyumen Region proper but in the Khanty-Mansiysk Autonomous Region-Yugra.

The growth of towns in the north was strongest in the 1980s, and workers of all backgrounds and parts of the Soviet Union were lured to them by high wages and the possibility of quick promotion. It was oil that bankrolled the Soviet Union in the 1970s, and it was oil that both provided the foreign reserves and hid the problems of the Soviet economy during its latter years. When oil prices began to fall in the 1980s, this had a destabilizing effect on the USSR and hastened its collapse. Today, the Russian state budget is drip-fed by the region's oil, and one of the greatest challenges of post-Soviet Russia has been to balance out its economic dependence on Siberia's resources.

Environmental damage caused by development was the dark side of the boom during the Soviet era, and although companies operating in the region today present themselves as good corporate citizens, the region to the north is obviously sensitive to any kind of development. This is especially the case in the far northern Yamal-Nenets Autonomous District around Salekhard, which in addition to the Khanty-Mansiysk-Yugra Autonomous District, comprises a semi-independent region in Tyumen Region and is nominally based around its indigenous population. The Yamal-Nenets Autonomous District is predicted to experience the largest growth in oil and gas production over the next decade. Tyumen itself is expected to double in size from its present 600,000 inhabitants by 2030, largely due to people moving to the capital from the surrounding villages—a fact of life for most Siberian provincial capitals these days and one reason why villages in Siberia are dying out at an alarming rate—but also due to migration from outside the region.

From Fortress to Metropolis

Tyumen was founded in 1586 as a fortress, five years after the Cossack Yermak took the Tartar town of Chimgi-Tura, situated on the banks of the Tura. The two men responsible for its foundation were the military governors (*voevody*) Vassily Sukin and Ivan Myasnoy, who were among a series of governors sent to Siberia by Moscow to secure Yermak's conquests.

Jeremiah Curtin (1835-1906), a diplomat, folklorist and traveller who spent several years in Russia in the 1860s attached to the American legation and at one point as consul-general for the US in Russia, gives a good account of these early days of colonization. Curtin was a gifted linguist, and it is said he learned the Buryat language to a high level of competence in just a few weeks (by his own admission he had already learned Latin and Greek in just seven months in order to enter Harvard College). He collected folk tales on his travels, and in his *A Journey in Southern Siberia*, dating from 1909, he explains that after Yermak's death Siberia lapsed back into the hands of the Tartar rulers and "was lost to Russia for a season. In Moscow no one knew what had happened in far-off Siberia."

Realizing the hopelessness of the situation, Curtin remarks, the 150 soldiers remaining from Yermak's group and those others who had arrived later with a government official by the name of Prince Bolkhovsky fled by boat and crossed the Urals back into European Russia. In 1585 Tsar Fyodor I (1557-98), the son of Ivan the Terrible, sent another official to replace Bolkhovsky, a man by the name of Ivan Mansurov who established a winter stockade (it was too late in the season to return to Moscow) at the confluence of the Irtysh and the Ob rivers near the present-day town of Khanty-Mansiysk. The Siberia he found was a cold place entirely devoid of Russians. He and his party of Cossacks managed to repulse attacks by the Khanty who lived there, and at the first opportunity Mansurov also set off west back over the Urals. Tsar Fyodor, having heard of this development, dispatched the two commanders to re-establish a Russian presence. "In July of that year, 1586," says Curtin, "Sukin founded Tiumen on the Tura, and, not venturing to move farther on toward Sibir [the Tartar capital, near Tobolsk], he extended Moscow rule over tribes in the region around him. He was not too far from the Urals, hence safe. The position was good, geographically."

According to Curtin, Tobolsk was established in early 1587 when a contingent of 500 men was dispatched from Moscow to Sukin and Myasnoy in order to found a second city, which they did near the mouth of the Tobol. Construction of the *krepost* (fortress) in Tyumen began in late July 1586 on a stretch of the Tura where the smaller Tyumenka flows into it. The site of the fortress is today part of several interconnecting squares near Historical Square (Istorichesky Skver).

In its earliest days the fortress was a rudimentary wooden construction with a small church and a few administrative buildings enclosed by log ramparts, but gradually it outgrew its ramparts and by the turn of the seventeenth century the population of Tyumen had risen to almost 2,000. In 1616 its first monastery was founded. Almost a century later, in 1715, this institution was reconstructed in stone and renamed the Holy Trinity Monastery (Svyatoy Troytsky Monastir).

Around the same time as the monastery was founded numerous other buildings rose up in the vicinity of the Tura, including warehouses that served as the local treasury. The town grew quickly, largely thanks to the merchants who lived and traded there.

As in Tobolsk, Tyumen's merchant tradition goes back to a time before the arrival of Russians. The Khanate of Sibir was a culturally rich feudal state, and because of the Bukharan traders it had access to goods traded along the Silk Road to the south. It was the Bukharans, too, who provided the religious education for the khans of the Siberian Tartars, although the population itself remained largely pre-Islamic or practised an interwoven form of Islam and shamanism that to a certain extent survives today. Trade, therefore, was important to the growth of Tyumen from its earliest days, and in the late sixteenth century tax concessions were ordered by the tsar for the Bukharan traders and a settlement was established for them across the river from the fortress. This is still the Tartar quarter of town today.

As well as its trade links, Tyumen had the advantage of being on the road leading into Siberia. Indeed, it likes to call itself the "gateway to Siberia", and for good reason: the Sibirsky Trakt entered town at the foot of the Holy Trinity Monastery and all travellers, settlers, exiles and goods crossing the Urals into Siberia passed through here. This traffic included peasants who, having been freed from bonded labour by the reforms of Alexander II, would try their luck in Siberia from the mid-nineteenth century.

By the 1890s Tyumen had undergone large-scale industrialization and was an important centre for food processing (for several decades before the First World War much of the butter served at the tables of Britain and several other western European countries was produced by Danish butter manufacturers in western Siberia). Other important industries were timber, animal hide processing, glassmaking and shipbuilding. It is said that of the almost 200 steam ships that plied the Ob-Irtysh river system in the early twentieth century about two-thirds were built in Tyumen shipyards. Although Tyumen was located some distance from these two great rivers of western Siberia, it became instrumental in the growth of inland shipping on such waterways. The wealth of its merchants spilled over into the cultural life of the town, and Tyumen's first professional theatre was founded in the 1890s.

Like Tobolsk, Tyumen played a minor role in the tragic final drama that culminated in the execution of Nicholas II and his family. The royal entourage arrived here by train in August 1917 and was transferred to a ship, the *Rus*, which sailed down the Tura and Tobol rivers to Tobolsk. In 1918 the tsar and his family returned, this time as the family, travelling separately due to Alexei's illness, edged towards its fate in Yekaterinburg.

In March 1918 the city—for almost two decades now a strategic point on the Trans-Siberian Railway line and a convenient springboard into the north—fell to the Bolsheviks. Fierce battles took place in and around the city during the civil war between Bolsheviks and White forces. As in Yekaterinburg, a Czech-Slovak Legion of First World War prisoners was involved in fighting, having become caught up in the turmoil and deciding to fight their way home across Siberia on the side of Admiral Kolchak and his counter-revolutionary forces. Tyumen was finally won back by the Bolsheviks in August 1919.

During the Second World War the population of Tyumen swelled due to the flow of refugees from other parts of Russia and its role as a centre for prisoners of war. Here, as in many other Siberian towns, local industry received a boost from the transfer of strategic industries from central Russia and the Ukraine, with some 22 large factories resettled to maintain the production of vital goods during the war. But it was another piece of valuable freight, Lenin's conserved body, that arouses more curiosity. In an unusual move in July 1941 Soviet authorities placed the embalmed revolutionary on a special train and dispatched him from his mausoleum on Moscow's Red Square to the local agricultural college in Tyumen, where he was safely stored and guarded until March 1945, when he was loaded on a train again and sent back to Red Square.

In August 1944 a new Tyumen Region was carved out of parts of Omsk Region, and Tyumen became the capital of its own region, sealing its fate as Russia's "Dallas" when a resources boom got underway.

Today the standard of living in Tyumen is said to be second only to Moscow (and comparable with Poland or Hungary), and in some ways it does have the feel of a down-sized capital. At the same time, it retains the typical architectural characteristics of a Siberian metropolis. Here you find shimmering high-rise buildings stamped out of the earth since the collapse of the Soviet Union; grey fringe areas and Soviet-era *mikrorayony* (suburban regions) with their lines of drab concrete housing estates; timber houses, which are mostly situated around the waterfront just along from Historical Square; historic merchant houses; and a heavy sprinkling of Soviet-era administrative buildings with monumental intent.

Modern travel writing or guidebooks usually portray Tyumen as a grey, somewhat unprepossessing and sprawling city. Of these descriptions the latter probably best characterizes it. It is certainly not an easy place to walk around, and a bicycle or driver can come in useful; to really explore the city properly, a walk will have to be divided over a couple of days.

HOLY TRINITY MONASTERY: MISSIONARIES AND INDIGENOUS COLONIZATION

One place to begin exploring Tyumen is at the Holy Trinity Monastery (Svyato-Troytsky Monastir), located on an inauspicious section of ulitsa Kommunisticheskaya. The complex was founded in 1616 by the monk Nifont and originally contained a Transfiguration Monastery (Preobrazhensky Monastir), which, like all buildings in the monastery complex before the eighteenth century, was constructed of wood. Building in stone began under the metropolitan Filofey Leshchinsky (1650-1727).

The early eighteenth century marked a time when the Orthodox Church vigorously sought to convert the indigenous peoples. The man entrusted by Peter the Great to do this was the Ukrainian-born Leshchinsky. Having already been forced to pay *yasak* (tribute) to the tsar and thus far in their history having avoided being drawn deeply into the Islamic faith of the khanate, Khanty and Mansi were now being coerced into converting to the Orthodox faith.

Armed with decrees from the tsar, Leshchinsky's churchmen fanned out over western Siberia in the early 1700s and set about reinforcing the religious basis of their colony. In many instances those who resisted were threatened with death. According to James Forsyth's *A History of the Peoples of Siberia*, officials tracked down heathen idols and burned Khanty and Mansi sacred structures. Faced with the prospect of religious subjugation, Khanty and Mansi carried their figures of worship to safety deep in the taiga and in some cases simply migrated to new grounds, where the Khanty, for instance, mingled with Selkup and Tartar populations.

This phase was one of several transformations that occurred in the religious colonization of Siberia. These are described in interesting detail by historian Yuri Slezkine in a chapter of the book *Between Heaven and Hell*. It is a complex process, but Slezkine distils some key attitudes.

Paradoxically to modern eyes, when the Church first arrived in Siberia it found indigenes whom, because they were not Orthodox, it saw as "foreigners". But converting indigenes to Orthodoxy brought a problem: once converted, a male indigene was no longer obliged to pay tribute. Because only adult males were required to pay tribute, the result was that most of the earliest indigenes converted were women. This in turn helped provide wives and sexual partners for the Cossacks and early settlers in a Siberia that suffered from a chronic shortage of Russian women.

When Filofey Leshchinsky arrived in Tyumen in the early eighteenth century he spearheaded the new approach in which being Russian was defined by the borders of the nation and not by having converted to Orthodoxy. The result was that the tsar's men could convert a native without this person being freed of an obligation to pay tribute. As Slezkine explains, "the citizen of a great power could no longer be a pagan... Russians were to become Europeans, the native Siberians had to become Russians." The idea of the age, therefore, was that if the "pagans" were Russian in one sense because they lived within the borders of the Russian Empire, but their being pagans cast doubt upon this fledgling European empire, then Russia needed to convert its pagans. As well as promoting conversions of the type using Leshchinsky as his extended arm, Peter the Great abolished the position of patriarch—the head of the Orthodox Church— in 1721 and replaced it with a synod overseen by a state official.

In the late eighteenth century a new attitude arose when the state stopped supporting missionary work altogether in Siberia. This brought a lull in activities and left Siberia with populations of Orthodox natives who paid tribute, and a Church that had fallen into disrepute. With the arrival of German-taught missionaries, however, definitions assumed more of an economic character. In the early nineteenth century indigenes were considered foreign and culturally inferior if they were engaged in "savage" kinds of economic lifestyles: reindeer herding, for instance, was labelled "backward". Tribute could also be demanded of such people, and as

Slezkine observes, the notion of progress (becoming Russian) was based on a rather vague idea of adopting agriculture and being Christianized.

In the late nineteenth century missionary activities were stepped up and a new phase was ushered in: missionaries, long seen in Siberia as drunks and good-for-nothings, diligently began learning native languages, establishing schools and converting indigenes in their native tongue. The reason was not entirely altruistic, as an important factor behind this new bout of missionary activity was a perceived Muslim threat. But converting Siberia's entire native population was an enormous or even impossible task, so efforts centred mainly on Muslim populations and more politically significant groups like Buryats, who were shamanists and Buddhists. The smaller groups were often ignored. Nevertheless, efforts at conversion are said to have been by and large of very limited success.

The last stage before the revolution of 1917 was one characterized by what Slezkine calls "abomination". Everyone was equal in God's eyes, the thinking went, but what was to be done with an indigene who bought and sold his wife, herded reindeer and believed in shaman spirits or idols? Such a dilemma posed ethical problems for the Church. At the same time, indigenes had developed a fondness for Christian symbols such as crosses and icons, which—to the horror of the Church—they liked to integrate into shaman rituals. During this phase of Siberia's religious colonization, atheistic Bolsheviks seized power.

Although the Soviet system officially propagated atheism, the Second World War brought a more ambivalent attitude than earlier policies that saw Stalin's men tearing down Russia's churches. This ambivalence is generally seen as being rooted in Stalin's need to encourage loyalty to a Russia at war. A new patriarch was elected, after the position had been reintroduced on the eve of the Bolshevik revolution and abolished again in 1925. It is from this position of ambiguity between patriarch and State—involving at times the persecution of religious figures by the State, but also said to involve a certain amount of cooperation by patriarchs—that post-Soviet Russia later picked up the pieces.

Back in early eighteenth-century Tyumen a process of replacing wooden churches with new ones of stone began under Leshchinsky. His opus magnum in Tyumen was the Holy Trinity Monastery complex consisting of three stone churches with bell towers within a compound, completed largely by Ukrainian craftsmen, some brought in from Tobolsk. The

Holy Trinity Monastery Tyumen

complex includes one of the earliest surviving stone churches in Siberia, but not the first to be built, as an Annunciation Church (Blagoveshchensky Sobor) was erected in 1704 across the Tura. It was razed, however, in the 1930s.

The first church in the monastery complex was the Cathedral of the Holy Trinity, finished in 1715. It was crowned by three large cupolas and two smaller ones, reminiscent of the Ukrainian style of the day, and decorated with icons—now lost—by Kiev artists. In the 1850s the walls of the church were adorned with frescoes depicting Biblical scenes.

The second church in the ensemble was the Church of the Forty Martyrs (Tserkov Soroka Muchenikov) from 1717, which had a tower alongside it where Leshchinsky resided for much of the time between 1711 and his death in 1727. This church was demolished when flood protection work was carried out in 1945. The third church is the Peter & Paul Church (Tserkov Petra i Pavla), which rose up along the southern boundary of the monastery from 1726. This is believed to have been based on the design of the Georgevsky Church (part of the Vydubetsky Monastery complex) in Kiev. A 130-foot bell tower was added in 1741, and the buildings themselves were finished in 1755. From 1760 work got underway again, this time on uniting the two separate buildings of the Peter & Paul Church. This brought a new architectural dimension, with hints of a turreted Russian country-mansion style. When fire raged through Tyumen in 1842 much of the church was destroyed, but restoration began about a decade later, giving us the church's current appearance.

From 1924 the Peter & Paul Church deteriorated into a disused, crumbling relic on a patch of wasteland, but in the 1980s it was decided to restore and recreate the building as a museum. Not surprisingly, much of the exhibition space was devoted to a Soviet-skewed history of Christianity in Siberia. There was a section on the church building itself, and another section with exhibits that included manuscripts and rare books, gold embroidery dating from the seventeenth to the nineteenth century, and Siberian icons from the early seventeenth. Some of these exhibits will probably wind up in a new museum complex taking shape at ulitsa Sovietskaya 63, near ulitsa Ordzhonikidze.

The Holy Trinity Monastery is closely connected to the fate of the German naturalist Georg Wilhelm Steller (1709-46), who participated in the Second Kamchatka Expedition led by the Danish Commander Vitus

Bering in 1733-43. This expedition was an ambitious undertaking that saw parts of the northern and the north-east coastlines of Russia mapped, the discovery of Alaska by the Russians and the first concerted effort to gather detailed scientific knowledge about Siberia. Steller was sailing with Bering when his ship, the *Svyatoy Pyotr*, was shipwrecked off Bering Island and Bering fell ill in what became a horrific struggle to survive the winter. Steller cared for Bering and buried him after the commander died. Only about half of the original crew of seventy on board the *Svyatoy Pyotr* survived the winter. In one graphic passage of his journal, published in *Journal of a Voyage with Bering 1741-1742*, Steller writes:

> Even before they could be buried, the dead were mutilated by foxes that sniffed at, and even dared to attack the sick—still alive and helpless— who were lying on the beach everywhere without cover under the open sky. One screamed because he was cold, another from hunger and thirst, as the mouths of many were in such a wretched state from scurvy that they could not eat anything on account of the great pain because the gums were swollen up like a sponge, brown-black and grown high over the teeth and covering them.

In a bitter twist of fate, Steller himself fell ill while returning overland from the expedition in 1746 and died of fever in Tyumen. A Protestant and German by birth from Franconia, he was unable to be buried inside the grounds of the Russian Orthodox monastery and instead was laid to rest on an unstable patch of ground between the monastery and the Tura river. A tomb was erected, which survived for several decades and was visited in 1776 by the German geographer and naturalist Peter Simon Pallas. Some time afterwards, however, the river bank—and along with it the tomb—was washed away in a flood, so that today nothing remains of Steller's grave. Thanks to Pallas, we do know that it was situated directly in front of the Holy Trinity Church.

TOWARDS HISTORICAL SQUARE AND CENTRAL SQUARE

South of the monastery on the corner of ulitsa Lunacharskovo, where it meets the traffic-congested ulitsa Kommunisticheskaya just before Historical Square, is the Architecture & Civil Engineering Academy (Arkhitekturno-Stroitelnaya Akademiya), a good example of Russian neoclassical revivalism. Work began on the building in 1908 based on a design by Moscow-born architect and engineer Ivan Rerberg (1869-1932). Rerberg is better known for his contribution to the design of the Pushkin Museum building and what is now the TsuM department store, both in Moscow. He was assisted on this project by V. K. Oltorzhevsky, and once it was finished the academy won a gold medal as best design for an educational building at the World Exhibition in Paris in 1913.

In front of the academy is the Church of the Exultation of the Cross (Krestovozdvizhenskaya Tserkov; Nikolskaya) at ulitsa Lunacharskovo 1, built from 1774 and consecrated in 1791. Its lavish interior decorative features were removed during nineteenth-century restoration. Its demise was temporarily sealed when during the Soviet era crosses were removed and the entire church was turned into a social club; in the 1990s it was restored and re-consecrated, replete with a new seminary building.

Further south, you arrive at a series of adjoining squares, beginning with a small paved area and a stone that marks the foundation of Tyumen. Although nothing can be seen of the original fortress on this elevated rise of land between the Tyumenka river and the Tura, it was here that the military governors Vassily Sukin and Ivan Myasnoy laid the foundations of the new town. Directly to the west (left, facing the monastery) was the site of the Tartar town of Chimgi-Tura. The foundation memorial stone has a plaque inscribed with the simple words: "On this site on June 25, 1586 the city of Tyumen was founded." The square itself is planted with flowers in summer and beyond the foundation stone are views north to the academy and the golden cupolas of the Cathedral of the Holy Trinity.

Next up is the paved area with an obelisk (Obelisk of Victory) and eternal flame dedicated to fallen Soviet soldiers of the Second World War and south of here Historical Square itself and a small cross surrounded by a few granite rocks that form a memorial to Yermak. The site is otherwise unmarked and rarely appears on maps, possibly due to a lingering ambivalence among local Tartars, for whom Yermak's victories also signify defeat.

Across the road from Historical Square, at ulitsa Lenina 2, is the "City Duma" Museum (Muzey "Gorodskaya Duma"), with steps leading up to neoclassical Corinthian columns. The building dates from the early nineteenth century when it served as the city chambers. The museum is part of the handful comprising the Tyumen Region Local Studies Museum (Tyumen Oblastnoy Kraevedchesky Muzey) and focuses on the flora and fauna of the region. Museums in Tyumen are in a state of flux and plans are to house exhibits on the history of Tyumen city here and the nature collection in a new museum complex at ulitsa Sovietskaya 63. As well as the permanent collection inside the City Duma Museum, regular rotating exhibitions are held in two rooms.

The museum is part of the handful comprising the Tyumen Region Local Studies Museum (Tyumen Oblastnoy Kraevedchesky Muzey) and focuses on the flora and fauna of the region. As well as the permanent collection, regular rotating exhibitions are held in two rooms of the museum.

From here, most of the city's sights are situated on or just off ulitsa Respubliki, a rather clogged and noisy artery that runs through the heart of Tyumen and eventually leaves it to become the Old Tobolsk Trakt. The Sibirsky Trakt ran along the entire length of what today is ulitsa Respubliki. Before acquiring its Soviet name in 1917 it was called ulitsa Tsarskaya (Tsar Street) in honour of Alexander II (1818-81), who visited in 1837 prior to being crowned in 1855.

Directly opposite the museum and Historical Square is a modern pedestrian suspension bridge (Lovers' Bridge) connecting the Tartar lower town on the other side of the Tura with the business centre of Tyumen. Though the design is interesting in itself, the bridge is unusual for the tremendous number of locks attached to it by newly-wed couples—as elsewhere in Russia, this symbolizes eternal wedlock. The crumbling church seen across the bridge is the Ascension Church (Voznesenskaya Tserkov), consecrated in 1789 and for many years Tyumen's largest church. Today it is undergoing a long process of restoration, having also operated as a place where the town's curriers met and did deals. While this may at first seem odd for a church, it was entirely in keeping with its history. From its earliest days, local leather-makers funded the church, which was located in the Bukharan settlement, and the neighbourhood around the church is also where the Bukharan traders resided.

Further south along ulitsa Respubliki is the Tyumen State Agricultural Academy (Tyumenskaya Gosudarstvennaya Selskokhozyaystvennaya Akademiya) at no. 7, dating from 1879. Originally a vocational college, it was converted into an agricultural college in the 1920s and later enjoyed some fame as the place where Lenin's body was stored during the Second World War. The building itself is in Renaissance style and doubled as an attractive palace for the most famous deceased revolutionary in the Soviet pantheon. Lenin received the full treatment that he was accustomed to in Moscow, including his own guard of honour.

Outside the building is a bust of the Soviet spy and partisan Nikolay Kuznetsov (1911-44), who studied here for one year in the mid-1920s before moving to Moscow in 1938 and joining the Soviet secret service. Kuznetsov is known for his role as a partisan in the Ukraine and for plots to assassinate and kidnap Nazi officials during the Second World War. He died in fighting in the Ukraine when, incognito and in a tragic case of mistaken identity (he was wearing a German army uniform), his own people took him for a German and shot him.

Across the road from the Agricultural Academy is a building complex that is part of the Tyumen Region Local Studies Museum. Tyumen's regional museum was founded in 1879 and was housed in part of the Agricultural Academy building until 1922.

The building at ulitsa Respubliki 18 is today one of two forming the Museum Estate Kolokolnikovykh (Muzey-Usadba Kolokolnikovykh), named after the family that owned the building in the 1880s. This is known as The House of Ikonnikova (Dom Ikonnikova), dates from 1804 and was built by the Ikonnikov merchant family. Here are elements of neoclassicism, rococo and baroque, complemented by traditional Tyumen wood carving. In 1837 it rose to fame as the place where Alexander II stayed while visiting Tyumen. So, too, did the poet Vasily Zhukovsky (1783-1852), who is credited with ushering in the Romantic age of poetry in Russia. The house landed in the hands of the merchant I. P. Kolokolnikov, who later set up a committee here during the civil war, and it was here, too, that Bolshevik commander, Vasily Konstantinovich Blyukher (1889-1938), had his office in 1919. Today the exhibits have been revamped and the building houses the Museum of the History of the Household in the Nineteenth and Twentieth Centuries (Muzey Istorii Doma XIX-XX Veka). Excursions tell about the 200-year history of the building, focusing on the two merchant families who owned it and those who have used it. I. P. Kolokolnikov (1830-95) achieved fame for a monopoly on wholesale tea traded at Russia's largest fair, held in Irbit (in Sverdlovsk Region). The family poured some of the resulting wealth into restoring the building, giving it the appearance of a down-sized palace and adding decorative touches on and inside the building. The museum collection consists of displays of household objects and applied art.

The second building (ulitsa Respubliki 20) in the museum complex dates from the turn of the twentieth century and focuses on the merchant tradition of Tyumen.

One block west along ulitsa Turgeneva, at ulitsa Lenina 24, is the Museum "House Masharov" (Muzey "Dom Masharova"), located inside a late nineteenth-century mansion once belonging to the local manufacturer Nikolay Masharov (1865-1922). Masharov was the owner of a foundry that produced household goods and manufacturing tools, bringing to Tyumen a number of masters who were famous in the Urals for their Kaslinsk cast-iron techniques. The house has been restored, furnished and filled with exhibits to create a feel for merchant life at the time.

Back on ulitsa Respubliki, across the street from the Regional Museum (alongside the Agricultural Academy), stands the Memorial to the Revolutionary Fighters (Pamyatnik Bortsam Revolutsii) on a square now of the same name. During the early days of the civil war the Bolsheviks buried their dead here in mass graves, only to find the bodies dug up and transported out of town by the White forces when the latter gained control in July 1918. In a rather macabre act of revenge, the Red Army did the same, digging up the buried dead of the White forces when they returned to power in August 1919. The site was eventually marked by an obelisk and then later, on the fiftieth anniversary of the October Revolution of 1917, the statue one sees today.

Alongside the square, at ulitsa Semakova 10, is the main university building, and across the road Tyumen's prettiest piece of religious architecture, the Cathedral of the Holy Sign (Znamensky Kafedralny Sobor). This colourful Siberian baroque cathedral was built on the site of an earlier wooden church dating from 1624 but destroyed by fires in 1697 and 1766. Two years after the second fire, work began on the current cathedral, the first stage of which was completed in 1786, complete with its five cupolas and an iconostasis—traditionally the wall of icons and religious paintings that separates the nave from the sanctuary around the altar—created by the Tobolsk coachman Fyodor Cherepanov. No sooner was it "completed" than rebuilding began and continued over subsequent centuries, with new side-altars added and others removed, which explains the cathedral's rambling, jumbled appearance today.

Situated some distance from the other sights, the Tyumen Museum of Fine Arts (Tyumensky Muzey Izobrazitelnykh Iskusstv, at ulitsa Ordzhonikidzhe 47, was established in 1957 and is the city's fine arts gallery, with a collection of about 10,000 works that include painting, graphics, sculpture and the decorative arts, as well as the works of Russia's old masters and contemporary talent. Western European artists also get a showing here, as do traditional folk arts from the north of the region. A section of this museum is also dedicated to Russian gravure, which established itself in the seventeenth and eighteenth centuries as a form of early book printing. At the invitation of Peter the Great, numerous foreign experts brought foreign methods of printing to Russia, including woodcut techniques and metal engraving. Moris Bakua (1680-1747) is one such person who figures in the museum.

Among the Tyumen Region artists featured in the museum the best-known is perhaps Semyon Remezov (1642-c. 1720), often called the first portrait artist of Tyumen and better known for his cartographical works and for his greatest legacy to the region, Tobolsk's kremlin. Another is Ivan Kalganov (1845-82), who is often referred to as the "Russian Hogarth". He came from the town of Turinsk and after attracting the attention of one of the local merchants moved to Tyumen, where he became one of Russia's finest portrait artists, especially in his depiction of grotesque figures. He moved to Moscow, soon immersed himself in the vices of the capital (particularly a predilection for alcohol) and returned to Tyumen, where he died. The third in the triumvirate of local greats is the painter, graphic artist and photographer Vasily Federov (1857-1924), whose best work is considered to be on the themes of nature and peasant life.

Two other museums are situated further away from the centre. The Museum of Geology, Oil and Gas (Muzey Geology, Nefti i Gaza), ulitsa Respubliki 142, covers the opening up of the region's resources for development. Situated some fifteen miles out of town on the road to Yalutorovsk, the Archaeological Museum Reserve (Arkheologichesky Muzey-Zapovednik) is an unusual and attractive site where visitors learn more about finds in the region. It is located on Andreevskoe Lake, part of a system of lakes where the locals of Tyumen swim, sail, or picnic among the pines and birches. The founder of the Tyumen Region Local Studies Museum, Ivan Slotsov, began digging here in 1883 and found signs of settlement dating back to 5000 BCE. Cult finds belonging to Mansi indigenes have also resulted in an exhibition on the lifestyle, housing and spiritual life of the indigenes.

RASPUTIN: THE MYSTIC FROM POKROVSKOE

In the other direction, fifty miles along the road to Tobolsk, is the village of Pokrovskoe, which these days has a population of about 2,000 but is famous for one man: Grigory Rasputin (1869-1916).

Pokrovskoe, of course, long predates the mystic, having been founded in the 1640s when a small stockade and church were built, and it was long a staging post for exiles travelling towards Tobolsk, including the writer Fyodor Dostoevsky.

Rasputin was born in Pokrovskoe in 1869 and spent five years as a pilgrim, travelling as far afield as Mount Athos in Greece. Even in his very early years, however, he fell foul of the law; at the age of seventeen, charges were laid against him (unsuccessfully) in Tobolsk for drunkenness, theft and indecent assault. Also while young, he claimed to possess supernatural powers. In 1887, two years before he embarked on his pilgrimages, he married a local farmer's daughter. Three children would be born from the marriage.

In 1903 Rasputin broke out for St. Petersburg to attend a religious celebration and soon word spread about the self-proclaimed *starets* (holy man) and prophet, propelling the lad from Pokrovskoe into the higher echelons of Russian society. At one point he acquired the status of something of a holy man for the ladies of St. Petersburg's better salons, despite the "goat like" smell that supposedly clung to him. His first big break came in October 1906 when Tsar Nicholas II received him in the royal palace. An even bigger one followed when he was summoned to the palace to "treat" the tsarevich Alexei, who suffered from haemophilia, believed to have been passed on by his great-grandmother, Queen Victoria, the first known carrier in the line. Rasputin's presence alone is said to have had a calming or healing affect on the tsarevich.

Rasputin became a frequent visitor to the palace throughout 1907 and was even rumoured to have had a relationship with the tsar's wife, Alexandra. In fact, word about Rasputin's supposed sexual excesses spread like wildfire through high society, prompting instructions in the spring of 1908 to Nicholas' palace commander that he should look into this sordid matter. He in turn sought the help of the tsar's secret police, which delivered confirmation of gross debauchery. With the mood in the palace swinging against him, Rasputin returned to Pokrovskoe in 1908. By 1910, though, he was back in St. Petersburg.

Rasputin with military admirers, c.1905

After his return to the capital Rasputin's notoriety made him a controversial figure in the press and in Russian politics, with claims that he wielded a strong influence on the course of tsarist policies. In 1910 someone unsuccessfully tried to run him over with a car. Less than a year later, he became embroiled in a disagreement about the appointment of a new bishop in Tobolsk, and the Church's favoured man was passed over for a friend of Rasputin: "Barnabus, the ignorant gardener who was made by Rasputin Bishop of Tobolsk," as the *New York Times* remarked in March 1917, not long after the February revolution. The same article explained: "The arrest of the ex-Czar and Czarina causes general satisfaction. The Russians are not vindictive, but there is a flat refusal to have anything more to do with the family that has been the cause of such an immense tragedy to Russia, and a strong demand that they should not be permitted to do any more harm."

Rasputin's credentials were not good in ecclesiastical circles, and the man passed over for the job of bishop, Monch Iliodor, published a letter stolen from Rasputin's home in Pokrovskoe a couple of years earlier that seemed to prove sexual relations between the mystic and Alexandra. When forgeries of the letter, with vivid embellishments, did the rounds of the salons of St. Petersburg, Rasputin was once again obliged to flee the capital.

Again he bounced back. Rasputin was at the tsarevich's side once more in 1913, this time in Yalta in the Crimea, where the royal family had been holidaying when Alexei suffered a fall. The holy man only confirmed suspicion that he was embroiled in politics when he declared himself against involvement of Russia in war brewing on the Balkans. This was the final straw, prompting several new attempts on his life. He survived all of them. In 1914, while in Pokrovskoe, he was stabbed by a former prostitute. As a result, Rasputin was rushed to hospital in Tyumen, where he underwent surgery. Not surprisingly, the attack is said to have made him more disturbed, and afterwards he sought the solace of alcohol and women. This meant prostitutes, and his old trick of telling women the path to redemption was by immersing themselves in sin by having sex with him, and repenting afterwards. It was an inventive line that served him well. The excesses, though, added fuel to a raging political fire. The scandals and decline of the fortunes of the royal family continued until December 1916, when Rasputin was lured into a trap and finally disposed of by several nobles.

Whatever took place that night of 16 December 1916 is still unclear. Rasputin was probably poisoned, he was shot, he was definitely clubbed, and ultimately he was tossed into the Neva river. Yet he apparently survived each attempt to kill him and seems to have died of hypothermia. His emasculated body was hauled from beneath the ice a few days later and buried in Tsarskoe Selo, the tsar's summer palace outside St. Petersburg, from where he was subsequently dug up and disposed of in the local Petersburg woods following the revolution of February 1917 (the first, which saw the creation of a provincial government).

Little remains in Pokrovskoe from Rasputin's time. The house he lived in was demolished in the 1980s. Nevertheless, a Rasputin Museum has sprung up at ulitsa Sovietskaya 79 in one of the town's surviving historic houses, opposite the place where his home once stood. Bizarrely, an extravagant, flaccid object that is purported to be the mystic's penis is today housed in St. Petersburg's Erotic Museum.

Chapter Four

TOBOLSK: FROM "SODOM IN THE TAIGA" TO A CULTURAL HEARTLAND

Almost from its earliest days of colonization, Siberia was burdened with a reputation for debauchery. The view of Siberia as a hotbed of vice goes back to the arrival of the Church in the form of its first archbishop. In 1621, when Cyprian took up his post in Tobolsk, he reported (at the more harmless end of the scale) street fighting and stabbings and scarcely any attempt to bring the culprits to justice. As elsewhere, local officials were brutal and exploitative in their zeal to collect tribute from the indigenes. Few people in Tobolsk observed religious rituals, and Cyprian also complained about couples marrying without involving the Church; religious fasting periods passed unobserved or broken. If that had been all, Archbishop Cyprian could have counted himself lucky. Alas, it wasn't. Men were treating their wives as slaves, he reported, and selling them or lending them out to other men while husbands performed duty in the *taiga*. Incest had become a serious problem. Men, he believed, were marrying anyone who would have them—sisters, illegitimate daughters, even their own mothers. Alcoholism and theft were rampant, as were a myriad of lesser vices the Church liked to keep under control.

The shortage of women in Siberia was a recurring problem during the seventeenth century, and to redress it, about 300 women from north-east European Russia were dispatched across the Urals in the 1630s to marry Cossacks, who had long looked to the local indigenous populations for wives, sometimes killing Khanty and Mansi menfolk to take them. It was also apparently usual for Cossack detachments to demand (and receive) a contingent of local women from the indigenes wherever they stayed in Siberia. In eastern Siberia this practice is said to have survived well into the nineteenth century. Native boys were also being captured and sold as slaves.

In 1761, when the French astronomer Jean Chappe d'Auteroche (1722-69) arrived in Tobolsk to observe the passage of Venus, he not only collected knowledge like a two-legged encyclopaedia, but was propelled to strange heights of moral projection when he tried to turn his knowledge into a world view on love in a cold *taiga*:

> Almost all philosophers are of opinion, that the constitution has less
> powerful influence in the northern, than in the southern climates: the
> people of the north are less addicted to venery. Love is among them a
> chaste and lawful passion, while it is always criminal among the people
> of the south. The observations I have made in Russia are entirely con-
> tradictory to this opinion; they make the Russians an exception to this
> general rule: and it should seem that this apparent contradiction may be
> accounted for from moral causes. The women being left to themselves,
> and suffered to live in idleness, the effects even of their most trifling pas-
> sions must be powerful. Among the common people, men, women and
> children lie together promiscuously, without any sense of shame. Hence
> their passions being excited by the objects they see, the two sexes give
> themselves up early to debauchery. Although the baths weaken them at
> the time they make use of them, yet the flagellation they receive there
> promotes the circulation of the fluids, gives elasticity to the organs, and
> animates the passions. These particular causes must necessarily produce
> great alterations in the effects resulting from the climate.

Theories on climate were popular in Europe in the eighteenth century,
thanks to the Frenchman Charles de Secondat, Baron de Montesquieu
(1689-1755), so it is not surprising that d'Auteroche should struggle with
a few practical Siberian anomalies in theories of climate and morality. In
a footnote, d'Auteroche even tells us how flagellation also decreases sensi-
tivity of the nervous system, which would be destroyed if Russians did not
spend so much time in the *banya*.

Not surprisingly, modern Siberians take offence at the idea that they
are somehow more debauched than their counterparts in European Russia.
They also tend to see themselves as a better people, exposed to corruption
that comes mostly from outside the subcontinent. Writer Valentin
Rasputin defends Siberia's reputation in his *Siberia, Siberia*, quoting the
Siberian historian Peter Slovtsov (1767-1843) and, like Slovtsov, rushing
to the defence of his people by pointing to the vices of newly arrived de-
portees from European Russia, or to vice-ridden Moscow.

In other respects, too, the arrival of Cyprian marked a new stage in
Tobolsk's development, which had been founded near the site of the Tartar

Tobolsk, 1912

town of Isker (Qasliq or Sibir), the capital of the Khanate of Sibir, and become Siberia's most important town. Not only did he start whipping morally culpable Siberians into line, but he also began an ambitious period of building churches. Over the next one hundred years the historic core of today's Tobolsk gradually took shape around Cyprian's churches. Arriving by train or road from Tyumen today, the visitor may recognize elements within a brief description by John Bell of the picturesque view across the taiga and flood plain to the kremlin on its high bluff above the Irtysh river. He writes:

> ... about noon, we were in sight of the city of Tobolsky, though distant from us about twenty English miles. It stands upon a very high bank of the Tobol. The walls are white; and the crosses and cupolas of the churches guilded, and make a very fine appearance. Tobolsky is fortified with a strong brick wall, having square towers and bastions at proper

distances; and is well furnished with military stores. Within the town stand the governor's palace, courts of justice, several churches built of brick, particularly a large cathedral, and the palace of the archbishop. From the walls you have a very extensive prospect of a fine country, especially to the south. To the west the land is also flat, and overgrown with tall woods. The inhabitants are chiefly Russians, of different professions; many of them are merchants, and very rich, by the profitable trade they carry on to the borders of China, and many places of their own country.

They live mostly on the hill. Under the hill in the suburbs, along the banks of the river, are several large streets, called the Tartar-streets, occupied by the ancient inhabitants of these parts. Here, as at other places, these people enjoy the free exercise of their religion, and the privileges of trade. They resemble, in their persons, religion, language, and manners, the Tartars of Cazan and Astrachan. Their houses are very cleanly. They are very courteous to strangers, and esteemed honest; on which account they get great credit in their commercial affairs. Besides the fortification, formerly mentioned, about the town, the whole suburbs are surrounded with a ditch and palisades.

In 2003, during a visit by Russia's president of the day, Tobolsk was earmarked for development as the tourist capital of western Siberia. Since then, money has been poured into restoring the run-down buildings and putting back together this town by-passed by the Trans-Siberian Railway.

The task is enormous. This is one town in Siberia that is especially in need of repair and a good coat of paint. The lower town, the traditional Tartar quarter mentioned by Bell, unfolds across the floodplain of the Irtysh as a picturesque, romantic, but crumbling ensemble of stone mansions, semi-restored nineteenth-century administrative buildings and wooden Siberian cottages. In some parts, it offers hints of a shanty town. In the evening a seductive blend of birdsong, children's voices and dog barking descends over it. As I discovered in a near-bite, sometimes even the dogs descend on it too. The occasional heel-snapping Cerebrus (there are worse places in Russia for stray dogs, including the entrances to Moscow metro stations) fits well with another aspect of Tobolsk—its role as a religious centre for Siberia. An official programme for revival at one time bore the mind-boggling title of the "Rebirth of Tobolsk as a Spiritual, Moral and Cultural Centre of Siberia". It is an interesting turn of events for a town Cyprian found rife with alcohol, incest and moral abandonment.

All going according to plan, Tobolsk will grow from its historic, religious and cultural attractions. About 150,000 visitors currently arrive each year, of which the overwhelming majority are Russians.

THE KREMLIN COMPLEX

In mid-1587 a contingent of about 500 Cossacks arrived in Tobolsk and began building a new town. It is often said that the first stockade they built was made using the wood of their boats. The Cossacks were either desperate, thought there was no going back, or were retrospectively turned into material for epic, colonial legend. They were probably all of these things. The site they chose for the town was the top of the bluff above the floodplain of the Irtysh, since called Troytsky Mys (Trinity Cape). In 1594 the original stockade was replaced by a larger one, which in turn made way for a residence for the newly arrived Archbishop Cyprian from 1621 and was flanked by a new church, St. Sofia's Cathedral (Sofiysky Sobor). Numerous fires ravaged the town in the seventeenth century, and the result of one of these was that in 1643 Tobolsk had to be rebuilt completely from scratch. The following year, 1644, a large wooden kremlin with nine towers was erected on the site, along with a new incarnation of St. Sofia's Cathedral. Both fell victim again to fire in the 1670s—one of the six that destroyed or severely damaged wooden kremlins here.

By the late seventeenth century Tobolsk was a bustling capital of Siberia, with its own military governor, and it had also become an important ecclesiastical centre and stepping stone for the expansion of Russia and the Orthodox Church across the subcontinent. Its importance, coupled with the devastating fires, led to the decision to build a kremlin of stone. The person chosen for the job was Semyon Remezov, the cartographer, geographer and architect who descended from a family of Tobolsk cartographers. Remezov travelled to Moscow in 1698 to attune himself to the latest movements there and oversaw work on the first of the new stone buildings rising on Trinity Cape between 1700 and 1714, the year Peter the Great gave orders to stop building in stone outside St. Petersburg. Before the order was enacted, Remezov managed to complete an administrative chamber, as well as the Merchant's Yard (Gostiny Dvor) and the Treasury (Rentereya).

Situated left of the Holy Gate, the first gate seen when approaching the kremlin from the square, Gostiyny Dvor was the yard where merchants stored their goods safe from fire and thieves while in town. Yards such as these were a feature of towns all over Russia, and often they included quarters where merchants could sleep, a customs house where the government could collect revenue and cellars that served as warehouses. Inside the yard itself the merchants traded their goods. It was completed in 1708 and developed into one of the most important in Siberia. Later, the mostly Bukharan merchants established their own trader settlement in the Tartar lower town. As in Tyumen, this was a logical continuation of the trade tradition existing between Bukhara and the Tartars before the Russians arrived.

The Treasury was built in 1714-17 and is also known as the Swedish Chamber, because it was largely the work of Swedish prisoners of war who had been captured during the Battle of Poltava in 1709, a victory in Russia's war against Sweden (1700-21) that gave Russia dominance of the Baltic Sea. Their arrival had added a new layer to Tobolsk's colourful ethnic make-up. The Treasury is sunk deep into a natural cleft to join two hills and doubles as a bulwark for the kremlin ramparts.

By the mid-eighteenth century work had recommenced on the kremlin, but the days of kremlins serving purely as protective fortresses were numbered, and many different buildings rose up inside the walls, including the House of the Higher Clergymen (Arkhiereysky Dom), and the Cathedral Bell Tower (Sobornaya Kolokolnya), which today is flanked by the two other cathedrals in the complex: St. Sofia's Cathedral on one side, and the Intercession Cathedral (Pokrovsky Sobor) on the other.

St. Sofia's Cathedral, with its Renaissance geometric forms, is the oldest building in the complex and predates Remezov. Work on it began in 1681 after Tsar Fyodor III Alekseevich (1661-82) ordered a cathedral along the lines of the Ascension Monastery (Voznesensky Monastir) inside Moscow's kremlin. The foundation was laid but it took two years for the bricks to arrive. In mid-1684, due to a construction fault that became all too obvious as the cathedral neared completion, it collapsed and builders had to start again. In 1686 it was finally consecrated. In 1733 disaster struck again, this time in the form of a fire. The burned out wooden roof was replaced by one of metal, and its baroque aspects were created. Today, the sky-blue and glistening gold cupolas of the cathedral are the dominant and most spectacular feature of Tobolsk's historic skyline.

Other changes taking place over the centuries include the addition of a northern side-chapel and the replacement of the iconostases—the last time being in 1860, when the iconostasis from 1710 carved by Ukrainian craftsmen and commissioned by Leshchinsky was replaced. The darkest period came in the 1930s, however, when virtually all churches in Tobolsk were closed down. St. Sofia's Cathedral was requisitioned to hold exiled prisoners and anyone accused of being a *kulak* (those who were purged by Stalin as well-off peasants during the collectivization campaign). Around the same time the iconostasis and original crosses and religious paraphernalia vanished. The cathedral was re-consecrated in 1995.

BANISHING THE BELL

Adjoining the south-east corner is the cathedral vestry building dating from the late eighteenth century but only used as a vestry from 1840. South of the vestry, the 250-foot high Cathedral Bell Tower was completed in 1791-97 with neoclassical features. The largest of the bells, which weighs sixteen tonnes, was made in the Urals town of Nizhny Tagil.

Bells are a theme in Tobolsk, and the most poignant of the stories surrounding them concerns the so-called Uglich Bell, considered in popular myth to be the first "exile" in Siberia. The tower that once contained this famous bell is an inconspicuous building on the kremlin's southern perimeter alongside the House of the Higher Clergymen.

The Uglich Bell was exiled to Siberia in 1593. The story of its banishment dates back to the period of Ivan the Terrible (1530-84), who declared himself Tsar of all Russia in 1547 and descended from the Rurik dynastic line. When Ivan died in 1584, he left behind two sons, neither of whom was suitable to rule. One, Fyodor (1557-98), was feeble-minded and, ironically, earned the moniker of Fyodor the Bellringer for his habit of travelling the country ringing Russia's church bells. Although Fyodor became nominally the tsar, Russia was ruled by a council, eventually dominated by the regent, Boris Godunov (1551-1605), a boyar (a rank just below prince). The other son of Ivan the Terrible, Dmitry Ivanovich (1582-91), stemmed from Ivan's seventh marriage, and because the Church recognized only the first three marriages, he could not assume the title. Instead, he was bundled off to the town of Uglich, which had been endowed to him as an apanage. There the young Dmitry eked out a living from his bonded peasants.

Dmitry was accompanied by his mother (Ivan's seventh wife), Maria Nagaya. From Dmitry's earliest years his relatives instilled in him the idea of returning to Moscow to claim his rightful throne. Even worse, they believed he had been exiled to Uglich in a plot specifically to prevent him becoming tsar. In 1590 a plan was hatched around Dmitry to seize power from the half-brother, challenging the ambitions of Boris Godunov, who later successfully became Russia's first non-Rurik tsar. In 1591, however, Dmitry was found stabbed to death in obscure circumstances. Godunov and the council were suspected of being behind the death, although his nurse did claim that the young would-be tsar had unfortunately been playing a game with a knife when he suffered an epileptic fit.

When word of the death got out, the Uglich Bell was rung, the townspeople of Uglich rose up, ransacked properties and murdered a high-ranking official who had become unpopular for his zeal in collecting taxes. Moscow dispatched troops to Uglich and successfully quelled the uprising. Then came the reprisal: the tongue of the bell was removed so that it could never be rung again, and the bell itself was publicly flogged and taken to Tobolsk. It stayed here visible for all to see—including arriving exiles—until 1892, and from 1836 it hung in a small belfry in the corner of the kremlin. The stone belfry you see today dates from 1868. In 1890 Tobolsk's museum bought the bell and two years later it was returned to Uglich. A copy was made, however, which is now part of the museum's collection.

According to another version, the original bell from Uglich was destroyed by fire in 1677 and a new bell with the same weight but a different form was created in the eighteenth century.

The third in the triumvirate of cathedral buildings is the baroque Intercession Cathedral from 1746, erected once building in stone was again allowed. Inside is the crypt of St. John of Tobolsk (1651-1715), who replaced Filofey Leshchinsky as metropolitan in 1711 after the latter decided to return to Tyumen.

On the southern side of the kremlin, alongside the Intercession Cathedral, is the large House of the Higher Clergymen, which for many years was the main building of the local museum, the Tobolsk State Historical & Architectural Museum Reserve (Tobolsky Gosudarstvenny Istoriko-Arkhitekturny Muzey-Zapovednik). The simple façade and columns at the entrance suggest its neoclassical provenance. It dates from 1775, is the last

The Uglich Bell

of a series of structures built inside the kremlin to house the clergy, and is often cited as Siberia's first neoclassical building. Little of its outer appearance has changed since.

According to current plans, the Palace of the Governor (Dvorets Zamestnika) will be the main building of Tobolsk's state museum, but the museum landscape of Tobolsk will, if work continues according to schedule, not settle for some time. One idea is to turn the House of the Higher Clergymen into a museum on Siberian Orthodoxy.

Work on the Palace of the Governor began in 1780. This was built literally to accommodate new reforms by Catherine the Great that came into force in 1782. According to these, Tobolsk was the seat of one of three vice-regents ruling Siberia. The new palace of the vice-regent was built just outside the kremlin walls.

Siberian Administration

The administration of Siberia took numerous forms over the centuries. Early on, it was ruled from European Russia by a series of state departments. Later, from 1637, it was governed by a special Siberian Office (the Sibirsky Prikaz) that regulated the courts, customs, food supplies and key administrative functions—including the all-important Siberian fur industry. Below the Siberian Office, the day-to-day running of Siberia was conducted by a bureaucratic group of local military governors, sub-departments and chambers. A military governor (*voevod*) had almost unlimited powers within his county or district. This framework changed in 1708 when Peter the Great abolished the Siberian Office and created a single Siberian province with a governor based in Tobolsk, its capital. Although between the early 1700s and 1822 numerous other changes were made to Siberia's administration (the Siberian Office, for example, was revived in 1730-63), most had one aim: to reign in corrupt or brutal military governors, says James Forsyth in his *A History of the Peoples of Siberia*.

In 1763 the reforms of Catherine the Great divided Siberia into two large provinces, one governed from Tobolsk and the other from Irkutsk. This was changed to three provinces with vice regents in 1782-97: Tobolsk, Irkutsk and Kolyvansk (Kolyvan, in the Altai Region). Hence the new Palace of the Governor in Tobolsk.

In 1803 one governor general oversaw all of Siberia from Irkutsk, and Siberia was carved into the three provinces of Irkutsk, Tomsk and

Tobolsk. In 1822 reforms introduced by Mikhail Speransky (1772-1839), a key figure in Russia's liberal movement, returned the system of two provinces: Western Siberia, with its capital in Tobolsk (and from 1838 in Omsk) and Eastern Siberia (including today's Far East), governed from Irkutsk. Each province had its own governor general with full powers. These reforms survived with only minor changes until the Russian Revolution.

Today Siberia has over two dozen administrative boundaries, some of these a region (*oblast*), others an autonomous district (*avtonomny okrug*), and some a republic (e.g. the Altai Republic or Tuva). Above these so-called Federal Subjects are three Federal Districts (in all Russia has seven of these), a new level created in 2000, with an envoy who oversees various federal functions.

OUTSIDE THE KREMLIN: DECEMBRISTS AND DOSTOEVSKY

Opposite Gostiny Dvor is a monument dedicated to Semyon Remezov dating from 1993, and behind this and a little to the north is the former Prison Castle (Tyurmeny Zamok). The prison was built in the 1830s following a decision to make Tobolsk a transit point for criminals and political exiles. From here they were dispatched to other parts of Siberia. The largest single group of exiles were the Decembrists, exiled here and elsewhere in Siberia after a revolt in St. Petersburg in December 1825.

The Decembrists were military figures involved in an uprising against Russia's new tsar, Nicholas I (1796-1855), who succeeded Alexander I (1777-1825) to the throne after the natural successor, Nicholas' brother Constantine, had disqualified himself by marrying a Polish commoner. A great deal of secrecy surrounded events inside the royal palace leading up to the crowning, causing suspicion about the motives for Nicholas' succession.

The underlying cause of the Decembrist Revolt, however, can be found in a desire for a more liberal, more constitutional nineteenth-century Russia. Many of the officers, who in the repressive years of Alexander were active in secret societies, sought reforms that would place Russia on a par politically with the western powers and were disappointed when the crown fell to the arch-conservative Nicholas I. On 14 December, the day the military should swear allegiance to the new tsar, about 3,000 refused and staged the uprising. Nicholas responded by trying to convince the officers to lay down their arms, but when this failed he ordered his troops to open fire. The Decembrists were poorly organized and easily defeated, with the result that five surviving leaders of the revolt were executed. Others were banished to Siberia. Many of the Decembrists' wives followed their husbands into exile, and together they exerted an extraordinary influence on Siberia's cultural life.

One of the more famous transit prisoners—probably imprisoned in the oldest part of the complex, which is now the restored City Archive (Gorodskoy Arkhiv)—was the writer Fyodor Dostoevsky. In 1848 Dostoevsky, who had already published his novel *Poor Folk* and his "Petersburg poem" *The Double*, became involved with a group of liberals around the St. Petersburg intellectual, Mikhail Petrashevsky (1821-66). This loose group of dissidents was known as the Petrashevsky Circle and, like the Decembrists, sought liberal reform. In 1849 Dostoevsky and others from the circle were arrested, given a mock execution in St. Petersburg and sentenced to hard labour in Siberia. He was transported to Tobolsk and thereafter spent four years in prison in Omsk and another five years of enforced service in a Siberian garrison based in Semipalatinsk (Kazakhstan). He returned to St. Petersburg in 1859 and three years later published *The House of the Dead*, based on his experiences in prison.

Dostoevsky arrived in Tobolsk in early January 1850. He was presented to the authorities, searched and relieved of any money he still had after being fleeced in the villages and towns he passed through in European Russia. He and his fellow prisoners were taken into a narrow room where they found three straw mattresses on plank beds. The winter was typically harsh and temperatures fell to 40 degrees below during his six days in Tobolsk. One of the prisoners from the Petrashevsky Circle already suffered from frostbite on his toes, and Dostoevsky's face is said to have been covered in sores. Several Decembrists' wives visited Dostoevsky in prison and smuggled in money to help him. He writes:

> I would like to go into our six-day stay in Tobolsk and my impressions in more detail, but this is not the place for it. I will only say that the lively concern and sympathy blessed us with almost complete happiness. Prisoners from earlier times (or rather their wives) fussed about us as if we were part of the family... We only saw them briefly, we were

Dostoevsky, a 1929 woodcut by V. Favorsky

strictly confined, but they sent us food, clothing, consoled us and gave us courage.

One of the Decembrist wives, Natalya Fonvizina, gave Dostoevsky a copy of the New Testament with a ten-rouble note concealed in the binding, and he reputedly kept the book under his pillow for the four years in Omsk and for the rest of his life. It is one of only a few books that exist today containing notes written in Dostoevsky's own hand.

In 2008 a monument to Dostoevsky was unveiled in Tobolsk in a square named after the writer, located near the St. Peter and Paul Church (Tserkov Petra i Pavla; 1774; ulitsa Bolshaya Sibirskaya 2). The work is by Moscow-born Mikhail Pereyaslavets, one of Russia's most respected contemporary sculptors. It is the second of the sculptor's works to grace Tobolsk, another being a memorial to Pyotr Yershov (1815-69), a poet and the author of the tale *The Humpbacked Horse* (1834). This complements a cluster of sculptures along ulitsa Remezova depicting characters from the tale.

A short distance away from the kremlin, situated beyond the water tower on pereulok Sverdlovsky, is the Art Museum (Khudozhestvenny Muzey). The building itself dates from 1887 and has strong neoclassical aspects with Art Nouveau touches. It was erected on the 300th anniversary of the founding of Tobolsk—hence the date on the left-hand side when one faces the building—and was formerly the main museum building in town. Inside, the collection includes early nineteenth-century icons and paintings (there is an impressive painting of Yermak by an unknown artist), portraits of the Tobolsk patriarchs, some portraits by the regional artist D. P. Shelutkov, and ivory and bone carving dating from the 1870s to contemporary times (Tobolsk became known for its bone and ivory carving in the mid-nineteenth century, and carving is still carried out there). Several historic and modern landscape paintings offer a bird's eye view of Tobolsk in early and recent times.

South of here, off a road leading into the lower town, is Yermak Park (Sad Yermaka), with an obelisk dedicated to the Cossack.

THE LOWER TOWN
For views before descending into the Tartar lower town, you can walk behind the Palace of the Governor, with its line of cannons and spectacu-

lar panorama of the Irtysh flood plain. Flooding, in fact, was a major hindrance to the development of this part of Tobolsk, and it appears that the first Europeans to settle in the lower town were monks from the former Monastery of the Holy Sign (Znamensky Monastir), which is today situated south of the river station near the corner of ulitsa Lermontova and ulitsa Dekabristov.

From the kremlin, a walled path (Pryamskoy Vzvoz) beneath the Treasury and wooden steps lead down into the lower town some 200 feet below the bluff. Once at the foot of the bluff, turning left into ulitsa Rozy Lyuksemburg and following this to the red-brick church near the corner of ulitsa Alyabeva, the visitor finds the Polish Roman Catholic Church (Rimsko-Katolichesky Kostel), completed in 1909 and built by exiles and the descendants of the Polish Rebellion of 1863-65. Across the road at ulitsa Rozy Lyuksemburg 14 is a building (now a hospital) that was the Provincial Classical School (Gubernskaya Klassicheskaya Gimnaziya), built by a local merchant in 1770. About a decade later it wound up in the hands of the town administration and was briefly used as the governor's residence after fire tore through the kremlin in the 1780s. By the turn of the nineteenth century it was a boys' school and it was here that Pyotr Yershov (of *The Humpbacked Horse* fame) taught and later became school director. Dmitry Mendeleev (1834-1907), who was born in Tobolsk and achieved renown as the author of the first periodic table of elements, went to school here too. Further back along the street at no. 7 is the building that later became the Boys' School (Muzhskaya Gimnaziya). Mendeleev taught here, and today it houses a couple of faculties of the Institute of Pedagogy.

Development continues apace around ulitsa Rozy Lyuksemburg, with new buildings rising out of the muddy soil and landscaping work transforming the floodplain. The area around the creek near the vehicle bridge is earmarked as a small harbour for Siberian leisure sailors.

Crossing the bridge, one reaches Bazarnaya ploshchad (Bazaar Square), where at no. 5 stands the late nineteenth-century, two-storey Public House (Dom Piteynykh Zavedeny), and at Bazarnaya ploshchad 1 the historic bathhouse (*banya*), dating from the same period.

This particular bathhouse had not been built when Jean Chappe d'Auteroche visited Tobolsk in April 1761 to observe the passage of Venus, but Tobolsk bathhouses in general seem to have turned the learned astronomer into an enthusiastic anatomist. Again, there is a hint of Tobolsk as a kind of Siberian Sodom, as he writes:

> The men in Siberia are tall, flout, and well made, as they are almost all over Russia: they are excessively fond of women and drinking. As they are slaves to a despotic prince, they exert the same absolute authority over their slaves or inferiors, with still greater severity. The women are in general handsome at Tobolsky: their skin is exceedingly fair, and their countenance agreeable; their eyes are black, languishing and down-cast; for they never dare look a man full in the face: they wear no caps, but use colored handkerchiefs, which they interweave so curiously among their hair, generally black and unpowdered, that this kind of head-dress gives them a very bewitching look. They all use paint, young girls as well as married women; and this custom prevails even among the servant maids, and some of the common people.
>
> The women are commonly well-made till the age of eighteen or twenty; but their legs as well as their feet are always large. Nature in this respect seems to have had in view the bulk they usually acquire; which seems to want very firm supporters. The baths, they use twice a week, contribute chiefly to spoil their shapes: they cause such a relaxation in all the parts of the body, that the beauty of the women is quite gone before they are thirty years of age.

Alongside the bathhouse is the Church of Zacharias and Elizabeth (Tserkov Zakhariya i Elizabety). This church, which dominates the area of low buildings between the bluff and the river station, was completed in 1776 in a late-baroque style and is the first of a swathe of buildings situated along ulitsa Mira that have been restored or will be in the future. At ulitsa Mira 4 is the House of the Merchant Volodimirova, a two-storey stone merchant's dwelling dating from 1760, also incorporating baroque features, whereas the traditional wooden house at ultisa Mira 8 is one of several in the lower town that may one day be turned into a small hotel.

The large city administrative building at ulitsa Mira 10 is the former governor's residence, and it was here that the Romanov family spent their final months before being taken to Yekaterinburg. Upstairs, one room of the building (the tsar's study) is now a small museum dedicated to the Romanovs, although very few of the exhibits actually belonged to the family. We are told that the exhibition may be expanded at some point.

The royal family arrived in Tobolsk in August 1917 on the steamer, the *Rus*, and took up residence on 26 August on the first floor of the building, after spending a week on the steamer moored at the river station while—following a complaint by Nicholas II—their future quarters were improved. Their servants occupied the ground floor. There the family read, played draughts or cards in the evening or performed banal household duties like chopping wood while civil war raged outside and the Bolsheviks, who had now overthrown the provisional government in the October Revolution of 1917, argued about what to do with them.

According to *The Last Days of the Romanovs*, a book published in the 1920s by a former Russian Justice Minister, George Telberg, and London *Times* reporter, Robert Wilton, which relied on accounts of soldiers and others who had contact with the Romanovs at this time, "People passing by could see into the lower rooms. It became a custom to bow to any member of the family who happened to be visible, and some of the citizens would demonstratively make the sign of the cross. Behind the governor's house was an immense enclosure, surrounded by a high wooden fence. Here the family took their exercise; here the ex-Tsar chopped and sawed wood, and here he built a sort of wooden terrace, where the captives loved to sit whenever the weather permitted." One of the most famous photographs of the period shows the family sitting on this terrace.

Wild rumours spread about the royal family and attempts to free them, and one of these, according to Telberg and Wilton, concerned "a bold Englishman ascending the Ob and Irtysh from the Arctic Ocean and wafting away the prisoners." In April and May 1918, on the orders of Sverdlov to bring the family to Moscow, the family left Tobolsk in two groups. Although their destination was Moscow, rivalry and distrust between Bolsheviks in Siberia resulted in a second order to take the family to Yekaterinburg, where they met their fate in Dom Ipatiev.

Across the street from the former Governor's House is Alexander Gardens (Aleksandrovsky Sad), where a small chapel was erected in 1887 to commemorate the 300th anniversary of the founding of Tobolsk and the fiftieth anniversary of a visit to Tobolsk by the future tsar, Alexander II.

East of here on the corner of ulitsa Kirova and ulitsa Lenina—and visible from the bluff in the foreground if you look from there—is the baroque Church of the Archangel Michael (Tserkov Mikhaila Arkhangela), one of the earliest churches in the lower town, dating from 1745-48.

ABALAK AND THE "PIOUS WORK"

Since the collapse of the Soviet Union, Tobolsk and its outlying villages have indeed re-emerged as a hub of religion in Siberia—which should come as no surprise, as the region's history has long been imbued with a sacred character. This process is especially interesting because it has happened so relatively recently, beginning roughly from the arrival of Cyprian in the early seventeenth century. The *Remezov Chronicle*, which came later and is dated at around 1700, illustrates the mystical side of Siberian history with some colourful details about Yermak's demise. According to the *Chronicle*, Yermak's body floated to the surface of the Irtysh one week after he drowned in battle—the day after the remnants of his band fled Siberia and Sibir fell briefly back into the hands of the Tartars. One day, a Tartar fishing on the Irtysh noticed Yermak's legs in the water and lassoed the body out of the river. The tell-tale coat of mail revealed the Cossack's identity, but fresh blood gushed from the corpse when the Tartar tried to remove the armour, suggesting eternal life. All and sundry flocked to see the miracle, which it was generally believed was intended to prove the power of one Christian God. When someone stabbed the Cossack with an arrow, fresh blood flowed again. He lay there for six weeks. Not even the birds dared touch him. Later, Kuchum arrived with some princes. Some of those present experienced visions, others grew insane, until in the end they decided to lay him to rest.

Tobolsk's religious upswing fits comfortably with its other role as the tourism capital of western Siberia, and no place illustrates this better than the small settlement of Abalak, situated some twenty miles upriver (southeast) of Tobolsk on the northern bank of the Irtysh. The village owes much of its unusually picturesque setting amidst taiga, bluffs and floodplains to being where Yermak won a decisive battle over Kuchum in late 1582 after Kuchum and a group of Tartar troops tried to recapture the capital. The *Kungur Chronicle* describes how, after this final victory, St. Nicholas appeared to Yermak in a vision and declared that this site would become a "home" of God. The village sprouted out of the taiga, and in 1636 a local widow experienced another vision telling her that it needed a new church. The blind traveller, James Holman, described this religious phenomenon when he passed through Abalak. He mentions an annual event still held today, during which an icon of the Virgin Mary—the "pious work"—is carried to Tobolsk in a procession. According to Holman:

> The spot on which it [the monastery] was situated, was, nearly two centuries since, the site of a small village; it happened, however, about that time, that two images, one representing the Mother of God, the other, Mary of Egypt, made their appearance to an old peasant woman, and communicated their orders to take down the village, and build a monastery in the place of it, the whole of which was expressly directed to be accomplished by human labour alone, the assistance of every other animal being positively interdicted. The woman immediately set off to Tobolsk, and on her way was met by the Virgin Mary, who repeated the previous orders. In consequence the head prior of Tobolsk commenced, and completed, the pious work [the icon]; and the Virgin Mary has resided in the place ever since, excepting that she makes an annual journey to the city of Tobolsk, and is absent from the 6th to the 25th of July, visiting the churches and inhabitants of that place. Her journey, both to and from her favourite monastery occupies three days, and she is accompanied by an immense concourse of people, who carry with them the necessary provision for their subsistence. Many of these devotees, of both sexes, are said to indulge in every kind of excess; taking up their lodging during the night any whim that offers, or even sleeping on the bare ground. They are interdicted, however, from rambling into the woods, and if detected in an attempt to do so, the accompanying Cossacks immediately take them into custody.

The procession these days takes place on 21 July, when the icon is carried to Tobolsk to spend the next two weeks before being returned to the monastery.

The usual explanation for the procession is that it began when the church's icon (one of the Virgin Mary that promises healing for the ill, and specially created for the church) was carried to Tobolsk in 1665 to rescue the local harvest from failure after heavy rains. This intercession worked, apparently. In 1680 the original wooden church burned down and in its place the stone Church of the Holy Sign (Znamensky Tserkov) was erected in 1680-91, followed by the Church of St. Nicholas (Nikolskaya Tserkov) in 1750, and the Church of St. Mary of Egypt (Tserkov Marii Egipetskoy), before a fully-fledged monastery was founded in 1783. Predictably, the Soviet era oversaw its decline and the monastery was almost a ruin before being revived in the late 1980s.

The original icon from the monastery no longer exists, but historic copies do, including one that is now in the Orthodox Holy Protection Church in Cabramatta, Sydney (Australia). It was reportedly carried from Abalak to Shanghai after being entrusted to a White Guard during the civil war and was later taken to Sydney when the guard's daughter migrated to Australia.

Today, an upmarket tourist complex affiliated with Tobolsk's best hotel, the Gostinitsa Slavyanskaya, is situated near the monastery.

Chapter Five

TO THE FROZEN OCEAN AND
STALIN'S RAILWAY OF DEATH

Along with the Ob, the Irtysh is one of western Siberia's great rivers. It begins in the Chinese province of Dzungaria, where it is known as the Black Irtysh, tumbles out of the mountains and flows across the steppes of Kazakhstan and through Omsk, Tara and Tobolsk on a 2,600-mile journey to its confluence with the Ob, near the town of Khanty-Mansiysk. A couple of times a week in the navigation season from July to late September, passenger boats via Tobolsk ply the stretch from Omsk to Khanty-Mansiysk, the capital of the Khanty-Mansiysk-Yugra Autonomous Region (Khanty-Mansiysky Avtonomny Okrug-Yugra). The journey from Tobolsk to Khanty-Mansiysk takes about 28 hours. A short distance downstream from there the Irtysh joins the Ob, which continues to Salekhard, deep in Siberia's north.

Just south of Tobolsk, the Irtysh passes the historic site of Isker (Sibir), the stretch of riverbank where the Khanate of Sibir had its capital and where Yermak arrived to find a deserted city in 1582. A few years after Yermak's victory, the military governor Ivan Mansurov spent a winter at a stockade situated downstream on the right bank of the Ob, where the Irtysh flows into it, and by the 1590s new fortresses had been established at present-day Berezovo, Salekhard (Obdorsk) and Surgut. It was around this time that the Russians met stiff resistance from the local Khanty (earlier called Ostyak) and Mansi (Vogul) indigenes, today the main indigenous populations in the region, and several uprisings took place in the middle Ob region between 1606 and 1616.

The Russians pushed swiftly eastwards in the early seventeenth century, and by 1637 various postal stations had been established in this region for changing horses. One of these was so-called Samorovsky Yam, a place which developed into the town of Samarovo, laying the foundations for the creation of today's town of Khanty-Mansiysk. The earliest Russian settlers here were *yamshchiky*, fifty or so coach drivers who were brought across the Urals with their families from Perm and other towns. A century later, traffic across the north was so heavy that the coach drivers here numbered almost five hundred.

Samarovo, however, remained an otherwise undisturbed corner of the *taiga* for many years, which is perhaps unsurprising, given its location. Even so, the nineteenth century was not only the century of the railway—which had little impact in this part of Siberia—but also the age of the steamship. In 1858 a local merchant by the name of Ryazanov obtained the rights to ply the Irtysh and the Ob between Tobolsk and Berezovo, situated further downstream at a point where the Ob broadens into a mass of waterways before reaching the Gulf of Ob. Services began a couple of years later, and the village received the go ahead for its own telegraph connection after the governor general visited in the late 1870s; the difficult job of laying the line between Tobolsk and Berezovo, via Samarovo, was completed in 1910. Yet Samarovo continued to be essentially a small town on a large river in a monstrously vast, mosquito-infested region of taiga punctuated by swamps. There was little reason for the visitor to come here unless en route to somewhere in the north, exiled here, or looking to make money out of the region's forest animals.

Samarovo was so far removed from Russia's important towns that few of the historic events that rocked Russia had much impact. It received exiles over the years, but when the 1905 revolution shook St. Petersburg, news took so long to reach town that it was virtually too late for the locals to stage their own uprising. In 1889 Nicholas II travelled here, and in 1912 the town had three inns for travellers, a tea house, a tavern where they could get a drink, one church and a few chapels, one school, six trading stores, a blacksmith's shop to shod the horses, and its *raison d'être*— the postal station. Precisely 398 men lived along with 427 women in what was typically a small postal town out in the taiga.

The region is the traditional homeland of the Khanty and Mansi, as well as Nenets in the far north. Despite a stream of reforms introduced since the rule of Catherine the Great (from 1762 to 1796), it was a troubled time for these indigenes, whose land had been made formally part of Russia and who were still being forced to deliver tribute or to pay taxes to the tsar if they lived in towns. As James Forsyth writes in his authoritative *A History of the Peoples of Siberia*: "the norm in Siberian commerce in the nineteenth century was still, as it had been for 200 years, self-enrichment at the expense of the indigenous population." When the Bolsheviks took power they abolished *yasak* altogether and cancelled the natives' debts to traders, while also providing help to communities through the period of chaos after the revolution. When they were not being philanthropic, however, the Red Guards of the civil war period were heavy-handedly trying to make Bolshevik comrades out of the indigenes.

In the 1920s and early in 1930 new reforms changed the lives of the indigenes everywhere in Russia, including those in the Ob river region around Samarovo: national territories were created for the indigenous peoples. While this policy was "enlightened" in theory (literacy programmes were started, and the languages were given a written form for the first time), in practice it was also part of a paternalistic approach during Stalin's era to bring the indigenes into the Soviet fold, especially once his collectivization drive moved into full swing. Fishing, limited livestock farming and vegetable growing had been the main industries in Samarovo until then, but in the 1930s a collective fishery industry became an important part of the local economy. At the same time, campaigns were started to stamp out shamanism, and some children from the north were forcibly removed from their families and put into boarding schools.

Collectivization here followed the pattern of elsewhere, with cultural bases founded to encourage indigenes to settle in village-style communities with communal services. But this meant abandoning the forests and often a decline of traditional languages or bans on their use. In some cases, the traditional heads were branded *kulaks* and persecuted, as happened in the region around the Kazym cultural base. Khanty and Nenets rose up there in 1933 and staged the Kazym Rebellion, which was quashed by the army, in some parts by using aircraft. Afterwards, repression of indigenous rites and celebrations was stepped up, including the banning of bear funeral rites. This struck at the heart of indigenous culture, as Khanty and Manis see themselves as descendants of the bear, and killing one involves a complicated ritual of seeking the bear's permission before holding the bear festival. Following the rebellion, practising the rites could be punished by ten years' imprisonment.

KHANTY-MANSIYSK: BOOM TOWN

After an Ostyak-Vogul National Region was created in 1930, the Soviet authorities had to find a capital. Some of the choices for consideration were Oktyabrskoe, Surgut and Berezovo, but all were thought too distant from the Khanty and Mansi heartlands. The authorities also considered a location at the confluence of the Ob and Irtysh, where Ivan Mansurov had built his winter stockade, but ravines there did not lend themselves to development. In the end, they chose another site in dense cedar forest three miles north of Samarovo, behind Mount Samarovskaya.

The indigenous settlement was given the name Ostyako-Vogulsk, and was changed to Khanty-Mansiysk in 1940. By the 1950s it was a small town, but once oil and gas were discovered in the region it boomed and expanded in a crescent shape around a hairpin bend in the Irtysh river as the capital of the newly-named Khanty-Mansiysk Autonomous District-Yugra.

The fortunes of Khanty-Mansiysk and its 68,000 inhabitants are closely tied to the oil industry in a region that today is home to about 1.5 million people. In the 1920s over forty per cent of the population were indigenous Khanty, Mansi and Nenets. Today, due to the arrival of Russian and foreign workers to extract the vast reserves of oil and gas from the taiga, this figure has plummeted to less than two per cent.

Despite its unusual location in the northern taiga—for a long time its only transport connections with the outside world were by river or seaplane—the capital is growing rapidly. The resources boom has brought relative prosperity, evident in the glistening office blocks rising out of the

Khanty-Mansiysk: futurism in the *taiga*

taiga, and in one building especially: a futuristic environmental tower de-signed by the firm of the renowned British architect Norman Foster. The space age tower, which resembles a cut diamond and whose interior is lit by natural light, was being built in 2009.

Khanty-Mansiysk's cultural scene very much reflects its wealth, and the town has several museums of which one is dedicated to the indigenes of the region. Situated in forest in the south-west of town at ulitsa Sobyan-ina 1, the open air museum "Torum Maa" seeks to recreate through dis-plays of clothing, housing, totems and artefacts the traditional life of the Khanty and Mansi. The State Museum of Nature and Man (Gosu-darsvenny Muzey Prirody i Cheloveka), situated in the heart of town near the central square at ulitsa Mira 11, has three core elements: a section on the natural environment on the theme of the rhythm of the biosphere, another on the theme of historical times, and a third relating to an in-digenous rendering of history in mythological time. Mythological figures and themes are presented without beginning or end, representing cyclical time, contrasting with a linear representation of time to be found in the historical section, which deals with the people and events that have shaped the region.

BEREZOVO AND SALEKHARD
From Khanty-Mansiysk, the Ob meanders north towards Berezovo, situ-ated on the left bank of the Northern Sosva river 26 miles from the con-

fluence; the latter flows east from the flanks of the Urals and in the sixteenth and seventeenth centuries was used by Russian hunters and traders as one of the main rivers into Siberia. The town was founded in 1593 as a stockade for collecting tribute and as a local trading post. The Bukhara traders also travelled this far, and in its early days Berezovo grew to become one of Siberia's most important trading centres, largely thanks to the lightning growth of the town of Mangazeya situated on the Taz, one of the rivers flowing into the Ob estuary. When Mangazeya fell into decline from the 1640s, so too did Berezovo.

For better or worse, Berezovo was also used as a convenient place to deposit anyone who had fallen out of favour or required removal from the capital. Prince Alexander Menshikov (1673-1729), a friend of Peter the Great and the tsar's second wife, Catharine I (1683-1727; she had been a mistress of Menshikov), was dispatched here after he fell from grace for his legendary corruption and vice.

Menshikov in Berezovo (1888) by W.I. Surikov

Menshikov, who died here, was not the first notable to wind up on this quiet stretch of the Ob, nor would he be the last, for Decembrists and twentieth-century revolutionaries also filled its prison over the years. The town's regional museum covers some of this history, and in 1993 a monument was erected to Menshikov on Historical Square (Istorichesky Skver).

Further downriver, the town of Salekhard, with almost 40,000 inhabitants, nestles on the Arctic Circle. A monument marks the spot. Today it is the capital of the Yamalo-Nenets Autonomous Region. Salekhard was founded near a settlement going back about 2,000 years that once belonged to an obscure race of northern people who probably mingled with Nenet and Khanty populations over time. Cossacks arrived here in 1595 and built a fortress near a Khanty settlement and it became known as Obdorsk. This is the same Obdorsk that crops up in the Dostoevsky novel *The Brothers Karamazov* in the form of the "travelling Monk of Obdorsk".

In its early days Obdorsk was a seasonal fort that was abandoned in winter and resettled each year in June once the ice broke up and cleared from the river. The Russians set up a tax collection post here, ostensibly to control trade between the Khanty and the coastal dwelling Nenets (whose homeland spans the Urals), and Cossacks used to sail down from Berezovo regularly to collect the proceeds. Obdorsk was also on one of the routes used to transport goods to Mangazeya.

From the early nineteenth century it became famous for its trade fair, described in some detail by the nineteenth-century German explorer Georg Adolph Erman (1806-77), who combed Siberia noting down magnetic observations on his world journey in 1828-30. According to Erman, the fair at Obdorsk attracted indigenes from as far west as Archangelsk in European Russia and far east as the Yenisey river who came to barter for Russian goods. Erman writes: "All these various nations and tribes can make themselves understood to one another, and also to the traders of this place, who make use of the Ostyak [Khanty] exclusively, as the commercial language; only a few Kosaks [Cossacks] understood the Samoyed [Nenet] language also." The Russians traded flour and bread, metal decorations, scrap iron such as old sabres which the Khanty reworked into their own decorations, cloth, tobacco and alcohol. In exchange, they received furs and walrus tusks.

Today the town goes by its modern name of Salekhard and has

become better known for the extraction of natural gas, which began in the region in the 1960s. It is one of Russia's fastest developing regions for gas—about ninety per cent of the gas Russia produces comes from the Yamal region; the region also produces about twelve per cent of Russia's oil.

THE RAILWAY OF DEATH

Salekhard was closely tied into the Soviet gulag system, being used as a hub for distributing prisoners into the scattered taiga camps. But it is one project in particular, the so-called "Railway of Death", that has put Salekhard on the map of Stalinist horrors.

The history of the railway goes back to the early post-Second World War period when the communist authorities decided to create a large sea port on the Gulf of Ob and connect this by railroad to Vorkuta in European Russia. Indeed, a section of line north through European Russia to Labytnangi, across the river from Salekhard, was completed in 1948 and went into service in the mid-1950s, and today the "Polar Arrow" train completes a journey between Moscow and Labytnangi in about 45 hours.

However, the government abandoned plans to develop Salekhard as a port for large vessels when it was realized that the gulf was too shallow. Stalin decided to locate the port instead at Igarka, situated on the Yenisey, and build a 800-mile trans-polar railway to connect it with Salekhard. This was seen as the beginning of a larger project to create a railway across the entire breadth of the north to the Pacific Ocean and run a line south to the Trans-Siberian.

On paper at least it looked like a good idea, and it is interesting to speculate today how this early attempt to industrialize the far north would have changed the region had it been successful. For better or worse, it failed, however, and it cost a still unknown number of human lives.

Between 60,000 and 120,000 labourers—women as well as men, most forced political prisoners or criminals—were involved in the project, which began in mid-1949. Gulag 501 worked eastwards from Salekhard, and Camp 503 westwards from Igarka. Conditions were, as can be imagined, atrocious. The prisoners were driven hard, and in summer the mosquitoes, gnats and other parasites made their lives unbearable. It is said that even the sentries were committing suicide under such extreme conditions. Machinery was difficult to transport to the sites, and some of the

rails used were second-hand taken from track damaged during the Second World War.

Even before the magnitude of the technical problems associated with the frozen earth became all too obvious, official enthusiasm for the project waned. Who was going to use the new railway? What would it transport? In 1950 work was advancing at great speed, but by early 1952 resources were already being diverted to more viable projects. The new line began to fall to pieces in the tundra. Gullies formed around the rails as the permafrost melted and land subsided, and clearings of forest vegetation quickly deteriorated into swamp.

About 450 miles of line had been completed by March 1953—just under half the distance from Vorkuta to Igarka—and trains at that time were already plying the stretch from Salekhard to Nadym (about 200 miles) once a day. The line stayed in operation until the 1980s before being shut down and partially dismantled for scrap.

It is impossible to say how many lives were sacrificed for the railway. Camps were located about every three to six miles along the line, filled with common criminals, political dissidents and men and women convicted of petty offences such as stealing grain. One report suggests about 300 prisoners died each month. Only signs of their labour can be seen today in Salekhard, but in 2003 a memorial to the victims of Camp 501 was erected—in the shape of the steam locomotive that once ran between Salekhard and Nadym.

Chapter Six
OMSK AND THE BARABA STEPPE

"It was on the night of Wednesday, August 28th [1901]—after I had watched the sun set like a huge crimson balloon behind the line to the far rear of us—that the conductor came and informed me we would be at Omsk within the hour. I intended to halt there for a day. So I threw my belongings together... and then looked out the window. We were going at a dead crawl. But far ahead I could see the moon-like glow of many electric lights. We rumbled across a huge girder bridge, 700 yards long, spanning the Irtish—the mast gleams of many boats at anchor, and the red and green lights of a steamer churning the water to a quay side, showing far below—and we ran into a big, brilliantly lighted station, crowded with people and with the grey and red of military uniform everywhere."

John Foster Fraser, *The Real Siberia*, 1901

While northwards of Tobolsk the Irtysh flows into country traditionally inhabited by the Khanty and Mansi (and further still, by the Nenets), upstream it passes through a string of settlements once predominantly inhabited by Siberian Tartars.

The Scottish physician John Bell noted the Tartar presence in January 1720 in his *Travels from St. Petersburg* while tracing a course along the frozen Irtysh towards Tara, today the largest river town between Tobolsk and Omsk. It is an interesting account because Bell gives us a glimpse inside a Tartar house and something that was common in Siberia at the time among the Tartars: using ice as "glass" for windows in winter.

We passed through many Tartar villages, and at night lodged in one of their little huts, and warmed ourselves at a good fire on the hearth. These houses consist generally of one or two rooms, according to the ability of the landlord. Near to the hearth is fixed an iron-kettle to dress the victuals. In one end of the apartment is placed a bench, about 18 inches high, and six feet broad, covered with mats, or skins of wild beasts, upon which all the family sit by day, and sleep by night. The walls are built of wood and moss, consisting of large beams, laid one above another, with

Wogulski Tartars on the
Frontiers of Siberia

Ostiacks on the Banks
of the River Oby

Nisovian Tunguzians in
their Summer Dress

A Nisovian Tunguzian
in his Winter Habit

"Wogulski Tartars on the Frontiers of Siberia", 1740

a layer of moss between every two beams. All the roofs are raised. A square hole is cut out for a window, and to supply the want of glass, a piece of ice is formed to fit the place exactly, which lets in good light. Two or three pieces will last the whole winter. These Tartars are very neat and cleanly, both in their persons and houses. They use no stoves, as the Russians do. Near the house there is commonly a shade for the cattle.

Almost all travellers who passed through the region in this and other centuries were surprised by the honesty and hospitality of the western Siberian Tartars. Bell was fortunate not to be around a couple of years later; in 1722, following a decree issued by Peter the Great demanding that all subjects swear an oath of allegiance to the tsar, conflict broke out in Tara and about 500 buildings were destroyed, with brutal Russian reprisals. Later, during the reign of Elizabeth Petrovna (1709-62) between 1741 and 1762, a campaign was conducted to force Tartars to renounce Islam. The price for refusal was a beating or imprisonment.

The Tartars living along the Irtysh fished the rivers, caught fowl, hunted in the forests and to a limited extent farmed the land. Tara itself was established as a fort in 1593 and benefited greatly from being on the route for Bukharan traders from Central Asia.

About 250 miles upriver from Tobolsk is the much younger town of Omsk. Omsk was founded in 1716, just four years before Bell travelled through the region, on the western edge of the Baraba Steppe. This is a wild, flat and mostly unspectacular region of marshes that extends north and south of the Trans-Siberian Railway line between the Irtysh at Omsk and the Ob at Novosibirsk. For most people travelling on the railway it is a drab stretch of country punctuated by small towns glimpsed from the window. While short stops at towns like Tatarsk and Barabinsk offer a chance to stretch legs, the only surprise the Baraba offers at first glance is that of fish, inexplicably the main foodstuff peddled by the middle-aged women working the station platforms. Lakes in the region, though not always obvious, are numerous. It is how Siberia is commonly imagined: large, unchanging and, in winter, a snowy "wasteland". And it is also how Siberia is less commonly imagined: stifling hot in its brief, glowing summers.

If you look closely you will see telltale miniature pillars of earth held together by tufts of grass, suggesting that a swamp is not too far away.

Several lakes come into view as you cross the steppe. North of here between the Irtysh and the Ob is the largest swamp system in the northern hemisphere—the Great Vasyugan Mire. If the Baraba is a purgatory—and most early travellers had good reason to see it like that—the mire is hell itself.

As early as 1628 the Russians had grown concerned about the brittle southern edge of their newly acquired lands, prompting two military governors of the region to travel to the capital with a request to establish a fort on the Irtysh where it meets the Om. Nothing came of the proposal.

Almost a century later, his treasury depleted by war with Sweden, Peter the Great gave orders in 1714 for Ivan Buchholz (a German by descent) to embark on an expedition in search of gold. Armed to the teeth for his dangerous voyage, Buchholz set off from Tobolsk in boats with a contingent of 2,932 men, sailed via Tara down the Irtysh along the fringe of the insect-ridden Baraba and to the border of Dzungaria in northern Kazakhstan, where he began building his fortress. Unfortunately for Buchholz, just as his masterpiece was nearing completion, 10,000 Dzungar (variously referred to as Oirat or Kalmyk) horsemen laid siege, prompting Buchholz and what was left of his men (about 500-700 in the end) to beat a retreat to the mouth of the Om, where, seeking new orders, he established a fortress to keep the raiding Kalmyks at bay and to protect the local Tartar and Russian population. This fortress became Omsk.

The first fortress built by Buchholz was located on the left bank of the Om about a quarter of a mile upstream from the Irtysh, but some fifty years later it was replaced by another on the right bank, situated directly at the confluence.

❧

Omsk grew strongly throughout the eighteenth and nineteenth centuries, becoming a city in 1782, and then the capital of Western Siberia from 1838 after administrative reforms in 1822 had divided Siberia into two separate provinces. (Although Tobolsk was formally capital of Western Siberia in 1824-38, the governor-general resided mostly in Omsk.) Omsk remained the capital until 1882, the year another Siberian reform relegated it to the capital of a separate Steppe Province. It received Decembrist exiles following the uprising in St. Petersburg in 1825, but its most famous exile is the writer Fyodor Dostoevsky, who was imprisoned here for four years.

Many of the older travel writers do not mention Omsk. There are two reasons for this omission: it was founded relatively late and either did not exist or was too small to interest early travellers; also, until the early nineteenth century the Sibirsky Trakt (the Great Siberian Post Road) veered off north towards Tomsk well before reaching Omsk. As a result it only found a place on the traveller's itinerary once the Sibirsky Trakt was relocated south, and later with the construction of the Trans-Siberian Railway. Today it is still often overlooked as nothing more than a place for train travellers to stretch their legs. In fact, it is a fascinating town, even if it is necessary to delve deep below its industrial surface.

REVOLUTION AND CIVIL WAR

One famous figure who did more than stretch his legs was the leader of the White Russian forces during the civil war, Admiral Alexander Kolchak (1874-1920).

When the February revolution of 1917 in Petrograd (St. Petersburg) brought down Russia's monarchy, the governors of Siberia tried to hush up the news. It was a pointless and foolish exercise, as by early March word had trickled through, mainly to those towns situated on the main railway lines. The news was greeted with celebrations among Siberians. Virtually all public officials, but especially the tsar's governors, were promptly thrown out of office, and special committees were created to keep law and order and to carry out reforms. At the same time, revolutionaries set about establishing soviets (councils of workers and soldiers). Thanks to the exile system, Siberia was one place with revolutionaries in abundance, and soon they were setting their sights on dominating the committees. It would take the civil war before they succeeded.

The revolution in Siberia was characterized by two trends. One was Siberian autonomy which was favoured by so-called regionalists backed by moderates and industrialists; they managed to create regional rural bodies and even organized a conference in Tomsk in early October 1917 to pave the way for a constitution and independence. The other tendency was driven by comparatively moderate Bolsheviks, anarchists and Mensheviks. Unlike their more radical counterparts in European Russia, these groups even supported in principle the newly created provisional government in Petrograd, but their members were divided on the question of Siberian autonomy. While on the whole the political tone in Siberia tended to be more moderate than in Petrograd, exiled Bolsheviks did form their own Siberian branch of a Central Committee that was affiliated with Petrograd's. Once the Bolsheviks in Petrograd formally resolved to seize power, cooperation among the various groups in Siberia broke down. Through propaganda targeting a large number of reservist soldiers in Siberia, the Bolsheviks were able to create a small division of Red Guards (the military mainstay of the Bolsheviks) in Siberia to support their bid for power and unite a majority of other party members behind their call for "all power to the soviets".

The Bolsheviks remained a small and unpopular minority among ordinary Siberians, but from the revolution in October 1917 they stepped up efforts to seize control. They were mostly able to exploit divisions to get their way without violence, but Omsk resisted, with the result that Red Guards had to be brought in from European Russia to bring it under the Bolshevik wing.

The average Siberian had numerous practical reasons for withholding support from the Bolsheviks. Although the Bolsheviks handed over all state-controlled land to the peasants, it did not really mean very much locally because Siberia had almost endless land. Peasant debts were cancelled, but this, too, was insignificant as no one in Siberia was repaying their debts by that time anyway. Furthermore, policies such as fixing grain prices artificially low at about one-sixth of the market price or trying to ban any kind of trade in food products were anathema to the Siberians, who lived from the flourishing small farmers' markets. Coupled with the diminishing prospect of autonomy, such policies fuelled opposition, and before long the Bolsheviks were forced to use their Red Guards yet again to quash resistance. The first uprising against the Bolsheviks took place in Irkutsk in December 1917, but the largest underground movement—like the others at that time, fuelled by the idea of Siberian autonomy—formed in Omsk.

Full-scale civil war raged all over Russia, but Siberia became the most important showplace of this conflict. Escalation was gradual. The Bolshevik fighters consisted of Red Guards as well as a volunteer "Red Army" that had grown out of imperial Russia's forces and prisoners of war from other nations captured during the First World War and sympathetic to the revolution. Resisting them were a detachment of Cossacks, former soldiers and volunteers that had formed under a Cossack officer by the name of

Grigory Semyonov (1890-1946), who led repeated forays into Russia from Manchuria across the border. They were partly armed by the Japanese, who saw an opportunity to get a foothold in Siberia and were augmented by various local underground groups such as the one in Omsk.

But it is another group that aroused the most interest, and gave Britain, the US, Japan, France and China a pretext to become directly involved. This was the so-called Czech Legion, some 40,000 Czech and Slovak soldiers, most of them prisoners of war, who supported an independent Czech-Slovak state (at that time part of the Austro-Hungarian Empire) and in the First World War fought as a separate unit alongside the Russians. After Russia signed the Treaty of Brest-Litovsk, ending hostilities with Germany, Leon Trotsky, Russia's war commissioner, gave the legion permission to cross Siberia (the only way out at the time) to board boats bound for Europe in order to fight the Allies on the Western Front. However, while the legion was travelling by rail to Vladivostok, Trotsky issued an order to disarm them. Learning of Trotsky's order and with relations between the legion and the Bolsheviks already poisoned by distrust, the legion rebelled in May 1918 while scattered throughout various parts of Siberia, triggering full-scale uprising against the Bolsheviks. After the legion and the underground White forces took Omsk in June 1918, uprisings occurred elsewhere, so that by late 1918 the Bolsheviks had lost virtually all of Siberia.

The seizure of Omsk was the beginning of a chain of events that turned the city into a focal point during the civil war. After the overthrow of the Bolsheviks a provisional Siberian government was established, and by this time Siberia even had its own flag—a rectangle divided diagonally into green and white sections, standing for taiga and snow. When in October 1918 a new all-Russian provisional government formed to oppose the Bolsheviks was forced to flee the Urals town of Ufa ahead of advancing Red Guards, it went to Omsk, where the St. Petersburg-born Alexander Kolchak was installed in a military coup in November 1918, thus being appointed to the position of "Supreme Ruler" of Russia. Though vesting himself with the powers of a military dictator, his plans for post-civil war Russia were vague and, in reality, he had trouble controlling some of his own forces.

Estimates put the number of foreign soldiers in Siberia at about 100,000. Eighty per cent of these were Japanese, who at one point occupied all of the Transbaikal (beginning on the eastern shore of Lake Baikal) and the Amur Region. It was also in their interests to encourage Siberian Cossack *atamans* (military leaders) there to act independently (this usually meant ruthlessly), causing some of the worst atrocities in the civil war.

Russia's self-styled Supreme Ruler had a strong aversion to the Socialist Revolutionaries (the party Siberians had favoured in the all-Russian elections), and not being from Siberia himself, he vehemently rejected the idea of autonomy. Neither of these traits increased his popularity. He tried but was unable to bring the Cossack atamans under control, and he boosted the ranks of his army by forcing peasants to serve in it. Soon his forces had gone from being saviours to pariahs and Siberians were engaged in a guerrilla war to overthrow him, opening the way for the Red Army to cross the Urals and fight its way back across Siberia. In November 1919 Kolchak was forced to flee eastwards as the Red Army advanced on Omsk and took the "capital". Other towns fell, and Kolchak was eventually arrested in Irkutsk and executed.

All foreign powers except Japan abandoned intervention from late 1919; by early 1920 the civil war was a lost cause for the Whites, and

Kolchak's troops, 1919

throughout 1920-21 soviets were re-established across Siberia and the period of "Red Terror" began. Again, Siberians rose up, this time in peasant revolts, due to the Bolsheviks' policy of confiscating surplus produce and because of their claim to a monopoly of power, accompanied by rigged voting in the soviets. Many Siberians were now calling for "soviets without communists".

Similar uprisings occurred throughout Russia, and events in Siberia were a significant factor in prompting Lenin to introduce his New Economic Policy to free up the economy. But Lenin also sent in army reinforcements and secret police to crush the Siberian uprisings. Again, Omsk played a role, as a large group of Cossacks had been based in Omsk Region at Ishim, and these regrouped with other White forces to launch guerrilla attacks from across the border in China, leading to protracted fighting in the Far East. By late 1922, however, all of Siberia had fallen to the Bolsheviks.

EXPLORING OMSK

Omsk is not a city that inspires love at first sight. But it is Siberia's second-largest (after Novosibirsk), and if you ask someone east of the Urals which city is the most Siberian of all on the subcontinent, he or she may well say Omsk or Krasnoyarsk. Both are situated on one of the great rivers. Both were founded as fortresses and both are old enough and large enough to capture the drama of Siberia's history. While Irkutsk (because of Lake Baikal) and Novosibirsk (due to its size) draw large numbers of visitors or new arrivals, Omsk and Krasnoyarsk have grown organically to become significant metropolises.

The heart of the old town is ploshchad Sobornaya (Cathedral Square). Today this is the site of the Assumption Cathedral (Uspensky Kafedralny Sobor), reconstructed in 2007 on the site of a former cathedral from 1898. The original was hailed as being among the most majestic of the nineteenth-century churches in Siberia—it featured Byzantine "Russian revivalist" elements—and was inspired by St. Petersburg's Resurrection Church (Christ-on-Blood), where Alexander II was fatally wounded in 1881. The foundation stone of the Assumption Cathedral was laid by his grandson, Nicholas II, but the cathedral's fate was sealed in 1935 when the city council demolished it and turned the site into Pioneers' Square. The bells were removed and sent to the smelters for recycling. This was how

Assumption Cathedral, Omsk

things stayed until 2005, when the go-ahead was given for reconstruction. Architects faced a difficult problem, however; the original cathedral had been built using few drawings, and none survived, so they resorted to old photographs. Then, during excavations, archaeologists discovered the original foundations, which allowed a precise reconstruction of the cathedral's shape. Interior decorations today are entirely the work of local artists and the historic lower level has been earmarked to become a memorial hall with a museum and shops.

On the western side of the cathedral is the Composition of the Golden Marathon Runner (Skulpturnaya Kompozitsiya "Zolotoy Marafonets"), dating from 2003 by the Moscow artist Vadim Kirillov. It celebrates the tenth anniversary of the Siberian International Marathon held in Omsk each year in August.

Directly opposite the cathedral is the Omsk Region administration, inside the former House of Justice building at Krasny Put 1. Work began on a new justice building on 20 November 1914 when a foundation was also laid for a monument to Alexander II on ploshchad Sobornaya as a memorial to the tsar who reformed the tsarist judicial system to bring Russia closer to the European legal systems of the late nineteenth century. Events soon overtook the planners, however. The revolution of 1917 meant that the memorial stood on the square for less than a year before being dismantled, transferred to the site of a local factory, and around 1928 disappearing altogether. The building itself was scarcely used for its intended purpose. It was, however, occupied by Admiral Kolchak, who was sworn in and governed from this building as Supreme Ruler of Russia during the civil war. With the return of the Bolsheviks in 1919 it became the headquarters of the Communist Party and the nerve centre for governing the Omsk Region. Notable or notorious figures who have passed through the portals of this three-storey brick building with its attractive combination of porticos, dome, pediments and inner courtyard include Joseph Stalin (1878-1953), Felix Dzerzhinsky (1877-1926; founder of the "Cheka" secret police) and former Soviet head Mikhail Kalinin (1875-1946). In 1991 it became the seat of the Omsk Region administration.

South of here on ulitsa Lenina is a picturesque square with a small fountain and a memorial stone to the victims of Stalin's regime (1991) and behind it Tara Gate (Tarskaya Vorota). The gate, also dating from 1991, is a reconstruction of the original fortress gate from 1792. It stands on what was the main thoroughfare leading into town from Tara. Dostoevsky passed through it in January 1850 as the second station of his journey into exile, but these days it is better known as a venue for open air music.

The building situated at ulitsa Lenina 2 on the northern side of the square is the Omsk Region FSB (Federal Security Service) headquarters— known locally as the "grey house"—and even better known as the former KGB headquarters for the region. This is an ensemble of several buildings dating back to the turn of the twentieth century, when a bishop's house and consistory were built on the site. From 1920 it was used as a psychiatric hospital before the two buildings were reconstructed in the 1930s, taken over by the security service and used by the KGB (called OGPU at the time) as a headquarters and prison for detainees.

Continuing along ulitsa Lenina one reaches an ugly memorial to Fyodor Dostoevsky from 2000 and the more attractive Academic Drama Theatre (Akademichesky Teatr Dramy) at ulitsa Lenina 8a. Even in its very early days Omsk had a lively theatre scene, but it long lacked a first-class venue for performances. This changed in 1905 when, at the instigation of local artists and theatre-goers, a new theatre building was opened, designed by I. G. Khvorinov (1835-1914). Khvorinov also designed the impressive historic department store at ulitsa Lenina 5. The Drama Theatre, however, is considered his masterpiece, was one of the largest in Siberia at the time, and is a revivalist blend of classical and baroque motifs, with sweeping balconies, ionic columns and an attractive domed roof.

This stretch of ulitsa Lenina was formerly known as Lyubinsky prospekt and is remarkable for its early twentieth-century buildings and what some may recognize as a turn-of-the-century New World feel. Anyone familiar with inner suburbs of Melbourne, Australia (such as Carlton or Fitzroy), will notice uncanny similarities, including the preponderance of expensive boutiques.

Across the road from the Drama Theatre at ulitsa Lenina 3 is the Mikhail Aleksandrovich Vrubel Museum of Fine Arts (Muzey Izobrazitalnykh Iskusstv imeni Mikhaila Aleksandrovicha Vrubelya). The museum is housed in two buildings; this one, the Vrubel Building (Korpus Vrubelya, inside a former trading store from 1914), contains Russian paintings from the eighteenth to the early twentieth centuries and a collection of about 300 paintings by mostly minor Western European artists working from the sixteenth century onwards. The second building is inside the former House of the Governor General, across the bridge at ulitsa Lenina 23, and holds the museum's collection of decorative arts.

The museum was founded in 1924 and has grown over the years to house over 25,000 items. It benefited greatly from the period when Omsk was the capital of Western Siberia, while other works were either transferred here from various museums in Omsk, from Moscow and St. Petersburg, or were bequeathed or bought from private collections. In all, the collection is excellent, with eight canvases by the avant-garde artist Alexei Yavlensky (1864-1941), as well as works by fellow abstract expressionist Vasily Kandinsky (1866-1944), and the Russian Cubist artist Natalya Goncharova (1881-1962). Ilya Repin's (1844-1930) portrait of the Russian expressionist playwright Leonid Andreyev (1871-1919) is another highlight of the collection, as is Nikolay Rerikh's painting *Boats*. Rerikh (1874-1947; sometimes written as Nicholas Roerich), the St. Petersburg-born theosophist and painter, travelled through Omsk in mid-1926 on his way back to Moscow from his Himalayan expedition.

Other Russian masters who have a place in the collection are landscape painter Ivan Shishkin (1832-98) and Konstantin Makovsky (1839-1915). Both of these belong to the so-called Peredvizhniki (Wanderers) movement of realists who wandered the Russian countryside in the late nineteenth century holding exhibitions, enabling them to escape the artistic restrictions of the academies. The Krasnoyarsk-born Vasily Surikov (1848-1916), famous particularly for his painting *The Conquest of Siberia by Yermak* (from 1895 and today in Moscow's Russian State Museum), is also represented here, and last but not least are works by the museum's namesake, the Omsk-born Symbolist painter Mikhail Vrubel (1856-1910).

The museum itself is flanked by parkland, and alongside it is a collection of iron sculptures by the Omsk-born artist Alexander Kapralov. The ensemble includes his complex *Scales of Life* (1998) and has artistic allusions to literary figures, particularly Don Quixote.

A short walk south brings the visitor to a small chapel reconstructed in 1995 on the site of an original from 1867, erected when a religious procession was held to rid the city of cholera. Across the road from the chapel is one of several statues of Lenin in Omsk and behind that, at ulitsa Lenina 10, the building of the First Women's School (Pervaya Zhenskaya Gimnaziya) dating from the early 1880s with neoclassical influences.

Running east off ulitsa Lenina is a street formally known as ulitsa Gasfordovskaya, after the governor general of Western Siberia from 1851-61, Gustav Gasford, and today renamed ulitsa Karla Libknekhta. It is an attractive street in parts with a collection of neoclassical buildings near the corner that combine well with the architectural unity of ulitsa Lenina. Two of these buildings are the former House of the Russian-American Fellowship "Triangle" (Treugolnik, from 1915) at ulitsa Karla Libknekhta 2, and the former building of the Salamander Insurance Society at no. 3 from 1914. Both are the work of the architect N. N. Verevkin, who seems to have done well out of the company, having had a hand in designing their offices on St. Petersburg's prestigious ulitsa Gorokhovaya, as well as other contemporaneous buildings on that street.

Ulitsa Karla Libknekhta is also the site of two more recent sculptural additions to the Omsk cityscape. One is the so-called Plumber Stepan, a sewage worker peering cheekily out of a manhole, a copy of a sculpture in Bratislava, and across from this Lyubochka, the Siberian (second) wife of

Plumber Stepan

Gasford and something of a society and cultural figure in nineteenth-century Omsk. She died of consumption in 1852 and, along with her colleague looking out of the manhole, was immortalized in iron in the late 1990s.

Further along ulitsa Lenina stand the domed Moscow Trade Rows at no. 14, dating from 1904 and Omsk's equivalent of the GUM trading rows in Moscow, and a building next door at no. 16 from the same year that belonged to the industrialist V. Morozov. Situated alongside this where ulitsa Lenina and ulitsa Partizanskaya meet is the monumental former Hotel Rossiya (now Hotel Oktyabr), also dating from 1905, where the Czech writer Yaroslav Hašek (best known for his *The Good Soldier Švejk*) lived for a while in 1919-20. From here, turn right (west) into ulitsa Partizanskaya, where the hotel building connects to what was the Crystal Palace Theatre in 1916 and today is a cinema.

At ulitsa Partizanskaya 14 is the former Guardhouse (Zdanie Byvshoy Khauptvakhty), Omsk's earliest surviving building. Built in 1781-85 within the second fortress on the north side of the parade ground, its baroque features are more austere than usual due it having been a military building that was originally constructed to house the fortress guards and administrators, but also contained cells for keeping soldiers who had stepped out of line. Upstairs rooms in the guardhouse were used as a school for the children of soldiers and Cossacks, and interestingly, it became an early language institute: in the late eighteenth century, when interpreters were trained in Central Asian languages. Once Omsk's fortress became redundant, the guardhouse was used for housing civil prisoners.

Near the guardhouse is a second statue of the writer Dostoevsky, and through the park, towards the river, is the House of the Commander (Komendatsky Dom), at ulitsa Dostoevskovo 1. Dating from 1799, this building was originally used by the commander of the fortress, and later by officers before being restored in the 1980s and converted into a literary museum. Dostoevsky is the main focus of many of the displays (it has a death mask of the writer); the collection is quite modest but interesting, and in the claustrophobic cellar of the building, reached via a trapdoor, various torture gadgets and other prisoner paraphernalia have been assembled. They include a daunting brush-like nail stamp used to tattoo the letter "K" onto the foreheads of the unfortunate inmates—standing for *Katorzhnik* (prisoner condemned to hard labour).

From the museum, walk to the bank of the Om and follow this back to the bridge (Yubileyny Most) and the small Serafimo-Alekseevskaya Chapel (Serafimo-Alekseevskaya Chasovya), a reconstruction of the chapel that stood here between 1907 and 1928. The resurrected version dates from the 1990s and, like the original, is of red-brick in a revivalist style hinting at a traditional Russian wooden church.

Across the bridge and just south of the square on ulitsa Lenina is the Palace of the Governor-General (General-Gubernatorsky Dvoretz), today housing the collection of decorative arts from the Fine Arts Museum, flanked by the ugly modern appendage of the State Historical-Local Studies Museum (Gosudarsvenny Istoriko-Kraevedchesky Muzey) at ulitsa Lenina 23a.

The Palace of the Governor-General was built on the site where originally a guesthouse stood for ambassadors arriving from Central Asia. In 1823, however, fire engulfed Omsk and the opportunity was taken to rethink its urban topography. Interestingly, one person who played a role in this was the architect William Hastie (1755-1832). Like the traveller John Bell, who left Britain and ended up on the payroll of a tsar, Hastie was born in Scotland; he eventually headed the office of town planning under Tsar Alexander I and shaped many of Russia's towns in the early nineteenth century. He was not the only Scot with a hand in Russian architecture. Another, Charles Cameron (1745-1812), was invited to Russia by Catherine the Great in 1779. Cameron worked on Tsarkoe Selo, the tsarist summer palace outside St. Petersburg, and in several other towns and he was joined by Hastie, a trained mason, who answered an advertisement in 1784 to come to Russia.

Hastie eventually rose to become chief architect of the palace from 1808-32 after capturing the attention of Catherine the Great during the last years of her reign, and his brief was extended to town planning and development. Between 1811 and 1830, his influence was such that he could make or break virtually any decision on town planning in Russia. After the 1823 fire in Omsk, plans for rebuilding found their way to Hastie, who considered them flawed and promptly redrew them, with the result that Omsk's original layout remained mostly intact and the new concept allowed public squares to be integrated into the architectural whole.

Gasford initiated construction of the palace, which was completed in 1862 and became the residence of the governor-general before changing hands several times during the civil war. The Red Army moved in after it took Omsk in 1919, but by 1925 the town's museum was already located on one floor as well as a roads planning authority. By the 1980s the Fine Arts Museum occupied the whole building.

This stretch of ulitsa Lenina is a main thoroughfare and unattractive for the most part, but it does have a couple of buildings from the mid- and late nineteenth century, such as the former Society Assembly building (Obshestvennoe Sobranie) at no. 25 and the Hotel Sibir at no. 22. Further along at no. 27 is St. Nicholas Cossack Cathedral (Nikolsky Kazachy Sobor), a neoclassical cathedral dating from the 1840s in which the original pennant belonging to Yermak was housed before it vanished during the civil war.

When the British traveller and writer John Foster Fraser arrived in Omsk in the autumn of 1901 during a journey through Siberia and Manchuria "on a mission of curiosity", he described the cathedral as "an imposing bulb-towered edifice of bedizened Byzantian architecture". He writes: "I went to see the church just as the congregation was dispersing. The ladies were more or less fashionably dressed in bright summer costumes and beflowered hats, and had gay parasols. Summer dresses and parasols in Siberia—there was something incongruous in the idea!" Omsk was the place where Fraser began to see in Siberia much more than a "frigid desert", a frozen heart of darkness. His change of perception was perhaps partly due to the ladies leaving the cathedral, but it also had something to do with the appearance of Omsk as "not unlike a West American town", with its mixture of stone buildings and ramshackle wooden houses. Fraser writes:

> It was while at Omsk that I awoke to the fact that my previous idea about Siberia was marvellously wrong. It was, of course, the popular idea, which is more dramatic than the actual condition. Siberia, to that useful but ill-informed individual, "the man in the street," is a horrible stretch of frigid desert, dotted with gaunt prison houses, and the tracks over the steppes are marked with the bones of exiles who have died beneath the weight of chains, starvation, and the inhospitable treatment of savage Russian soldiers. I had not, however, been long in Siberia before I realised that the desire on the part of writers to give the public something dramatic to read about had led them to exaggerate one feature of Siberian life and to practically neglect the real Siberia, full of interest but lacking sensation. So let me try to wipe from the public mind the fallacy that Siberia is a Gehenna-like region.

Like others who visited around the turn-of-the-century, Fraser found a Siberia with a bright future and "ripe for agricultural projects". He met a Danish butter manufacturer in Omsk who was exporting 30,000 buckets of butter per week to England, and he met one of eight Americans in Omsk at that time selling agricultural machinery: "One, the representative of the Deering Manufacturing Company, said to me, 'Sir, I have been all over the United States, and this is my third summer visit to do business in Omsk. I tell you Siberia is going to be another America.'"

It might have been, but it never happened. In the end, it was not agriculture but oil and gas that turned Siberia into Russia's post-Soviet cash cow.

From the St. Nicholas Cathedral on ulitsa Lenina it is just a short walk west to the banks of the Irtysh, from where you can follow the promenade north to the river station and ploshchad Bukhgoltsa (Buchholz Square). It was here that Ivan Buchholz set up his first camp after being driven back by the Kalmyks. Today, the river station is the departure point for cruises along the Irtysh as far as Salekhard during the season.

The Baraba Steppe

The Baraba Steppe is western Siberia's unspectacular agricultural heartland and today scarcely a shadow of its former self. This wooded steppe dotted with hundreds of lakes—the largest of which is Lake Chany, an important habitat for water birds—was long considered the wildest and most dangerous part of Siberia. Even well into the nineteenth century it was not the safest of places in which to set foot. This was one region where if the bloodthirsty insects did not attack the unfortunate traveller, rapacious bandits would.

The problem travellers here faced did not stem from the local Tartar population, but from Kalmyks (Oirats) or in some cases Kazakhs riding up from the south. In fact, many of the towns passed on the train between Omsk and Novosibirsk—including the largest one, Kuybyshev, known as Kainsk when it was founded in 1722—were founded to shore up the southern steppe from Oirat and Kazakh horsemen, who were not averse to taking hostages. "It is generally reckoned," writes John Bell about the

Swampy terrain in the Baraba Steppe

Baraba in the 1720s, "that more robberies are committed in the Baraba, than in any country on the road to China."

Bell describes the Baraba Steppe in his day as a vast marshy plain full of lakes and overgrown with aspen, alder, willows and birch trees. The lakes, he said, abounded with pike, perch, bream, eel and a fish he calls "karrafs", caught by the Baraba Tartars in summer and dried for the winter.

> I have eaten it often, and thought it not disagreeable. In winter they [the Baraba Tartars] use melted snow for water. They are very hospitable; and desire nothing in return of their civilities, but a little tobacco to smoke, and a dram of brandy, of which they are very fond. The dress, both of men and women, consists of long coats of sheep-skins, which they get from the Russians and Kalmucks [Oirats], in exchange for more valuable furs. As they wear no other apparel, not even shirts, they are very nasty. Their huts are most miserable habitations, and sunk about one half underground. We were glad, however, to find them, as a baiting-place in such a cold season.

The blind traveller, James Holman, had a slightly different angle on the Baraba when he sniffed and touched his way across it in the early 1820s and recorded his experiences. Like Bell, he notes the risk of being robbed. He writes:

> ... we began to enter upon the Barabinski Marshes, the very water of which is so noxious as to act as a deadly poison on the stomachs of those animals who drink it. So frequent were the deaths from this source, that an eminent medical man was sent by the government to investigate the cause, when it was ascertained to depend upon the qualities of a poisonous species of hemlock... the fact was proved by direct experiments made on dogs...

Guards, he says, had since been placed around the lakes to prevent the cattle drinking the water. He likens the Baraba to "tartarus", the abyss or dungeon in Greek mythology that forms part of Hades:

> ... the insalubrious quality of its atmosphere, loaded with malaria, or miasmatic impregnation, is not only abundantly productive of typhus

and intermittent fevers, but gives rise to a disease peculiar to this horrid steppe. This is a tumour, that commencing on some part of the head, but more commonly on the cheek, continues to enlarge until it bursts and frequently proves fatal.

This district gives birth also, to immense swarms of poisonous flies, like other insects, that almost literally overwhelm the unfortunate subject exposed to their attack; they penetrate into the mouth, ears, eyes, or any part that is not carefully guarded against them; the irritation of their bites is so great that the face of the traveller requires to be covered with gauze, to protect him from serious injury.

For Holman—though it should be kept in mind that his experience was somewhat quixotic, as he could only rely on other people's visual accounts—the Baraba was "a dreary pestilential country—a country so ungenial as to be only inhabited by wild animals, reptiles, and a few sickly Tartars, and which my imagination, excited by the accounts it had previously imbibed, did not fail to represent to me as the counterpart of the territory of the baleful Upas [a poison] itself."

One person who did see the Baraba was Georg Adolf Erman (1806-77), the German physicist and geologist with a special interest in magnetism. From 1828 Erman spent two years travelling around the world taking measurements, and these measurements formed the basis for Carl Friedrich Gauss' groundbreaking theory of terrestrial magnetism. Following his return, Erman wrote a two-volume account of his journey, called *Travels in Siberia*, in which he recounts in the second volume his trips up the Ob river to Obdorsk (today Salekhard) and across the subcontinent. He described the Baraba in winter as distinguishable by a "more regular outline of the monotonous waste of snow", mentioning wide tracts of reeds penetrating the snow and the swamps that "render the vicinity extremely dangerous for summer residence, and cause much annoyance, even to the traveller, at that season. The flies and gnats become then so tormenting, that it is impossible to venture abroad without a covering for the face, and the cattle even are obliged to be smeared with tar."

Like Holman, Erman found Kuybyshev (Kainsk) unimpressive, dismissing it as "gloomy and repulsive": "It contains nothing but mean and ill-built huts. I determined to remain there a short time, in the hope of being able to make some astronomical observations, but was disappointed by the sudden outburst of a snow storm." While there, he stayed in the hut of a Russian peasant (not a Tartar). "The settler's dwelling in which we were lodged, was far more dirty and miserable than those of the generality of the Siberian boors. The whole family lay crowded in a single apartment, furnished only with the common boiler, and encumbered with confused heaps of old peltry [animal pelts] and articles of clothing." Yet once he reached Lake Ubinsk (Ubinskoe Ozero), close to Novosibirsk on the eastern edge of the Baraba Steppe, Erman discovered an idyllic scene of villages dotting the landscape and rows of peasants' houses and larger villas with balconies and enclosed courtyards.

This region Erman refers to around Lake Ubinsk is the southern wedge of the Great Vasyugan Mire, the Northern Hemisphere's largest swamp, combining forested swampland, fens and bogs. The eastern section has been nominated for inclusion on the list of Unesco World Heritage sites.

Chapter Seven

OVER THE TOP:
THE NORTHERN SEA ROUTE

In mid-August 1894 the *New York Times* ran a small article on its regular "Her Point of View" page for women. Among pieces that tell us "in sultry autumn weather fruit water ices are more cooling than richer creams" and that "a dentist advises that acids are even worse than sweets", the article stands out as frighteningly portentous. It reads

> The Princess Alix of Hesse is finding that her coming greatness—that of a future Empress of Russia—is already casting long shadows before her. She has finished her course of religious education necessary to be received into the Russian Church... is now being instructed by a Russian tutor to the imperial family sent from St. Petersburg for the purpose... and recently a cordial letter from the Czar asked her what especial "act of mercy" she would like to have "ukased" in honour of the important event, "the pardoning of a thousand persons" being suggested by way of example.

The "Czar" mentioned is Nicholas II, while "Princess Alix" is none other than Alexandra Fyodorovna—later to be killed on the night of 16 July 1918 in Yekaterinburg.

While Alexandra was beginning to grasp what she might be letting herself in for by marrying Russia's last tsar, this same edition of "Her Point of View" reviewed a modest literary work under the headline "Woman at the Far North". It begins: "As every field is tempting women nowadays to an invasion, it is not surprising that the sombre and uncertain one of polar exploration finds its devotees among the fairer sex."

The woman at the far north was Helen Peel, daughter of Sir Robert Peel (1788-1850), the former British Home Secretary and Prime Minister who created London's police force. She had just published a book entitled *Polar Gleams*, which the newspaper thought "lacked the tragic element" of another, rival book but nevertheless evoked the "poetry of Arctic life". The editorialist of "Her Point of View" was apparently disinclined towards the notion of women travelling this far north. Helen Peel was, we are told, "only distinguished as any pretty, well-born, young woman is distinguished, in her social circle, until this fondness of travel and love of adventure led her to accept an invitation to join a party of voyagers to the far north."

The far north in question was the Arctic Ocean on the shores of Siberia's northern coast, and what Helen Peel had done was to join a party of six ships that in 1893 sailed across this ocean to the Yenisey river. From the article we learn that the voyagers had been contracted by the Russian government to carry 1,600 tons of rails to the "mighty Yenisei River".

A small fleet of Russian steamers, and its officers were amazed to find that Miss Peel had not provided herself with any furs, her costume consisting of a blue serge skirt, an unlined jacket to match, a red flannel skirt, and a straw sailor hat. The young Arctic voyageuse says, however, that she scarcely suffered from cold at all.

Siberia has always attracted its share of thrill-seekers. One of these was undoubtedly James Holman, the blind Englishman who breezed through on his "world tour" and wrote a journal that, as his contemporary Siberia traveller, John Dundas Cochrane, remarked, "certainly cannot be of ocular evidence." Cochrane, in fact, seems to have been envious of

Holman rising to fame on the strength of a disability, and he harboured grave doubts that anything could come of the venture. He comments wryly that Holman not only had the disadvantage of being blind and needing to rely on hearsay to fill his pages, but could also hardly speak a word of Russian. The military captain concluded: "Who will then say that Siberia is a wild, inhospitable country, when even the blind can traverse it with safety?"

Yet Cochrane himself, a straight-laced and proper captain of the British Navy who walked across much of Siberia, was also driven by the "freakish". Even in the nineteenth century when transport was more rudimentary than today, going by foot across Siberia was an unlikely challenge, and his regret is tangible when he writes that the fact that his journey "has only in part been performed on foot is to be attributed to the liberality of the Russian government, as well as to the hospitality of its people." Perhaps he should have tried walking to China blindfolded.

Someone who was neither straight-laced nor proper was the Connecticut-born John Ledyard, a maverick explorer who decided it would be interesting to cross the United States to the eastern seaboard on a land route starting in the other direction—via Siberia. Even in a part of the world where the outlandish is often met with a tolerant shrug, with well-meaning condolences for being foreign or with wry earnestness, Ledyard ran into snags and was escorted out of Siberia against his will by the Russian government. The experience of most people at the time, of course, was to be escorted against their will into Siberia by the Russian government. Put in this context, a group of high-kicking society figures sailing a dangerous stretch of water full of icebergs and polar bears—one known for being impassable rather than as a venue for musical frolics under a midnight sun—ranks as being only marginally beyond the norm.

EXPLORING SIBERIA'S SEAS

Four seas lap the northern coastline of Siberia. Helen Peel sailed one of them, the Kara Sea, which stretches from the Urals (marked by their seaward extension, the Novaya Zemlya or New Islands) to the Severnaya Zemlya (Northern Islands). Historically, this piece of coastline was important because when ice-free it offered access into western and central Siberia via the Ob and the Yenisey rivers. Farther east, the Laptev Sea begins at the Taymyr Peninsula and ends at the Novosibirskye Zemlya

(New Siberian Islands), receiving the waters of the Lena river, which provided a navigational link between inland eastern Siberia and the ocean. The other two seas, the Eastern Siberian Sea and the Chukchi Sea, proved even more difficult to navigate and flank areas that even by Siberian standards remain remote and wild. Despite this remoteness, the rivers that flow into the Eastern Siberian Sea, especially the Indigirka and the Khatanga, developed into important transport routes used by very early explorers to travel overland to Kamchatka.

It is likely that Norse seamen of the ninth century were venturing to the cusp of Siberia when they travelled the Barents Sea in search of seals and walrus. They either harvested the walrus tusk ivory themselves or traded for it with the coastal inhabitants, but it is less likely that they penetrated into the Kara proper. From about the twelfth century Novgorod sailors were also plying the White Sea in European Russia, but it was not until about 400 years later that anyone ventured into the seas of Siberia. It was probably also around the sixteenth century that local Nenets tribes moved into the coastal region of the Kara Sea and assimilated earlier indigenous peoples living there.

This was a time of change. From the 1500s Russian traders from the White Sea coastal regions (called the Pomore) sailed small boats (*kochy*) to the Gulf of Ob and beyond along the so-called Mangazeya Sea Route. This involved ocean travel (but occasionally portages by Russians) to round the Yamal Peninsula into the Gulf of Ob before mariners sailed up the Taz river to the boomtown of Mangazeya, founded in 1601 on the Taz to exploit walrus ivory and fur in the region.

Dutch and English seafarers were also attracted to the region, and not just because of the possibility of exploiting its riches, but also through their interest in finding a route across the top to the Pacific Ocean, from where they could reach the Indian Ocean. Theories about a passage across the north had been raised in 1527 by a British merchant Robert Thorne, who was based in Seville in Spain and wrote a letter to Henry VIII proposing the north-east passage as a viable alternative to the southern route into the Indian Ocean around the Cape of Good Hope. The Portuguese and Spanish controlled the African ports with fresh water supplies in the sixteenth century, and Britain, which was only beginning its rise as a maritime nation, desperately needed an alternative route in order to challenge the colonial achievements of Spain and Portugal. As a result, from the 1550s

British navigators were active in the northern seas and initiated the first formal contact between Russia and Britain.

The Dutch cartographer and sea captain Willem Barentsz (1550-97) thought the summer night-time sun might keep a passage ice-free. He was woefully wrong. On his third expedition into the region he reached Novaya Zemlya and, convinced there would be less ice at the northern tip of the islands, became unexpectedly caught in pack ice as he tried to force his way through. He died June 1597 after a bitterly cold winter spent on the ice.

The Dutch had lagged behind the British in their quest for new routes into the Orient, but Barentsz and his crew of the third expedition would press their noses ahead in one unusual respect, unwittingly becoming the first known Europeans from outside Russia to have wintered on Arctic ice. Their dramatic tale of being enclosed by mountains of ice and wintering in cold darkness of the north is captured in a vivid account of Barentsz's voyages by the carpenter Gerrit de Veer, who kept a diary of the third voyage. Some of de Veer's details are questioned, but his *The True and Perfect Description of Three Voyages by the Ships of Holland and Zeland*

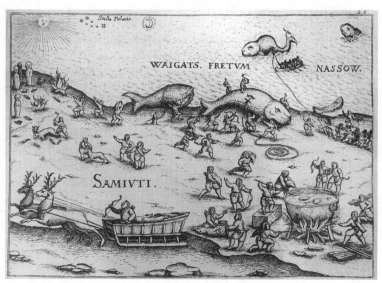

Illustration from Gerrit de Veer's diary

(1609) remains a fascinating early description offering an insight into the Arctic elements: most notably, the power of ice as it drifts and encloses the vessel within a jagged landscape of white mountains that leave the frightened men no other option than to hold on helplessly to their vessel and pray that they will soon be released. In late January, one of the sixteen-man crew opened the door of their makeshift 32-foot long hut built from the wood of the ship to house them for the winter and sees, for the first time in months, the sun peeking over the white horizon. After that, the men began going for walks as the light gradually returned and then equipped small boats in order to sail back to Vardø (Wardhouse) in Norway. Barentsz was ill by this time and asked de Veer to raise him while rounding Novaya Zemlya if Ice Point, its most northerly headland, became visible. The boats were caught in floes, however, and the men, suffering from scurvy, were forced to clamber onto one and camp there, where Barentsz died on 20 June, seven days after the group had set out. Seven weeks later the surviving twelve men reached the mainland at the Kola Peninsula.

Weakened by an interregnum in the early seventeenth century (the so-called Times of Trouble), Russia watched while British and Dutch merchants increased trade in the White Sea, but when the ships of foreign powers started appearing on the Mangazeya Sea Route, the route was closed down completely by Russia from 1619, and the land route became the only way to reach resource-rich Mangazeya.

The closing of the sea route dampened large-scale exploration of the northern coast for a century, and activity on Siberia's northern seas from that time was limited to coastal navigation between the great rivers by Cossacks. A voyage around the eastern tip and into today's Bering Sea by the Cossack Semyon Dezhnev in 1648 was the most successful of these, but Dezhnev's record of the journey lay lost in an archive in Yakutsk for almost a century before being unearthed by the German academic Gerhard Friedrich Müller (1705-83) from the St. Petersburg Academy of the Sciences. It was partly because of the loss of Dezhnev's account that the Dane Vitus Bering had to repeat the exploration of the Bering Strait on his First Kamchatka Expedition.

The Second Kamchatka Expedition
Peter the Great, who had founded the Academy of the Sciences by decree in 1724, instigated the next important step when he commissioned Vitus

Bering to lead an expedition to explore and map the northern coasts of imperial Russia. Bering had already tried to find out whether Russia and America were connected by a land bridge, but his next expedition took on a completely different scale. Known as the Great Northern Expedition or the Second Kamchatka Expedition, it comprised four marine detachments under Bering's command and a land-based academic group that included members of the St. Petersburg Academy of the Sciences. It lasted from 1733 to 1743, and cost the lives of Bering himself as well as numerous other expedition leaders and their crews.

In one way or another, about 3,000 people were probably involved in the expedition, which was so large that it completely disrupted the lifestyle of some indigenes who had been coerced into service, causing starvation in some indigenous communities as a result. While Bering led one of the marine detachments in exploring the waters around Kamchatka and the Bering Strait between Alaska and Russia, a Pacific Group sailed along the east coast of Siberia from the Sea of Okhotsk to Japan under the command of another Dane, Martin Spanberg. Meanwhile, a Northern Group had the responsibility of mapping the northern coastline from Archangelsk in European Russia to the Anadyr river, north of Kamchatka. It was a complicated venture. Expedition planners decided that this group should build ships upstream on the Ob and the Lena rivers and sail these to the ocean and explore pre-assigned sections of coastline. One of these ships, built in Tobolsk, was to sail eastwards along the Kara Sea coast and meet up with another, the Lena Westward group, sailing west from the Lena. A third, the Lena Eastward group, would sail eastwards from the Lena to Kamchatka.

This was easier said than done. Under the leadership of Dmitry Owzyn, the Ob group needed four attempts before it finally reached a storehouse placed especially for it on the Yenisey, battling ice and scurvy that broke the boats and the health of the crew along the way. Other groups had it no less difficult. The Arctic explorer Nils Adolf Erik Nordenskjöld gives an interesting account of the fate of the two Lena groups in his *The Voyage of the Vega round Asia and Europe*.

According to Nordenskjöld, the Lena Westward and the Lena Eastward groups set out from Yakutsk in 1735, sailing down the Lena towards the delta. The westward group was under the command of the marine lieutenant Vasily Pronchishchev, while the eastern group was led by Lieutenant Pyotr Lassinius. "The river," Nordenskjöld writes, "was from four to nine fathoms deep, and on its banks, overgrown with birch and pine, there were numerous tents and dwelling-houses whose inhabitants were engaged in fishing, which gave the neighbourhood of the river a lively and pleasant appearance."

The Lena is treacherous to navigate, splintering at its delta into five major arms before flowing into the Laptev Sea. The lieutenants chose as their route the easternmost arm. Here the two groups parted. Pronchishchev anchored near a group of islands and sought refuge in hunters' huts, where he, his wife (they had recently married, so she accompanied him) and his crew saw out the winter. Almost a year later, in August 1736, they set sail west, reaching the Khatanga river on the eastern side of the Taymyr Peninsula, where on land they found some bread and a few dogs that seemed to belong to a group of hunters away at the time. They continued along the coast, only to become surrounded by dense floes of ice. Luck was on their side, however, for while they were trapped, winds rose up, pushed them south and unexpectedly freed them. They sought refuge in the mouth of the Khatanga, but this, too, was iced over. They had no choice but to press on across the ocean. As Nordenskjöld explains, they were "exposed to cold and wet, and worn out by exertions and privations of every description. Pronchishchev, who before had been sick, died of his illness... He was newly married when he started. His young wife accompanied him on his journey, took part in his dangers and sufferings, survived him only two days, and now rests by his side in the grave on the desolate shore of the Polar Sea."

The mate, Chelyuskin, took over the command, organized the burial of the dead on shore and brought his crew through a severe winter. When summer arrived, they abandoned their attempt and struggled back to Yakutsk.

In St. Petersburg, however, the admiralty decided to launch a new attempt, and chose Chariton Laptev to lead the expedition. Laptev left Yakutsk in mid-1739 and built a high signal tower at the mouth of the Lena for travellers who came after him, turned left and headed towards the Yenisey. Again, the bays, including the Khatanga river mouth, were freezing over or packed with ice. He decided to see out the winter upriver on the Khatanga with local natives. In spring he sent a group out to map the coast from the land, using dog sledges and assisted by local Samoyeds. Having decided he would not get any further due to permanent ice,

Laptev turned back for the Lena but was caught in ice as soon as he reached the ocean. He and the crew crossed the ice to land and dug pits in the frozen earth, taking turns to lie in them for shelter. They also retrieved rations from the ship regularly until one day, tragically, the ice broke up and the vessel drifted away from them. It is difficult to imagine the torment they must have felt at the sight of their ship slowly vanishing in the grey sea.

Without a boat, they had no choice but to walk through the tundra. Laptev and his crew needed 25 days to cover the 300 miles to the station where they had spent the previous winter upriver on the Khatanga with the indigenes. Twelve men died en route. In a "plan B", Laptev and his team spent the next few years wandering about the Taymyr Peninsula exploring and mapping it.

Meanwhile, Lieutenant Lassinius of the Lena Eastward group had the task of sailing east to the Anadyr. Lassinius covered about 75 miles from the Lena Delta channel before ice and scurvy struck. Lassinius and almost all his crew died. Hearing about the disaster, Bering dispatched a relief party to find survivors. Of the 53 men only a priest, the mate and seven sailors from the Lena Eastward group were still alive, and more died later. Bering then sent a new crew for the ship and Dmitry Laptev (1701-71), a cousin of Chariton Laptev, was appointed captain. In mid-1739 they set off but immediately encountered ice. Laptev and his crew turned back and wintered in the grim cold of the delta, keeping scurvy at bay by drinking an extract made from cedar cones. Deciding, however, that a passage across the frozen ocean did not exist, Laptev returned—with Bering's permission—to St. Petersburg. Although the Admiralty sent him back on one more attempt, Laptev failed to round Cape Baranov into the Pacific. Concluding once and for all that there was no navigable sea route, he crossed Chukotka by land and spent two years surveying the Anadyr.

NORDENSKJÖLD'S EXPEDITIONS

Despite the failure to find an ice-free route over the top of Siberia, the Great Northern Expedition from 1733 to 1743 was a landmark in polar exploration and helped pave the way for further attempts to find a northern sea route. It took 36 years before anyone successfully found a way through, and the man who did it was a Finn by birth (at a time when Finland belonged to Russia) who left home for Sweden and worked for twenty years at the Swedish National Museum of Natural History. His name was Nils Adolf Erik Nordenskjöld (1832-1901).

Nordenskjöld, a mineralogist and geologist by training, arrived in Stockholm in 1857 after upsetting the Russian authorities with his patriotism, and used the museum as his base for numerous expeditions to study the north. For one of his expeditions to the Yenisey he enlisted the support of Sweden's wealthiest businessman of the day, Oskar Dikson, after whom Nordenskjöld named an island at the mouth of the Yenisey in 1875. It was on this expedition that Nordenskjöld sailed to the Yenisey and began rowing upriver in a small boat, attaching himself to a larger vessel after a few days and allowing himself to be towed to Yeniseysk (north of Krasnoyarsk).

One of Nordenskjöld's aims had been to see whether goods could be transported into central Siberia from the north. His experience convinced him that it would even be possible to reach the Pacific. The Swedish monarchy liked the idea, contributing along with Dikson and the Russian sponsor Alexander Sibiryakov (1849-1933) to finance a new voyage in 1878. Sibiryakov owned gold mines in Siberia and, along with another important Siberian industrialist Mikhail Sidorov (1823-87), was behind a spate of attempts from the mid-nineteenth century by Russians as well as foreigners to explore and open up a route across the Kara Sea into Siberia. This was Nordenskjöld's ninth Arctic journey, and the ship he used was the *Vega*, a 150-foot wooden-hulled sailing barque with a sixty horsepower steam engine, built in Bremerhaven, Germany. Three other ships accompanied the *Vega* some of the way; two of these carried cargo up the Yenisey, and the third sailed up the Lena to Yakutsk.

After parting from the third ship at the Lena Delta, the *Vega* continued along the coast through shallow waters, managing only a few nautical miles each day and making continuous soundings to avoid running aground. Just a couple of hundred miles before reaching the Bering Strait, however, Nordenskjöld committed an unusual error of judgement by tying up to a large ice floe for the night. By morning, the waters had become clogged with floes and the *Vega* was stuck.

In a re-run of the horrors experienced by those who had tried to find a passage before them, Nordenskjöld and his crew spent the next nine months confined by ice. They fetched ice from the land to melt for drinking water, and small guiding fences were constructed across the five-foot thick ice so the crew could find their way back in blizzards. About a mile away from the *Vega* they built land laboratory huts and passed the winter and spring measuring wind speed, temperatures, humidity and snow depth, sticking to a strict routine in order to overcome boredom. One day a Chukchi native passed on his way to the town of Anadyr and took a message with him from Nordenskjöld. Once word of the explorers' plight spread, the Chukchis became frequent visitors, often bringing their families to meet the crew. By July 1879, about one year after setting out, the *Vega* freed herself of the ice and at 11 a.m. on 19 July entered the Bering Strait to become the first ship to complete the entire Northern Sea Route.

JOSEPH WIGGINS AND HELEN PEEL

Nordenskjöld was an academic with good connections to the Swedish monarchy. Around the same time as he was undertaking polar expeditions, another very different individual, an eccentric Englishman by the name of Joseph Wiggins, was plying the northern coasts and rivers of Siberia with middling success, spurred on, like Nordenskjöld's sponsors, by the idea of making money out of Siberia's trade and resource potential. Wiggins, in fact, would lead the expedition that took Helen Peel across the Kara Sea.

Wiggins was born in Norwich, England, in 1832 and his father drove coaches until (in an ironic twist, it would later turn out) the age of the railway put an end to coach-driving. His father then ran a pub in Bury St. Edmunds. Wiggins, his mind set on going to sea, left school at fourteen and by the age of 27 was master of the *Victoria*, the world's largest steamer in its day. He married in 1861 and worked at the port of Sunderland for a time. After failing to obtain a place on Arctic expeditions, he began organizing his own. The explorer Henry Morton Stanley (of the famous phrase "Dr. Livingstone, I presume") almost joined him, but could not persuade his employer, the *New York Herald*, that the expedition was worthwhile.

On this first expedition in 1874, Wiggins reached the Gulf of Ob but was prevented from going further due to ice and the deep keel of his vessel, the *Dianna*. A year later, he was back there, sailing this time on the *Whim*, a smaller ship whose name seemingly reflected his state of mind. He knew the Russians had sometimes portaged across the Yamal Peninsula to the Gulf of Ob, and he wanted to see whether building a canal across it would be feasible, thus making it unnecessary to sail around the peninsula. On this occasion, storms in the Barents Sea drove him back.

Despite such setbacks, Wiggins continued to harbour the dream of a new trade route into Siberia, and his next attempt was a resounding success. He set off in 1876 in his steamer, the *Thames*, with the aim of sailing up the Yenisey—like Nordenskjöld, to illustrate the feasibility of carrying goods into central Siberia from the north. Wiggins surveyed the region west of the Ob (where he still wanted to build his canal), then was forced by difficult wind conditions to skip the Gulf of Ob and sail directly into the Yenisey. By doing so, he took the first fully-fledged ocean-going vessel upriver to Yeniseysk, where he received a rousing welcome from all and sundry before going overland to St. Petersburg and lecturing to learned societies on his achievement.

In 1878 he returned once more in the company of the naturalist Henry Seebohm (1832-95), hoping to sail the *Thames* downstream, but they ran aground and had to abandon the vessel, eventually selling her for scrap. That same year, however, he successfully sailed into the Ob from the west and brought back a load of wheat—the first time produce had been carried out of Siberia using the northern route. Yet when he tried to repeat the experiment a year later with a fleet of merchant ships, success turned into failure; 5,000 tons of produce was transported down the Ob to the arranged meeting point, but the fleet, which consisted of ships with deep draughts, could not negotiate the shallows. This debacle brought an end to Wiggins' Siberian travels for almost a decade, and the route became discredited by the setback. In the late 1880s, however, Wiggins was back with new syndicates and, despite the earlier obstacles, the Yenisey was again seen as a potentially viable way of carrying cargo into Siberia's interior.

Wiggins' most ambitious venture took place in 1893—the expedition that included Helen Peel. The 1893 voyage was an unlikely undertaking that began when a yachting enthusiast by the name of Francis Leyborne-Popham established a syndicate to sail to the Arctic. Gradually it took on the character of a business venture, coinciding with the construction of the Trans-Siberian Railway and the need to transport rails purchased in Britain into Siberia. The Russian government released funds to find out whether this would be feasible, and what began life as a pleasure cruise evolved into a fully-fledged expedition of six ships under the command of Wiggins. They flew Russian flags and were bound for the Yenisey, with one, the *Orestes*, carrying a cargo of rails.

Leyborne-Popham's yacht, the *Blencathra*, was a gunboat that had been converted into a pleasure craft. He strengthened its hull and equipped it with an ice ram for the Arctic. On board were Leyborne-Popham himself (whose chief aim was to enjoy sailing across the Arctic), his guests the society couple, Mr. and Mrs James, and Helen Peel. A fifth person sailing with Wiggins on the *Orestes* was Frederick G. Jackson, an Arctic explorer preparing for an expedition the following year to the extreme north, harbouring an ambition to beat Norwegian polar explorer Fridtjof Nansen (1861-1930) to the North Pole. His true desire, Helen Peel explains, was to "plant the standard of his native land and sing 'God save the Queen'." Jackson, as it turned out, would disembark at the Yugor Strait, just south of Novaya Zemlya, and explore Vaygach Island for the season with a Nenet guide and the guide's wife.

In the opening chapter of *Polar Gleams* Helen Peel writes:

> The terrors of the sea to an inexperienced and bad sailor are no doubt formidable draw-backs, but they were overborne, as were all other anticipated dangers, by a weird resistless impulse to sail through the icebergs of the Kara Sea, up the mighty Yenesei River, and to be the first of my sex to do so. All this was sufficient to determine me to accept an invitation for such an enterprise, even though we should not exactly reach the goal of so much ambition, and solve the problem whether or not we might feast on strawberries and cream at the North Pole.

Before setting out, Peel met Wiggins, her future commander, in Bideford, North Devon. Wiggins left behind a good impression, and Helen Peel effuses over his qualities:

> In the conference room of the Royal Hotel, which dates from 1688, we discussed our Arctic expedition with Captain Joseph Wiggins, the wellknown Sunderland navigator, whose name and established reputation are widely recognised. Discoverer of the ocean route to Siberia in 1874, he is a man of great nautical experience and genius, and of delightful conversational powers; his characteristic physique testifies to an enterprising nature, and to thorough acquaintance with the perils and dangers of Arctic sea life.

Wiggins was, in fact, something of a happy-go-lucky sailor who did not care much for logbooks or maps. A Russian academic Vladimir Semyonov complained of another of Wiggins' voyages that the plan had been primitive and that a couple of hundred years earlier those sailing the coasts in kochas were using the same principles as Wiggins, who had not even bothered to compile rough charts from earlier voyages. Meanwhile, after just one night at sea, Helen Peel, for other reasons, harboured doubts about having left civilized England: "Dreams and nightmares also capped my imaginings, revealing before my eyes visions of waves mountains high, gales, polar bears, icebergs, and myself denuded of nose, ears, fingers, and toes, and consequently exiled as a recluse from all social intercourse for the rest of my days." Going to bed beneath a near-midnight sun was, she says, reminiscent of the early hours of the morning after London dances.

Yet they were a long way from London society. The ships met up at Vardø in northern Norway, on a little island described as having "fishy attractions", where Peel and her fellow tourists spent two weeks before continuing on to the Yugor Strait in late August 1893; there she found the surrounding scenery "dismal and gloomy in the extreme". The socialites drank champagne with the captain of a Russian man-of-war that had sailed to the strait to deliver provisions to one of the fleet, and then "at early dawn on the 29th August our little fleet weighed anchor and steamed cautiously through the Straits."

The Yugor Strait is a narrow passage about 22 miles long and just two to six miles wide between Vaygach Island and the mainland. Approaching it from the west in clear weather, the low hills of Vaygach Island come into view from about twenty miles away, providing orientation for passage. As Peel passed through she could see the small Arctic outpost of Khabarova, inhabited at that time by Russians and local Nenets who seemed to recognize Wiggins from earlier expeditions (after so many, it was probably difficult not to) and clambered on board the ships. The party then landed at Khabarova and Peel was taken on a reindeer sledge across the snow-less tundra by a Russian merchant dressed in skins:

> ... heedless of obstacles, we bumped and jolted in the most fearful manner, so much so that to prevent being thrown off the sledge I had to cling with both my arms round my companion's neck. The soil was very marshy and undulating, but nothing seemed to slacken the speed

of the reindeer, so I shouted at the top of my voice, in response to which the Russian kept soothing me in terms unfortunately unknown to me.

Back on board, they sailed on through the Kara Sea, gliding between the bluish-green floes of ice in splendid weather, and settling in for musical evenings. Leyborne-Popham proved to be especially adept at playing a violin while simultaneously squeezing windpipes between his knees, while Peel hammered away at the piano, Mr. James puffed into his flute and the unmusical Mrs. James was condemned to the role of audience. In this spirit, the party high-kicked till midnight each bright evening, sailed past the Yamal Peninsula upon glassy seas and spotted hundreds of walruses lounging on ice floes. Instructions were given not to shoot, the crews and passengers having already frightened off a first group of walruses with a spontaneous fusillade:

> Mr. Popham, however, had the dinghy lowered, then sprang into it armed with a gun and rowed off towards the scene of action. The great art in striking the animal a fatal blow is to shoot it in the nape of the neck, death being the instantaneous result. The walrus, however, were not to be tampered with. They raised their heads, and upon seeing the enemy plunged, one and all, into the water. The small boat was instantly surrounded by dozens of huge beasts, but Mr. Popham, with the cool calm manner and careless intrepidity so characteristic of him, showed no fear of the impending danger.

The intrepid Popham safely back on board from killing a walrus, the party sailed forth and by 2 September 1893 had reached the mouth of the Yenisey and the outpost of Dikson. From there they pressed slowly upriver against the current through a flat, dreary landscape towards Golchika, several hundred miles upstream. "A dull barren coastline was alone distinguishable, and a few wooden houses and reindeer tents constituted the small village of Golchika. Situated on an island at the mouth of a small tributary stream on the right bank of the Yenesei, it lies at a distance of 200 miles up the river."

Helen Peel and her companions spent three weeks on the Yenisey river at Golchika, weeks that she said would "ever remain a memorable feature of my youthful days, and in years to come will form an enduring and eventful episode in my life. My mind had certainly grown richer by a thousand new impressions, never likely to fade."

Meanwhile, Wiggins was unloading his rails, plagued by furious storms that made transferring them to barges difficult. Half the barges sprang leaks while being loaded. One, loaded with 1,300 rails, sank unceremoniously to the bottom of the river, and a couple of days later, a further 1,500 disappeared into the cold, murky depths. Only about 1,600 were safely unloaded in the end, and Wiggins was even forced to leave 1,100 on-board, carrying these back to Europe on the return voyage of the *Orestes*. Despite the losses, the experiment was judged a success, although the sea route would never establish itself as a means of transporting rails.

Soon after, Wiggins and his tourists were on their way home. They stopped in at Khabarova again, bumping into Mr. Jackson, fresh from his explorations with the Nenet guides. "Mr. Jackson," Peel writes, "dined and slept on board, which he seemed thoroughly to enjoy after such a long spell of roughing it."

NANSEN AND THE DRIFTERS
The Norwegian Arctic explorer Fridtjof Nansen (1861-1930) was a nose ahead of his British contemporary Jackson, although Jackson made many important discoveries in his own right and is credited with having saved the lives of Nansen and fellow Norwegian explorer Fredrik Hjalmar Johansen (1867-1913) during Nansen's 1893 expedition to test theories of polar ice drift across the Arctic Ocean.

Nansen passed through the Yugor Strait just a couple of weeks before Helen Peel, in the *Fram*, a round-hulled vessel built to cope with pack ice. Whereas Mr. Popham had his sights set on walrus and Helen Peel was living it up in unusual circumstances with the Jameses, Nansen deliberately locked his vessel in pack ice and waited for it to carry him across the North Pole and beyond to a final position near Spitzbergen, off the Norwegian coast.

Realizing that the ice drift would not take them over the pole, in March 1895 Nansen and Johansen abandoned the *Fram* (the rest of the crew stayed on board and survived) and set out for the pole with sledges, dogs and two kayaks. At just north of 86° the two were forced to turn back, fought their way across the frozen landscape towards Franz-Joseph-

Fridtjof Nansen

Land, and by chance ran into their rescuer, none other than Frederick George Jackson.

On 17 June 1896 one of Jackson's men looked across the ice and saw a wild-looking figure approaching with dishevelled hair and fat- and blood-soaked clothing. This was Nansen, who never quite got over Jackson's self-portrayal as the Norwegian's saviour. Jackson's man rushed back to camp and Jackson himself looked through his spy glass and saw Nansen as well as a second figure in the distance alongside a mast. He set off across the ice towards the distant figures, directed by men standing on the roof of the hut. "On our approaching each other, about three miles distant from the land, I saw a tall man on ski with roughly made clothes, and an old felt hat on his head. He was covered in oil and grease, and black from head to foot."

It took some time for Jackson to recognize Nansen. He writes:

> It then struck me that his features, in spite of the black grease and long hair, resembled Nansen, whom I had met once in London before he started in 1893, and I exclaimed: "Aren't you Nansen?" To which he replied: "Yes, I am Nansen." With much heartiness I shook him warmly by the hand and said: "By jove, I'm d***ed glad to see you, and congratulated him on his safe arrival.
>
> Contrary to Dr. Nansen's experience, our sense of smell must have become considerably *lessened* by long absence from civilization, for, strain our noses as we may, we failed to discover the slightest trace of the "monkey" (or any other known) brand.

After the meeting on ice, the two explorers sat up for the next 48 hours talking, Nansen too excited to sleep. They abstained from political discussions, Jackson writes in his book *A Thousand Days in the Arctic* (1899), "as much as possible, as our views on the subject are diametrically opposed to one another." He describes Nansen as being fat and unwell, while Johansen, mentioned several times as a "capital fellow", is described by Jackson (who we recall had sailed on the yacht to Vaygach Island with Helen Peel) as a being "fit and well as he might have done had he just come off a yachting trip".

Nansen gives his own account of the meeting in *Farthest North* (1897):

Suddenly I thought I heard a shout from a human voice, a strange voice, the first for three years. How my heart beat and the blood rushed to my brain as I ran up on to a hummock and hallooed with all the strength of my lungs! Behind that one human voice in the midst of the icy desert—this one message from life—stood home and she who was waiting there; and I saw nothing else as I made my way between bergs and ice-ridges. Soon I heard another shout, and saw, too, from an ice-ridge, a dark form moving among the hummocks farther in. It was a dog; but farther off came another figure, and that was a man. Who was it? Was it Jackson, or one of his companions, or was it perhaps a fellow-countryman? We approached one another quickly. I waved my hat; he did the same. I heard him speak to the dog, and I listened. It was English, and as I drew nearer I thought I recognized Mr. Jackson, whom I remembered once to have seen.

I raised my hat; we extended a hand to one another, with a hearty "How do you do?" Above us a roof of mist shutting out the world around, beneath our feet the rugged, packed drift-ice, and in the background a glimpse of the land, all ice, glacier, and mist. On one side the civilized European in an English check suit and high rubber water-boots, well shaved, well groomed, bringing with him a perfume of scented soap, perceptible to the wild man's sharpened senses; on the other side the wild man clad in dirty rags, black with oil and soot, with long uncombed hair and shaggy beard, black with smoke, with a face in which the natural fair complexion could not possibly be discerned through the thick layer of fat and soot which a winter's endeavors with warm water, moss, rags, and at last a knife, had sought in vain to remove. No one suspected who he was or whence he came. Jackson: "I'm immensely glad to see you."

The meeting between Jackson and Nansen was an interesting encounter between very different characters in the Arctic. It is captured in a photograph taken at the time, showing a rather prim Jackson in Wellington-like rubber boots shaking hands with a bedraggled Nansen. This photograph is one of the most poignant images of Arctic exploration, but was in fact taken ten days after the men met in what was an interesting piece of dramaturgy on ice. According to Jackson's account: "Nansen re-dressed himself exactly as he was on that occasion and in every way the scene was exactly reproduced, except that his hair and beard had been cut and he was in a more cleanly condition." *Fram*, a play by the British poet and playwright Tony Harrison that premiered in London in 2008, takes a poetic look at the life and legacy of Nansen as man and statesman.

Nansen's expedition had been a courageous venture, and one inspired by the tragic voyage of the USS *Jeanette*, a refitted navy gunboat that left San Francisco in 1879 on an expedition to the North Pole, but also with instructions to see what had happened to Nordenskjöld and the *Vega*. The *Jeanette* sank in 1881 near the Lena Delta, and as a result of the tragedy, which saw the ship's wreckage carried in drifting ice to American shores, Nansen understood the significance of drifting polar ice. Later, when a Soviet icebreaker, the *Sidov*, was inadvertently trapped in ice and drifted for over 800 days from 1937, drifting ice stations became a feature of the Arctic.

With the collapse of the Soviet Union in 1991, the Northern Sea Route was formally opened up to international shipping, and there are signs now that this unusual stretch of coast is shifting back into international focus. As before, it is the shortest route between northern Europe and north-east Asia. As Billings and Dikson knew, it offers a short and convenient way out for Siberian resources, and this is especially true now due to the vast oil and gas reserves discovered in the north. With eyes now turning to the resources of the Arctic Ocean, Billings, Dikson and others like Vasily Pronchishchev and his young wife, buried on the "desolate shore of the Polar Sea", could also take heart posthumously from the route's newly found importance.

Chapter Eight

NOVOSIBIRSK AND THE
TRANS-SIBERIAN RAILWAY

The unusual incident occurred one night while I was travelling in eastern Siberia and happened to be staying in the annex of a large conference hotel, separate from the main building. Around midnight I was woken by loud hammering and went downstairs to find a woman standing in pyjamas, a Russian man in his late thirties and two cleaning staff. The sound of the banging from a nearby room was deafening. Everyone stood by perplexed, not saying a word.

"What's that?" I asked.

They shrugged. "We don't know."

"You don't know?"

The man shrugged. "No, we don't know either."

The banging grew louder. The security guard was so frightened that he refused to leave his cabin at the entrance of the building. After we had coaxed him out, he was too scared to put the key in the lock to open the door. Each time he tried, he froze with fear, his hand with the key poised at the keyhole. The banging continued. "Is that a single or double room?"

I asked the cleaning ladies. "Double," they replied. If a second person was inside, we were convinced he or she was already dead, the victim of some horrific crime committed by a deranged culprit. We asked the security guard to call his colleagues from the main building. They arrived, stormed the room and led out a pale and speechless middle-aged, half-naked Russian who had accidentally locked himself in the bathroom. This bathroom had no window. He had been so frightened he could not even scream or shout for help, so he hammered on the door, as if insane. We shook our heads and drifted off just as silently to our respective rooms.

It was an odd occurrence and I was impressed by the efficiency of the back-up crew when they stormed the room of the unfortunate man. I was also struck by the poetry of this situation: here, in the vast landscape of Siberia, a confined space, an interior world, had reduced a human being to frightened silence. I thought nothing more of it, however, until I chanced upon a passage in a book by the US writer and politician Lindon Wallace Bates Jr. (1883-1915), who travelled on part of the Trans-Siberian Railway and in 1910 published *The Russian Road to China*. The train worked out well for Bates, an unusually eloquent engineer, but he had less luck with ships; he was on the *Lusitania* when it was torpedoed by a German submarine in 1915. Bates wrote in a description of one day of his trans-Siberian journey:

> Slowly the daylight wanes. The gray darkness deepens steadily; it seems to gather in over the gliding snow, and the peculiar gloom of a Siberian winter's night closes down. At each track-guard's post flash with vivid suddenness the little twinkling lanterns of the wardens of the road. Involuntarily conversation becomes less animated and voices are lowered; the spell of the sombreness is over all. Soon the electric lamps are lighted, and from brazen ikon and sparkling glasses flash reflections of their glitter. Curtains are drawn, which shut out the enshrouding blackness. The piano begins tinkling again; the waiters come and go with tea and liqueurs; the babble of conversation rises; and the idle laughter is heard anew. Darkness may be ahead, behind, and beside, but within there is light—enjoy it.

After reading Bates, I wondered whether the grotesque—or burlesque— proportions of Siberia's landscape outside as much as the small bathroom had caused the man's panic. Bates captures this paradox of the inner and outer worlds, and I found his description also captured the poetry of train travel. Later, deciding to experiment with Bates' description by settling into the dining carriage of the Sibiryak—Novosibirsk's no. 25 flagship train—and waiting for darkness to descend, I even convinced myself that this poetry of Siberia might be a metaphor for the human condition. And if this was a metaphor for the human condition, then I could expect much. Perhaps I had spent too much time on trains. Perhaps my thoughts were running away with me. My outer darkness never descended, however—not on the train, at least. I was travelling in summer, and the experiment with Bates was pleasantly interrupted by a young French couple, Jean-Michel and Tiffan, whom I had met a few weeks earlier in Irkutsk and now turned up unexpectedly on the train. We rolled dice together, cautiously tolerated by the staff in the restaurant wagon where "games of chance" are prohibited. Before darkness fell outside and I could enjoy my "Batesian" moment, I reached my destination, Novosibirsk, and had to alight.

For many, the Trans-Siberian Railway is a weeklong alcoholic binge in a strange, entertaining or poetic setting. For others, it is a romantic train journey through a foreign and exotic land. For some it is a confined, sleepless process that begins pleasantly enough but gradually deteriorates into a harrowing routine of regular meals, irregular sleep and increasingly sporadic ablutions performed in poky bathrooms. The involuntary response of some human beings is to stop sleeping, stop eating and surrender to constipation. Most people doing the entire length of a route emerge at the end of it in worse shape than when they boarded. (The alleged "goat-like" odour of Rasputin comes to mind.) Bates writes:

> Looking long from the windows at this steppe, a drowsy hypnotism steals over the mind—a dull stupor of unbroken monotony. It is better to do as the Russians—pay no attention whatever to the landscape outside, but make the most of the life within the moving caravansary,—cards and cigarettes and liqueurs, tea and endless talk, with yarns that take days for the spinning.

When Harry de Windt rode the Trans-Siberian in 1901 on one of his Siberian journeys he described a monotony that became almost unbearable. "The landscape is dreary, of course," he remarks of the steppe in winter, "but most days you have the blue cloudless sky and dazzling sunshine, so often sought in vain on the Riviera. At mid-day your sunlit compartment is often too warm to be pleasant, when outside it is 10° below zero. But the air is too dry and bracing for discomfort, although the pleasant breeze we are enjoying here will presently be torturing unhappy mortals in London in the shape of a boisterous and biting east wind."

Another early Trans-Siberian traveller was Mrs. John Clarence Lee. Her book *Across Siberia Alone* from 1914 was subtitled "An American Woman's Adventures", but the claim to adventures is somewhat exaggerated, and anyone expecting a ripping yarn will be disappointed. For this and other reasons, the *New York Times* in July 1914 said it was "tempted to call her work a pleasing bit of fiction" and likened it to a dime novel. The paper adds: "Siberia, indeed, has been greatly maligned in the past, and it is time that she should win her rightful place among countries where life is not always a distortion from moral standards."

The *New York Times* had good reason to demand a less "distorting" picture of Siberia. The advent of the railway across Siberia triggered a boom in foreign travellers venturing onto the subcontinent, and more than a few of them, even when describing conditions that might have been real, did so by resorting to bigotry. The writer Archibald Colquhoun, for instance, unwittingly travels in the psychological footsteps of Siberia's first archbishop Cyprian, arriving to discover debauchery, vice, corruption and bloodshed. He writes of Siberia in 1898, which was then experiencing agricultural prosperity, as needing:

> ... the infusion of a new spirit from outside, consequent upon the opening up of the country to the world; new objectives and ideals, competition and rivalries, which will leave no room for the existing slothful debaucheries; new standards of morality, or, at the least, of commercial expediency, which will discredit as stupid and clumsy such a semi-civilized weapon as promiscuous lying.

If in the West the railway has been likened to an iron horse, and in China—as in the title of Paul Theroux's book—an iron rooster, in Siberia another animal image was popular. Mrs. Lee mentions at one point that a Russian she met called the railway "the track of the camel" because it runs through the wilderness and bypasses so many towns. This image crops up differently in another book, *Strange Siberia: Along the Trans-Siberian Railway*, written by the US theologian Marcus Lorenzo Taft (1850-1936) in 1911:

> The measured movements of these Russian express trains remind one of the camel, which for ages used to traverse these interminable wildernesses. Never do they deign to start like a thoroughbred on the instant the signal is given. Rather, grunting like a patient camel, they only begin to move after three distinct actions, similar to the jerky opening of the blades of a jackknife, reminding one of how first the camel rises on its knees, then straightens its hind legs, and finally its front ones.

BUILDING RUSSIA'S RAILWAY

Constructing a railway across Siberia from Europe to the Pacific only became feasible once the status of the Far East as a Russian possession had been formally acknowledged in treaties with China. Two treaties, the Treaty of Aigun (1858) and the Treaty of Peking (1860) recognized Russia's control over the Primorsky Kray (Maritime Territory), which was opened to settlement for landless peasants from the 1860s.

From the mid-nineteenth century early proposals for a railway trickled into St. Petersburg from Siberia and abroad, but nothing came of these until 1886, the year Alexander III gave his approval for construction. He had several good reasons for going ahead at that moment. The flame of Siberian regionalism was burning brighter, so a railway would—and did—pave the way for more peasants to cross the Urals from European Russia, helping to keep Siberia safely in the empire's fold. Indeed, accusations had surfaced among Siberian regionalists that St. Petersburg was even deliberately trying to keep Siberia dependent on European Russia by actively hindering economic development. Commerce was therefore an important factor, and creating a railway would allow goods to be transported across the subcontinent, especially into Asia. Siberian businessmen grasped it as an opportunity, even if its economic efficiency in those days remained a pipe dream.

Another reason was geopolitical, as the balance of power in Asia was changing. Japan was industrializing and acquiring influence in the region, while in China and the Pacific foreign powers such as Britain and France were keenly pushing their own interests. Siberia was a frontier territory, a "Wild East", and Russia now saw the need to shore it up.

From the late 1880s teams set out for different parts of Siberia to explore possible routes for the new railway. Finally, in 1891, work began from two directions. In May that year, Nicholas II laid a foundation stone in Vladivostok, in the Far East. As if to demonstrate how remarkable the venture would be, he travelled there on a steamer via the wonders of Egypt and India, but he also made sure he returned home through Siberia on the postal roads. While Nicholas II was digging up ground in Vladivostok, construction got underway on the western side in the Urals town of Chelyabinsk.

A key figure behind the building of the new railway was the tsar's finance minister Sergey Witte (1849-1915), a Russian of German-Baltic ancestry who after graduating in mathematics in Odessa rose to the position of director of the Odessa Railways and the South-West Railways (the latter connecting the Baltic and Black Sea). In 1893 he became Russia's finance minister and found himself having to bankroll an expensive railway on non-existent budget surpluses. In the end he financed construction using railway bonds issued on foreign stock exchanges, in particular France and Belgium. His trick was to declare the money from these bonds as state "income", but it was a dubious ploy and the Russian people would later pay for it in the form of higher taxes. The advantage of Witte's financial wizardry was that the tsar's railway remained a state undertaking, and the problems of a fragmented, non-integrated private rail network could be avoided.

Planners got to work by carving Siberia into three parts: a Western Siberian segment between Chelyabinsk and the Ob river (Novosibirsk), a mid-Siberian segment from the Ob to Irkutsk, and a third that included the Circumbaikal (around Lake Baikal), Transbaikal (east of Lake Baikal) and Amur and Ussuri lines in the Far East. As early as 1894 work was finished on the line to Omsk, and a year later the railway reached the Ob at present-day Novosibirsk. By 1895 a branch line connected Yekaterinburg to the mainline, and in 1898 trains were also arriving in Irkutsk from the west. The Ussuri line between Vladivostok and Khabarovsk was opened for traffic in 1897, and the Transbaikal line from Mysovaya on the eastern shore of Lake Baikal to Sretensk (east of Chita) went into operation in 1900.

In 1897 construction also began on the Chinese Eastern Railway, a single track line that ran from Chita via Harbin (on the Amur river) and through Chinese Manchuria to Vladivostok. This shortened by about 300 miles an original route along the Amur that had presented overwhelming technical problems. The following year work started on another branch (later known as the South Manchurian Line after the Japanese took control of it), this one through Manchuria between Harbin and Port Arthur on the Liaodong Peninsula. Russia was leasing the peninsula from China at the time and used Port Arthur as a naval base. Both Chinese lines were opened in 1901-2.

One of the last sections of the Trans-Siberian Railway to be built was in the Amur. Work on its completion only began after Russia was defeated in the Russo-Japanese War of 1904-5, a war that made all too apparent the perils of running tracks through foreign territory. Work began in 1908 and the line was finished in 1915.

The Baikal section of the line was another one that had railway engineers scratching their heads due to the mountainous terrain. After much debate it was decided to carve a route through forest along the Angara between Irkutsk and Port Baikal, where the locomotives and carriages would be put on ships and transported to Mysovaya on the eastern shore of Lake Baikal. From there, the journey continued on rails along the completed Transbaikal segment. Specially constructed ice-breakers began plying the lake in 1900. When the ice was too thick to crash through, as happened during the Russo-Japanese War, tracks were laid across it and the locomotives were drawn by horses. Rolling stock was lost, however, when it broke through the ice. The Russo-Japanese War thus also showed how important it was to keep one's train on the rails, and the decision was taken to build a railway line (the Circumbaikal) around the southern shores of Lake Baikal. This section, which included 39 tunnels and over 400 bridges, was finished in 1904. When the Angara was dammed in the 1950s, the Irkutsk-Baikal line was relocated away from the river and the Circumbaikal stretch fell into disuse. Today it is used mainly by tourist excursion trains.

Like the Great Siberian Post Road, the "Trans-Siberian" route has never been static, and the term itself has variously been used to describe the mainline between Moscow and Vladivostok, the trains that service the line, or loosely as the network of three major lines. It is usual to consider the Moscow-Vladivostok route to be the Trans-Siberian proper. Another route is the Trans-Manchurian, which follows the main line to Tarskaya, veers south to the Russian border post of Zabaikalsk, crosses to Manzhouli and continues via Harbin to Beijing. The third major route, the Trans-Mongolian, turns south from Ulan-Ude to Ulaan-Bataar in Mongolia and also terminates in Beijing.

In 1984 a new line came into operation, the Baikal-Amur Magistral (BAM), which passes along the north shore of Lake Baikal via Tynda to Sovietskaya Gavan on the Pacific coast. Constructing the line was a monumental project instigated in the 1930s, but because of technical difficulties the BAM only began to be used without hindrance from 1989 and in its final form from 2003, when the last section—a nine-mile tunnel that is Russia's longest railway tunnel—finally came into service.

Constructing these lines presented an enormous challenge for man and machine, especially given the schedule involved. Roubles and time were saved by accepting deficits in quality. The beds for the rails were narrower and thinner than usual, lighter-than-usual rails were employed, and sleepers were placed sparingly under the tracks. Wooden bridges were foreseen for the majority of river crossings, but these had a habit of catching fire from locomotive sparks and burning down. Tunnels were avoided wherever possible, with the result that the lines were built with numerous tight curves and steep gradients, reducing the speed of travel.

Less than one in five of the workers employed to build the lines came from Siberia. The further east the construction, the higher was the percentage of casual workers on two- or three-year contracts from China, Korea and Japan; but even labourers as far away as Turkey and Persia found their way to Siberia to work on the lines, and about a quarter of all workers were foreign casual labourers. About 20,000 prisoners were also used over the years, and a year was knocked off their sentences for every eight months of labour on the lines. At the height of construction in 1896, about 90,000 workers were cobbling together the tracks, including a large number of Italian stonemasons employed to work on tunnels.

The conditions under which the men worked were extraordinarily harsh. Free Russian workers could always buy food and clothing from stores, but the prisoners lived on rations of tea, porridge and soup. It is said that in some cases the Chinese workers survived from eating grass. Cholera and typhoid were rampant, afflicting about one third of the workers.

Prisoners at work in the Amur

Technically, the railway was the first major achievement of the new century, and one aspect in particular—the building of bridges across the major rivers—was truly remarkable. Economically, it opened the way for a flood of new settlers in the south of Siberia, but it also changed the way the outside world saw Siberia. For the first time, the western European shores of the Atlantic were connected with the Pacific. This new vision flung foreign powers into a state of consternation and expectation. North Americans began to imagine Siberia as a highway across which they could transport their goods, and as a boom region where they could sell them. They also worried about possible competition from western Siberian grain fields.

Meanwhile, the French dreamed of connecting Paris with New York. Together with the Russians they explored possibilities and mapped a new railway route along the Pacific seaboard from the Amur via Okhotsk to the Bering Strait, where a tunnel would link the continents. Revolution killed the idea of a railway connecting Russia and North America, and the idea sank into oblivion for almost a century—until the early 1990s, when the project was revived. This time, engineers proposed a route that would run through British Columbia in Canada, the Yukon to Fairbanks in Alaska, and then across the Bering Strait by tunnel. From there the line was to continue south to Magadan and west to Yakutsk, where the northern branch line of the Baikal-Amur Magistral would complete the intercontinental connection.

Many engineers say that, though difficult, the technical means are today available to fulfil this dream.

NOVOSIBIRSK: BRIDGE OVER THE OB

Kolyvan, situated some thirty miles north of Novosibirsk on the Sibirsky Trakt, is a sleepy town of about 11,000 inhabitants reached in about an hour by bus or collective line taxi. It has a small market stacked with cheap, Chinese textiles, and a grid of tarred roads leading out from the centre and disintegrating into dirt on the edges of town. It is about two and a half miles west of the Ob river. Connoisseurs of small, dusty Siberian towns will like it. Much of the year, though, it is frozen in ice and snow.

Novosibirsk and its bridge

Kolyvan is one of the older towns in Siberia, but not to be confused with the Kolyvan in the Altai Region, which along with Tobolsk and Irkutsk was a key administrative centre with its own vice governor in 1782-97. Because it was on the postal road between Tobolsk and Tomsk, most travellers passed through it, including exiled Decembrists being transported to Irkutsk and beyond. The German scientist Georg Adolf Erman visited Kolyvan in the late 1820s just after the Decembrist Revolt, confused it with the other one, but wrote: "The next post station, Kolivan, has lost the dignity of the chief town of a government, which it enjoyed till the close of the last century. A few of the buildings lately erected, carry something of the air of a city; all the rest are mere log-houses, as rude and untrimmed as are to be found in the villages."

The log houses that gave Kolyvan a village feel in the 1820s are reason to visit today. Kolyvan also has a substantial regional museum at ulitsa Moskovskaya 34, located inside a former church. As well as the usual exhibits on the history of settlement and the region's natural environment, the museum has portraits of Decembrists transported through here.

But it was a bridge—or lack of one—that sealed the town's decline. Historic Kolyvan would have been the obvious place to build a bridge over the Ob for the new railway, but after surveying the site engineers decided the relief was unsuitable. The fact that it was not chosen led to the development of a new city south of the post road: Novosibirsk.

Founded in 1893 and therefore scarcely more than a century old, Novosibirsk is one of Siberia's younger cities and sprang up on the banks of the Ob at the site of the bridge. The region did contain a few villages, and a small one by the name of Krivoshchekovo already existed alongside the Ob before the work gangs and barges arrived. At first, most people lived on the south side of the Ob, but gradually the railway workers dispersed across the river on the north bank, laying the foundations for a new town. This changed names several times before it became Novonikolaevsk (after the last tsar, Nicholas II); from 1925 it was called Novosibirsk. Interestingly, right up to the early 1920s the two banks of the river were in different time zones.

The bridge was completed in 1897 to link the Western Siberian segment of the line with the mid-Siberian segment, and from that time the settlement developed into a bustling centre for trade, acquiring the status of a city within its first decade of existence. This had much to do with its location on the Ob and on the Trans-Siberian line. Novosibirsk became a natural choice for the establishment of new factories, and the city also began to specialize in the construction of agricultural machinery and operated as a hub for grain production and the butter trade with Europe. The population of Novosibirsk increased rapidly, rising to anything from between 80,000 and over 100,000 by the February Revolution of 1917 to make it the largest commercial and industrial centre of Siberia. This boom, along with its grid-system of streets, earned the city its sobriquet "the American city". But the civil war also marked the beginning of a low for the city, with outbreaks of typhus and cholera following terror perpetrated by both Red Guards and White forces. The all-important bridge was destroyed during fighting between Reds and Whites and had to be rebuilt. Conditions only began to improve again from 1921, with the introduction of Lenin's New Economic Policy (NEP).

During the civil war the Bolsheviks had pursued a policy of war communism, which saw the state seeking to directly control the economy. Shortages had been the norm, especially of foodstuffs, and the population abandoned workplaces in city factories and moved onto the land to survive. Strikes, peasant unrest and the revolt of the armed forces in Kronstadt (off St. Petersburg in the Baltic Sea) caused a rethink, and the changes introduced through the NEP in 1921 made it easier for peasants to sell their surpluses at markets, freed up nationalized industries and made investment more attractive. This brought a recovery in the 1920s, but the strategy was abandoned in 1929 by Stalin's so-called "Socialist Offensive" against wealthy peasants (kulaks) and those who had done well under the NEP in the cities.

Novosibirsk, which had been losing its population at a dramatic rate before the NEP, grew again and continued to develop in two parts: industry on the left bank (south) of the Ob, and administration, culture and commerce on the right bank (north). It remained, however, first and foremost a commercial centre. This changed in the 1930s, when Stalin focused on making Novosibirsk a large industrial centre for power, agricultural and mining equipment and metal and food processing industries.

The early 1930s, a period marked by Stalin's brutal collectivization of agriculture, brought a flood of new settlers fleeing famine on the land. About 180,000 refugees from the countryside arrived in Novosibirsk during this difficult time, settling in slums on the outskirts. During the

Second World War the city received a second boost through the relocation of about fifty strategic industries and a fresh wave of about 140,000 war refugees, laying the basis for post-war modernization and industrial growth. In 1957 Nikita Krushchev ordered the building of Akademgorodok (Academic Town), a leafy scientific research complex about twelve miles south of Novosibirsk. From that time on Novosibirsk became a scientific centre that brought some of Russia's finest researchers to the region. Because being far from Moscow meant greater freedom from kremlin ideologues, Akademgorodok's researchers enjoyed a relatively open and robust academic life on the banks of the Ob.

Novosibirsk was not, however, the natural candidate to become Siberia's "capital". While the railway was being built in Russia, entrepreneurs in the United States who envisaged new land connections opening up between America and Western Europe laid plans for regular shipping services from the West Coast to Vladivostok, and according to these, Irkutsk would become a booming transport hub with trade connections leading into Europe and Asia. This dream died with the birth of the Soviet Union, and it was Novosibirsk that was to fill the role of Russia's "third city".

For many decades it could quite rightly stake a claim to this title (it is still the third-largest, after Moscow and St. Petersburg) and no one doubted that it was the unofficial capital of Siberia. Foreign companies settled their managers here, and it was the natural place to exhibit goods at a trade fair. Today, however, Novosibirsk's status is less clear cut. Krasnoyarsk, with a population of just under one million, is gradually closing the gap in terms of size and foreign investment, while further west Tyumen is growing on the strength of the oil and gas industries.

AROUND NOVOSIBIRSK

A first glimpse of Novosibirsk, with its over-sized railway station, is impressive. The railways were the lifeline of Soviet industrialization, and by the late 1920s the existing station here, which survived the civil war intact, had become too small to cope with the traffic. In stepped the Architectural Society of Moscow, which held a competition for a new one that produced some unusual entries. One of these (the runner up) was from St. Petersburg architect Igor Yaveyn, who proposed a functional cube-form inspired by the late work of German architect Ludwig Mies van der Rohe. The jury was split on this design, however, and the job went to Nikolay Voloshinov, who had submitted a constructivist building which in its original form placed the station partly above platforms and tracks. The inspiration for his design was Cincinnati's Grand Union Terminal. Yet Novosibirsk's planners were not especially enamoured of the design, considering it too box-like and resembling a factory. In the end, a veritable brigade of architects worked on this vast anomaly, adding the arch and passage that leads from the lower level directly beneath the plaza and street. By 1939 the station was ready to receive trains, and today it is indisputably one of Siberia's best examples of station architecture.

From the railway station, Voksalnaya Magistral forms the main thoroughfare into the centre, terminating at ploshchad Lenina. Along the way, at no. 11, stands the Natural History Section of the Novosibirsk Region Local Studies Museum (Otdel Priroda - Novosibirsky Oblastnoy Kraevedchesky Muzey). It is one of the places in Novosibirsk where you can see a skeleton of a mammoth.

Continuing down Voksalnaya Magistral to Krasny prospekt and turning right, is the main building of the regional museum at Krasny prospekt 23, opposite the large Theatre and Ballet building. The main museum building was designed by Andrey Kryachkov (1876-1950), who between 1930 and 1950 headed what today is called the State Academy of Architecture and Fine Arts and whose socialist neoclassical buildings shaped Novosibirsk almost from the start. The museum building dates back to 1910 and was formerly the City Trade Building.

In 1908 the city authorities decided it was time to create a central administrative building and began looking for a location. Several were considered, but in the end they decided on one where the central marketplace stood. The City Trade Building was designed to be multi-purpose, holding offices, shops and the state bank. Its strict symmetry (softened by the red brick), central hall supported by neo-Corinthian columns and with space for 1,000 people, arched windows lighting the upper level and Gothic-inspired cupolas all reinforced its claim to being the most pompous building in pre-revolutionary Novosibirsk.

Inside the museum is a large section on shamanism, with exhibits such as shaman coats dating mostly from the nineteenth century. Shamanism is thought to have become established in Siberia during the Glazkov Culture about 3,500 years ago. The word itself is derived from the Tungus

(Evenk) language—the Glazkov people are believed to be the ancient fore-bears of Tungus—but practices and the nature of the shaman vary greatly in Siberia. In many regions a shaman inherits his or her role, while in others inheritance is unimportant. Everywhere, however, a shaman needs to show special abilities. She or he (there are also transsexual shamans) performs a special ceremony called the *kamlanie* or shaman's act of in-voking spirits by entering a trance and directly going into the spiritual world or allowing the spirits to take over. Birth, illness and death, time (past, present and future) and hunting are the most common aspects dealt with in the rituals. Some shamans are specialized in certain duties, while others will engage in a variety of tasks. The Koryaks of north-east Siberia, for instance, are said to distinguish between professional shamans who serve a broad group of people and family shamans who perform rites at family festivals and so forth. Among the Chukchi of the north-east, pro-fessional shamans would traditionally focus on communicating with spirits in rituals of ecstasy, on rituals of prophecy or on performing incantations that can induce harm or benefit. The Buryats, like many other groups, have white and black shamans, and folklore even suggests the first shaman was a woman who had sexual union with an eagle.

According to the anthropologist M. A. Czaplicka, the Buryats believe that white and black shamans "fight with each other, hurling axes at one another from distances of hundreds of miles." The black shamans serve the east and are feared for their powers to bring illness or death, and an aspen tree will shade the grave of a deceased Buryat black shaman, who is pinned to the earth with a stake from the tree. White shamans serve the west and conduct rituals surrounding major events such as births and deaths.

Not surprisingly, attempts by arriving Russians to convert indigenes to Orthodoxy coincided with moves to stamp out shamanism, and in the 1920s Soviet authorities officially banned shamanism. The Soviet author-ities made it illegal to perform the rituals in public and often they confis-cated paraphernalia such as the drums and coats. One problem faced by authorities, however, was that even tribal people who were officially "good socialists" continued to believe in shamanism. Shamanism penetrated vir-tually all aspects of life for the indigenes, and quite clearly this was not going to change simply by banning it or disseminating Soviet propaganda. Measures therefore had limited impact, and it was only when the lifestyle itself faced a serious challenge through collectivization and the forced settlement of nomads in the 1930s that shamanism began to seriously become undermined. Although many aspects of shamanism continue to exist in indigenous culture today, it tends to survive in a fragmented form or take a revived form, generally known as neo-shamanism.

In Tuva and elsewhere, neo-shamanism often takes the form of an organized clinical practice, and a system of accreditation was introduced there in the 1990s, replete, according to the ethnomusicologist Theodore Levin, who with Valentina Süzükei wrote an interesting book called *Where Rivers and Mountains Sing* (2006), with red cards modelled after Communist Party membership forms. The system, he was told by the chief architect of neo-shamanism in Tuva, Mongush Kenin-Lopsan, was intended to prevent charlatans from edging in. Levin even mentions a problem that he dubs an "animistic version of simony" (treating foreigners for money and neglecting the local community), in a reference to the Christian practice common before the time of the Reformation of priests getting rich on selling indulgences to exonerate sins.

Back in Siberia's largest city, on matters more earthly, anyone with a deeper interest in the architectural aspects of Novosibirsk will find it useful to visit the S. H. Balandin Museum of the History of Architects in the Novosibirsk State Architecture and Art Academy (Muzey Istorii Arkhetektury Sibiri Imena Balandina pri Novosibirsky Gosudarsvennoy Arkhitekturno-Khudozhestvennoy Akademii), situated at Krasny Prospekt 38. Much of the collection here was assembled by Sergey Balandin, a student of Kyachkov who later taught at the institute. This is as much an archive as a museum, and covers Siberian architecture as well as local buildings such as the Theatre of Opera and Ballet.

Ploshchad Lenina forms the centre of Novosibirsk and is where you find a large statue of a wind-blown Lenin, who gave his name posthumously to the square in 1924. The dominant feature of the square, however, is the enormous Novosibirsk Opera and Ballet Theatre—a building that, like the railway station, has a chequered architectural history.

In 1931 the foundation stone was laid for what was originally intended to be a multipurpose house of science and culture with a vast auditorium for theatre performances. It was also foreseen as a venue for mass events. Work began in earnest in 1933, but even while the building was rising up on ploshchad Lenina, architectural horses were being changed midstream.

The original constructivist design gave way to neoclassical revivalism, and the building lost its other purposes to become simply a theatre. The last architects to have a hand in the design were V. C. Berkenberg and L. M. Gokhman. It won a gold medal at the World Exhibition held in Paris in 1937. In 1941, however, Russia entered the Second World War, work stopped and treasures from Moscow's Tretyakov Gallery, St. Petersburg's Hermitage and other museums were freighted to Novosibirsk and stored inside the domed monolith. Another interesting aspect of the building's history is that the Leningrad Philharmonic Orchestra worked here "in exile" during the war. In 1944-5 it began operating as a fully fledged venue—the largest theatre in Russia, with a cupola of some 200 feet in diameter and a height of 115 feet, covered with thousands of iron "scales". Below the cupola a revivalist façade attractively combines circular and square neoclassical forms. Inside, the spaces between the upper galleries have been decorated with copies of sixteen ancient sculptures.

The scales were to become the theatre's problem zone. Almost as soon as it was finished the building needed repairs. In the 1980s and 1990s a complete overhaul saw the replacement of the scales, repairs to the façade and refurbishment of the interior, including the installation of new stage

Socialist-era sculpture, Novosibirsk

technologies. The original steel scales had been shaped by hand, but the skills needed had been lost in the Russia of the 1990s and new techniques and materials based on riveted aluminium placed over the wooden frame of the cupola were borrowed from the aircraft industry. Temperature differences between upper and lower layers of scales, however, caused deformities, and the scales had to be replaced again in 2004-05.

From ploshchad Lenina, Krasny prospekt leads south towards the Ob and its bridge. Just off Krasny prospekt at ulitsa Kommunisticheskaya 38 is a museum (Muzey N. K. Rerikha) devoted to the artist Nikolay Rerikh (1874-1947). Rerikh was born in St. Petersburg into a well-to-do family and dedicated himself variously to art, spiritual belief and philosophy, as well as ethnology and geography. He was a great admirer of the Russian and Ukrainian realist painter Ilya Repin (1844-1930) and created about 7,000 works in his lifetime. After graduating from St. Petersburg University and the Academy of Arts, he travelled widely throughout Russia, the US, Central Asia, the Himalayas and India, and established the Himalayan Research Institute and the International Rerikh Pact in his efforts to protect cultural heritage and promote peace. The pact later became the Hague Pact of 1954, which seeks to protect cultural monuments during times of war. Although works by Rerikh crop up in several other galleries in Siberia, this museum is the main one housing the artist's works.

Back on Krasny prospekt, the Novosibirsk Art Museum (Novosibirsky Khudozhestvenny Muzey) is situated inside another Andrey Kryachkov design, the three-storey former Revolutionary Committee (Revkom) building at no. 5. Foreign paintings—about forty works—make up a small part of the collection in the museum, which is largely dedicated to Russian artists. Icon paintings from the sixteenth to the twentieth centuries cover major schools such as the Moscow, Stroganov, Ural and Volga schools. The features to look for in trying to distinguish between the different schools are the use of colour and the form of figures. The Moscow school, for example, is typified by elongated figures and warm colours and a complex use of symbolism. Along with the Nevyansk school, the Stroganov school was the last major icon movement and tended to use smaller figures, plentiful gold and silver tints and occasionally fanciful landscapes in the background.

The most important paintings in the collection date from the eighteenth and nineteenth centuries, but Soviet art and modern Russian art from the late twentieth century are also well represented. Among the latter are Natalya Nesterova's *Prud* (Pond, 1976) and two works by Maksim Kantor. Important for the collection are sixty works by Rerikh, including some from his Himalaya series.

At Krasny prospekt 1a, the neo-Byzantine revivalist Alexander Nevsky Cathedral (Sobor Aleksandra Nevskovo) was completed in 1897 to celebrate the Trans-Siberian Railway. It is the work of the architect and engineer Nikolay Tikhomirov (1857-1900), a co-founder of the city. The cathedral was closed in the 1930s and re-consecrated in 1991, but the intervening years were not kind to Novosibirsk's first stone building: the steeple was blown up, the domes rotted, and of course everything inside was carted off and the interior left to fall apart. Today it has been restored and refurbished.

At the foot of Krasny prospekt is Novosibirsk's *raison d'être*—the railway bridge. Nothing but a small section of the original bridge remains today (situated on the river bank), as it was found to be suffering from metal fatigue and pulled down in 2001, just over a century after its construction.

The original bridge may be gone, but the railway heritage is not forgotten, as today two museums are dedicated to the history of the railways in Siberia. The most recent of these is situated outside town (near the Seyatel train station) on Berdskoe Shosse, the road leading to Akademgorodok. This museum (Novosibirsky Muzey Zheleznodorozhnoy Tekhniki imena N. A. Akulinina) displays a large collection of locomotives, including steam-driven models, as well as carriages; more recently it expanded its exhibits to include Soviet-made cars of various eras such as the Gaz, Moskvich and Zaz, as well as a few tractors and trucks.

THE MAMMOTHS OF AKADEMGORODOK

Meanwhile, deep in the leafy, suburban calm of Akademgorodok itself—Khrushchev's academic town on the shores of the Ob Sea—the Institute of Archaeology and Ethnology (Institut Arkheologii i Etnografii) has some mammoth skeletons displayed in the foyer of its building on the corner of prospekt Morskoy and ulitsa Tereshkovoy. One of these was discovered in Yakutia in 1971 and dates from about 40,000 year ago. This specimen was probably around 65 years old when it died, about ten feet high and weighed around five tonnes.

The woolly mammoth and other giant animals such as the woolly rhinoceros and giant deer roamed a vast region across the north of Europe, Asia and America. Mammoths themselves were gigantic herbivores belonging to the elephant family and probably diverged from the Asian elephant about 5.5 million years ago. The woolly variety, known as *Mammuthus primigenius*, was most likely the last of its species to evolve, probably some 400,000 years ago, and mainly inhabited Arctic regions. It was about the size of an Indian elephant and had long red-brown fur that grew to about twenty inches. Significantly for the early Siberians who sought suitable material for tools or to carve, an adult mammoth had fifteen-foot long tusks that curved around the trunk. The days of the woolly mammal were numbered, however, when temperatures rose during a period of climatic warming about 30,000 years ago. Hunters also became more adept at the task of bagging them. Scientists believe the process of extinction began during this period in the Crimea (southern European Russia), in the Caucasus region, and from about 12,000 years ago woolly mammoths were also dying out in northern Europe, Scandinavia and Siberia. Oddly, an oxymoronic "dwarf mammoth" species seems to have developed on Wrangel Island and survived until about 4,000 years ago.

The permafrost regions of Siberia are ideal places to find the frozen remains of woolly mammoth, and the Norwegian explorer Fridtjof Nansen recounts in his 1919 book *Through Siberia* how he was promised a meal of steak from a frozen mammoth that had been found near the mouth of the Yenisey in Golchika. He was reluctant to try the steak, though, especially because of poisonous amines released from the cadaver.

> For my part, though it might be quite amusing to eat a steak of such a strange animal, which moreover had lain frozen in the ground for so many thousands of years, I did not feel greatly tempted; I could not help thinking of ptomaine poisoning and other unpleasantness in connection with the big animal that had died a natural death.

Fortunately or not for Nansen, the mammoth barbecue was not to be: dogs had discovered the corpse and begun chewing it before they could organize the grill.

Today, scientists speculate on whether it would be possible to clone frozen tissue from a mammoth to reintroduce the species; some are already combing the tundra for frozen tissue or for mammoth sperm that they might introduce into an elephant mother to create a hybrid. All sperm found to date, however, has been damaged and unusable. One person with a promising idea is the Russian scientist Sergey Zimov, whose sixty-square mile Pleistocene Park in Yakutia is gradually being transformed into the willow-savannah landscape of the region 10,000 years ago. Here he hopes to reintroduce prehistoric bison, the Yakutian horse (the species exists in Yakutia today), moose and reindeer and other candidates that would help us understand the dynamics of the grassland ecosystem ten millennia ago.

An insight into the archaeological and ethnological aspects of prehistory can be gained at the Institute of Archaeology and Ethnology building situated at Zolotodolinskaya 4, where specimens have been assembled from various sites around Siberia, including finds dating from the Pazyryk culture, which existed in the Altai region around 500 BCE.

Chapter Nine

THE ALTAI REGION AND REPUBLIC: MYSTICS, MOUNTAINS AND NOMADS

In the north of the Omsk region, in the small town of Bolshie Uki, a museum dedicated to the Great Siberian Post Road offers visitors the unusual experience of what it was like to shuffle through Siberia in felt slippers and fetters. Instead of being flogged and cajoled along the twelve miles the prisoners were expected to cover in one day, visitors can get a taste of the exiles' hardship by walking about eighty yards along a snow-covered track that was once part of the eighteenth-century post road.

The myth of Siberia as hell was for exiles, of course, no myth but a very real conclusion one might draw from exposure to the harshest of suffering. Today—when circumstances are re-enacted as in Bolshie Uki—the idea of Siberia as an underworld survives as a phantom itch in the cultural imagination. Yet in contrast to this image of hell, Siberia's abundance and its history of offering freedom have also lent the subcontinent an aura of heaven. Serfs—and later poor peasants—belong to those who fled unfavourable conditions in European Russia and found a better life here. The author Harriet Murav says the Russian Romantic poet Nikolay Nekrasov (1821-78) thought of Siberia—albeit, from the distance of European Russia—as a source of purity because he idealized the common people of Russia, of which Siberia had many, and therefore it was a place where Russia might be reborn. For Decembrists, she observes, it was oppressive like hell but also exotic like heaven.

Contemporary Siberians could be forgiven for wondering what the fuss is about, especially in the more banal context of everyday life in the metropolises. In the 1990s, however, new life seemed to have been breathed back into the metaphor. Some Siberians in remote regions were cut off when infrastructure collapsed. They almost starved. Others sat in communal flats in Omsk and other cities during long winters watching the ice thicken and rise up alarmingly on the inside of their windows. Many Siberians had no choice but to resort to the seasonal abundance of the fields, forests and dacha gardens for subsistence. Stories circulated in the press of wages in Siberia being paid in the form of coffins and toilet paper.

Mountain lake, the Altai

In the city of Barnaul, capital of the Altai Region, employees laid off by the local matchstick factory were each given 5,000 boxes of matches.

The legendary hospitality of Siberians—another of the "myths"—also has a reality, one that partly arose out of the region's vast distances. Exiles begged their way across Siberia, seeking the generosity of villagers, herded together singing a beggar's song, described by the American George Kennan as "half sung, half chanted, slowly in broken time and in a low key, by a hundred voices, to an accompaniment made by the jangling and clashing of chains". He had never heard anything so mournful or depressing, he wrote.

The distances, the climate and the sheer remoteness of some towns and their lack of facilities for those journeying meant that Siberia was traditionally a place where the stranger might be given shelter and provided for. Even today, a bus driver who completes his last trip for the working day in a remote town without a hotel will have a long-standing arrangement to stay overnight (and pay for this) in the home of a local villager.

Although his connections were better than most, John Dundas Cochrane gave a good illustration of Siberian hospitality—even when he did not fit the part—in his *Narrative of a Pedestrian Journey through Russia and Siberian Tartary* (1824). He had just arrived in Tobolsk. "Upon my arrival I searched out the abode of Mr. Rosing, son-in-law to the Governor, and brother-in-law to my late kind host Mr. Berg in Perm," he writes, observing that he had been caught in heavy rains and arrived "half drowned and famished".

> The family were all at the Governor's, but receiving a note from me, they kindly invited me to dinner; my situation, however, rendered this impossible, as I was all but naked. My second apology brought the host himself, who ordered me every accommodation I needed. In the evening the whole party visited me, from the Governor's, observing, with much kindness, on the delay of the visit, and adding the proverb of Mahomet and the mountain. I gave myself up to the enjoyment of this delightful company, and of my pipe and a glass of punch, and could have fancied myself any where, rather than at Tobolsk.

Once upon a time the Great Siberian Post Road had post stations offering a samovar, basic quarters where the journeying could sleep and eat a bad meal ("I think the best dinner we got at a post station consisted of chicken soup, then the newly killed chicken that made it, and pancakes," says Henry Lansdell in *Through Siberia*). In settlements without post stations locals were legally obliged to provide horses at the official going rate of the ordinary post horses. The candle inside a post station had also by law to be kept burning all night, though the post master responsible for it might have been drunk. Today there are *komnaty otdykha* (rest rooms) at railway stations that function as places to sleep between train journeys. And more than elsewhere, Siberia depends on a private home-stay industry.

BARNAUL AND THE ALTAI

I found Barnaul, like other Siberian cities, friendly and hospitable—despite the reputation of its inhabitants for being reserved (and therefore being uncharacteristic of Siberians). This impression was not even dampened by a middle-aged man who turned a corner and briefly took his hands off the steering wheel of his imported SUV to deliver an obscene gesture (involving a fist and forearm) my way without apparent reason. Barnaul is the capital of its own Altai Region (Altaysky Kray), not to be confused with the Altai Republic (Respublika Altay)—the wilder, mountainous region situated to the south around a conflux of borders with Kazakhstan, Mongolia and China. It was settled earlier than the republic and attracted many Germans.

If all Siberian cities have their own character and setting, then Barnaul struck me as a cross between Omsk and Yekaterinburg. Like Omsk, it was once on the southern edge of the empire and had to cope with armed bands riding up from the steppe of the south. Like Yekaterinburg, it was founded as a mining town and gradually developed into an industrial centre. Yet unlike either of these, Barnaul was used as a storehouse for Siberia's gold and silver bullion before it was sent to St. Petersburg. I wondered whether being a Siberian Fort Knox on the Central Asian frontier is what possibly has given this city of 650,000 inhabitants its reputation for reserve or caution.

A "nervousness" arising out of this location is captured graphically in an incident that happened while the English architect and writer Thomas Witlam Atkinson was travelling through and sketching the Altai in 1850. The events began late one night when a party of Cossacks suddenly galloped into town with the news that 3,000 Asian invaders were approaching on horseback from the south to plunder the town's supplies of gold. At that time, Barnaul was known to be the bullion mustering point and, according to Atkinson, about 40,000 pounds of gold and another 29,000 pounds of silver were locked in the storehouses at the time, ready to be sent to St. Petersburg. "The shops and warehouses contained supplies of everything needed by the inhabitants, and an immense stock of vodky [vodka] was stored in the government cellars," he writes.

Barnaul braced itself for the onslaught. The officers were roused from sleep, and a force of about 800 men prepared to march at daybreak to defend the town. Word of the impending attack travelled to Tomsk and across western Siberia. The unwelcome news that a horde was launching an attack was broken gently to the ladies of Barnaul.

> The idea of being captured and carried away by the savage tribes, filled their minds with horror; as many traditions remained in Siberia of the barbarities inflicted by the Asiatic hordes in former invasions. When their husbands announced the orders they had received, the excitement increased; the news spread into every dwelling, as usual, much exaggerated on the transit. Many believed that the invaders were close at hand, and fear caused some to fancy they heard their savage cries.

Cossacks galloped to and fro, says Atkinson, giving orders to evacuate. Bugles and drums echoed throughout Barnaul.

> Just as dawn began to break in the eastern sky, two Cossacks dashed through the gate into Barnaoul, and galloped on to the house of the Director... the invaders were rapidly descending the Valley of the Bëa [Biya]... murdering every man, woman, and child they could lay hands on.

Their number had swelled now from 3000 to 7000 and many of them were armed with rifles.

> Further, this army of savages was led on by the Englishman Atkinson, a fact affirmed to be beyond doubt, as the writer of the dispatch stated that he had seen him. This account caused general alarm. Some thought that

the wild hordes of Asia were bursting forth, as in the time of Genghiz Khan, to spread desolation over the country on their march towards Europe.

No one doubted, Atkinson writes, that he was colluding with the invaders, "but not as their leader. It was thought that I had been taken prisoner in the regions to the south of the Altai, and being so well-acquainted with the passes in the mountains, it was supposed that the commanders of the hordes had compelled me to act as their guide. When this was made known, some of the ladies betrayed a gleam of hope, assured that I should try to save my friends. The officers were most anxious about my safety, and many plans of rescue were suggested."

The troops prepared to march. Meanwhile, the colonel prepared for the defence of the factory and barricaded himself in his house. One proposal was that the women should retreat to the governor's large mansion, which would become a kind of citadel. The tsar's valuables and precious metals would be placed on the ground floor, and the children would be given refuge on the upper floor. By ten o'clock that morning the number of the horde had soared to 10,000 and the inhabitants of Biysk and other towns were already fleeing with whatever belongings they could carry. Dispatches were sent informing the tsar. A contingent of Cossacks was also marching towards Barnaul from Tomsk as reinforcements. On their way, they saw people abandoning towns and villages. "On the fifth day the troops from Barnaoul reached Bisk [Biysk], and found the town deserted by all the inhabitants..."

They need not have bothered. Atkinson explains: "In the course of two days it was ascertained that that this alarming invasion had its source in a party of 40 Circassian prisoners who had escaped from the gold mines of Biriroussa [situated on a river between the departments of Irkutsk and Yeniseysk]... These fugitive Circassians had no intention of invading the Russian dominions, their object being to escape from the great Siberian prison to their far distant homes."

Things would end tragically for the prisoners. While escaping, they had taken a couple of their guards and forced these guards to lead them to the Chinese border. Once at the border, however, the guards knew nothing about the terrain on the other side and the prisoners therefore set them free. From that point on the prisoners' escape gradually deteriorated into a wild and meandering flight through wretched valleys and over raging rivers that brought them back into Siberia. Atkinson himself says of the high plateau around the Chuya river, a difficult section of terrain to the south of Barnaul that had to be crossed by the prisoners: "I had found this region a chaos of rocks, high precipices, deep ravines, and roaring torrents; often forming impassable barriers."

The escaped prisoners spent three weeks in this labyrinth. Siberia had become a gigantic maze. At one point they clashed with local Tartars, and a couple of Tartars died and several houses were burned down in the chaos. And so began the rumours of a marauding horde razing villages and killing the inhabitants. After several months on the run the prisoners were tracked down and finally ambushed by Tartars. All but a few died in the hail of bullets. Those who survived fled into a forest and were never found.

INDUSTRIAL HERITAGE

During the eighteenth and nineteenth centuries Siberia's main economic activity was agriculture, mostly based on the mild southern steppes. After agriculture, though, the non-ferrous and precious metals industry was the most important branch of the economy, and some of the largest deposits had been discovered in the Altai. From the 1720s Barnaul became the centre of their exploitation.

The stage was first set for mining development when in 1719 Peter the Great issued an edict to create a Department for Ore Mining Affairs, giving anyone the right to seek and exploit Siberia's minerals. Teams led by the father and son team of Stepan and Yakov Kostylev discovered copper deposits in the Altai and news of this trickled back to the Urals, where the Demidov family was busily earning its fortune from mining. The first smelters were established in Kolyvan (not to be confused with Kolyvan near Novosibirsk), on the southern border of the Russian lands, but the depletion of supplies there and the threat of marauding Oirat (Dzungarian) Mongols would lead to their abandonment.

With this in mind, the founder of the smelter, Akinfy Demidov (1678-1745), moved the headquarters of his works north, establishing a factory in 1739-44 where the Barnaulka river flows into the Ob. This was the beginning of Barnaul. Demidov was the son of the Urals mining pioneer Nikita Demidov, who died in 1725 and left the factories in the hands of his son. The factory was founded at the foot of what today is

Krasnoyarmeysky prospekt, on Demidovskaya ploshchad, as a copper smelting works.

Kolyvan, meanwhile, was gradually sinking into obscurity, and today it is best known for a couple of mining museums and the so-called "Tsarina of Vases", a nineteen-ton jasper vase now housed in St. Petersburg's Hermitage Museum. It was dragged to the capital of the day in 1843 by a team of 1,000 men and about 150 horses, and today figures on the heraldic shield of the Altai Region.

With the discovery of gold and silver in the Altai in the 1740s, events took an unfortunate turn for Demidov, with Tsarina Elisabeth Petrovna (1709-62) accusing him of secretly smelting silver in the Kolyvan works. She confiscated his factory, which he only recovered after paying a large bribe. He continued to process silver until 1744, when, caught red-handed again, he tried to get out of his bind by requesting his possessions be placed under the control of the crown. In 1744-5 a mining committee sent to the Altai had already discovered large deposits of silver in the region, and after Demidov's death in 1745 an edict transferred all mines to the state. This gave the crown *de facto* ownership of Siberia's mines. State mining, however, became unprofitable in the late eighteenth century; most of them had been shut down by the 1780s and numerous new ones had opened up in private hands.

From the 1850s, Barnaul was contributing to a thriving agricultural industry in western Siberia, particularly the butter industry. In 1917 a fire raged through Barnaul that not only changed the architectural face of the city but had newspapers proclaiming its "death". Indeed, fire destroyed a great deal of the town, including its business centre around prospekt Lenina. Reconstruction began in the late 1930s, but work was interrupted by the Second World War, and much of the rebuilding was carried out in the 1940s, based on plans that allowed for wide boulevards and a grid system of streets.

During the war the city had received an industrial boost, with about a hundred industries being transferred from European Russia. By the 1960s it was producing eighty per cent of the Soviet Union's tractor-drawn ploughs and about one-third of the country's railway carriages, and today machine building is still one of the major industries.

At first glance, Barnaul's urban landscape does not appear particularly attractive, and most travellers use Barnaul only as a springboard into the

Altai Republic to the south. But this is an interesting town in its own right. The most rewarding parts for visitors are on and off Krasnoyarmeysky prospekt, which runs from ploshchad Svoboda (Freedom Square) at the railway station south to the historic core around ploshchad Demidova; and prospekt Lenina, the main administrative and business street which runs parallel a few blocks to the north-east.

Barnaul's early development was governed by the Barnaul Silver Smelting Works (Barnaulsky Sereblavilny Zavod), located about half a mile upstream from the point where the Barnaulka flows into the Ob. From 1739 buildings were erected around a central dam. Directly alongside the dam was the main factory, allowing water to be channelled through wooden pipes to mechanical wheels inside the factory to supply power for production. Buildings on the site periphery included storehouses, a guardhouse and living quarters for officers. The only part of this very early factory still preserved is a section of the dam, dating from 1739, which was larger than its counterparts in the Urals.

In 1785 a general plan of urban development was introduced, the heart of which was the smelting works. Among the handful of buildings surviving on the site today are a blacksmith's workshop from 1784, as well as two smelting workshops built between 1809 and 1839.

This period also saw the improvement of what today is called ploshchad Demidova, with a line of neoclassical buildings standing around a memorial obelisk completed in 1844 to belatedly celebrate a century of mining in the Altai. The square was developed between 1820 and 1850, and used St. Petersburg squares as its role model. These buildings include the Factory Hospital (Zavodsky Gospital) at Krasnoyarmeysky prospekt 19, the Mining School (Gornoe Uchilishche), and the almshouse (Bogatelnya) of the Church of Dmitry Rostovsky. When serfdom was abolished in 1861 by Alexander II, so too was an industrial form of bonded labour that existed in places such as Barnaul, and the factory lost many of its master tradesmen, who were now free to leave if they wished. This exodus was accompanied by a decline in production, and finally the factory was abandoned in 1893. Later a sawmill opened up here, and in 1942, with Stalin moving important factories to Siberia, a matchstick factory was transferred to the site from Gomel in Belarus—explaining why the employees received payment in matches after a lay-off in the early 1990s. Today, there are all sorts of plans for the site—currently a wasteland—in-

Downtown Barnaul: prospekt Lenina

cluding an industrial museum complex.

Although the fire of 1917 destroyed most of Barnaul's wooden houses, a handful have survived near ploshchad Demidova. Three interesting museums are located in this area, too. Barnaul's flagship museum is the Altai State Local Studies Museum (Altaysky Gosudarstvenny Kraevedchesky Muzey) located at ulitsa Polzunova 46. The museum was founded in 1823 by the mining engineer from the Kolyvan works P. K. Frolov (1775-1839) and the explorer and entomologist F. V. Gebler (1781-1850). Gebler is the most famous of the early explorers of the Altai and its mountains; the glacier on Mount Belukha (14,783 feet) in the Altai Republic—the source of the Katun river—was discovered by him and is today named after him.

Another worthwhile museum nearby is the "City" Museum (Muzey "Gorod"), which takes a different angle on Barnaul by focusing on the people who have lived there, worked in Barnaul or passed through. It is situated at ulitsa Lva Tolstovo 24. The third museum is the State Museum of the History of Literature, the Arts and Culture of the Altai (Gosudarstvenny Muzey Literatury, Iskusstva i Kultury Altaya), situated further east at ulitsa Lva Tolstovo 2. Housed inside a neoclassical early nineteenth-century villa with attractive gardens, it concentrates mainly on the role of the Altai in the Russian arts. Three artists who figure prominently are Rerikh himself, the film director and writer Vasily Shukshin (1929-74) and the writer Georg Grebenshchikov (1883-1964).Grebenshchikov was born into a peasant family in the Altai and during the First World War was wounded while serving as an officer. Following the Russian Revolution, he migrated to Connecticut where he co-founded in 1925 the Russian artists' colony of Churaevka in Southbury. He later became a US citizen. A chapel that survives in the colony today was designed by Rerikh in 1933, and one of the tours conducted by the museum explains the life and work of the writer and academic. In his essay "Altai, Pearl of Siberia" he wrote: "Every time I hear or pronounce the word 'Altai', I even see its lilac-blue colour with white edges. And, of course, in all languages and for all people, the tender, musical harmony of the word must be understandable— Altai!—because it sounds like 'homeland'."

Shukshin was born in the village of Srostki near Biysk in the Altai Region and worked as a writer, director and actor. His father was arrested and shot in 1933 during the collectivization campaigns. He worked in odd jobs for some time before serving in the navy and later as a teacher and school director in his native village. In 1954 he studied cinematography at the Russian State University of Cinematography, founded in 1919 as the world's first cinematography institute and linked to directors like Sergey Eisenstein and Lev Kuleshov. After graduating in 1960, he went on to become one of Russia's leading directors in the 1960s and early 1970s.

PROSPEKT LENINA: URBAN ARCHAEOLOGY

Prospekt Lenina (under a different name) was one of the earliest streets in Barnaul and, like the others, was related in one way or another to the factory—a hospital, chancery and guardhouse were built on it, as well as houses for factory employees. In the 1780s it was carved to a width of almost 150 feet and became Barnaul's main artery. In the early nineteenth century it was part of the Sibirsky Trakt leading to and from Moscow, which explains why it was called ulitsa Moskovskaya; later it was turned into a leafy boulevard with a central nature strip, which is more or less the form it takes today in the town centre.

The legacy of reconstruction after the fire of 1917 is most apparent in a handful of buildings that provide a kind of linear archaeology of

Barnaul's urban development. Two buildings here, an administrative building at no. 6 (1940) and the Soviet-era constructivist Kinoteatr Rodina (1941), are the work of the architect G. K. Frenk. Another administrative building at no. 25 (1941) is the work of V. L. Kazarinov and is a good example of Soviet-era neoclassical revivalism. These, along with a residential building at no. 35 by the architect A. P. Bobrov, developed from original post-fire plans conceived in the late 1930s. Along the way, you pass the former seminary building at prospekt Lenina 17, which dates back to the 1870s. It suffered greatly in the fire and needed extensive reconstruction in 1923.

In the 1950s a second plan was implemented by the city authorities that led to the development of the ugly area around the railway station, which today is a jumble of bazaar-like stalls on one side of ploshchad Pobedy (Victory Square). In the 1960s and 1970s, however, large-scale reconstruction continued on prospekt Lenina and ploshchad Sovietov, where today the Hotel Tsentralnaya is located. Nearby is the neoclassical revivalist building of the Altai State University (Altaisky Gosudarskvenny Universitet) at prospekt Lenina 61. It was also during this wave of town planning that the city spruced up its parks and gardens; the fountain and pool between the statue of Lenin and the Altai Region administration building at prospekt Lenina 59 are good examples of the approach of Soviet town planners to public spaces.

At prospekt Lenina 88, directly east of the railway station vicinity, is the State Art Museum of the Altai Region (Gosudarstvenny Khudozhestvenny Muzey Altaiskovo Kraya). About 3,000 works on the Altai or by local artists are owned by the museum, and many of these understandably portray the landscape of the region. It has some seventy paintings and 1,500 graphics by the artist Grigory Gurkin.

Gurkin (1870-1937) was born in Gorno-Altaisk and worked on iconostases and icons before studying in St. Petersburg at the Academy of Arts. His paintings have an almost decorative character, and the spiritual emphasis that is common for Altai artists or artists painting Altai motifs. He was arrested during the civil war and imprisoned in Biysk, accused of being a separatist, and after he was released for lack of evidence he fled to Mongolia, travelling in 1920 to Tuva, and returning to the (present-day) Altai Republic in 1925. In 1934 he was arrested again, this time for Turkic nationalism and in 1937 he was executed.

THE ALTAI REPUBLIC: SPIRITUAL LANDSCAPE

Barnaul is the largest town on the M-52 highway between Novosibirsk and the idyllic mountains and steppe of the Altai Republic in the south. Before you reach the Altai Republic, you pass through Biysk, still part of the Altai Region, with about 220,000 inhabitants. Beyond Biysk, an invisible line runs through the landscape and demarcates a new understanding of it.

Perhaps it was no coincidence that Georg Grebenshchikov believed the name Altai is itself evocative of the land. The Altai landscape—meaning the region of mountain and steppe inside the Altai Republic—figures sharply in the imagination of Russians and Altaic people as a kind of mystical homeland. For Grebenshchikov, the name almost loses its arbitrary character as a geographical signifier and acquires a physical dimension of the landscape itself. Anyone travelling from Barnaul into the Altai Republic will notice the outward forms of this change in people and religious customs. The inner changes are more difficult to see.

The landscape of the Altai, or rather the understanding of it, is shaped by the beliefs and lifestyle of Inner Asian nomads. Similarities exist with a couple of other regions, notably Tuva and Buryatia (and across the border in Mongolia), but in recent years a unique idea of what the landscape means for the Altai Republic as a nation seems to have taken root.

In 2006 an interesting book on the Telengit people of the Altai appeared by the Warsaw-born social anthropologist Agnieszka Halemba. In *The Telengits of Southern Siberia*, she notes the Altai's reputation as a place of beauty and mysticism:

> If you happen to talk to someone with an interest in spirituality, personal development or mysticism, you can be sure to hear a longer narrative about the power and mystery of the Altai and the potential spiritual revival that awaits you through interaction with the Altai's natural and mystical qualities.

While travelling through the Altai, as in other regions where shamanism and Buddhism predominate, places of spiritual significance are obvious even to the casual observer because of the custom of tying pieces of cloth there (*jalama* or *kyira*), or piling rocks (*üle*) on each other at the location. You find them throughout Buryatia and in Tuva, along the shores of Lake Baikal, and in most other places where Buddhism is practised. Russian and foreign visitors sometimes copy the custom by tearing up pieces of cloth at these sacred sites and attaching them to trees and so forth. This, Halemba says, is viewed as misguided by the Altai people, who believe it diminishes the power of a site by polluting it. In some cases, she observes, it is even seen as a dangerous for anyone who does not believe in the religion of the Altai or who fails to carry out the ritual properly, as it is said to pollute their soul. There are special customs to adhere to, such as the specific colour of the cloth or the cloth being clean and not just a strip torn from an old shirt. At a spring Halemba visited white, yellow or blue fabric was required, while at a mountain pass another sign explained that the colour should be white. At one site she visited a sign even warned visitors against doing anything at all, lest they harm the landscape and pollute their soul.

The cosmology of Inner Asia and Siberia is usually described as having three "worlds", each of them inhabited in one form or another. The middle world of the Siberian steppe nomads is the home of living people, and the upper one is seen as equivalent to the sky. Halemba believes the Altai people have reinterpreted this, and they have done so through an Altai expression, *Altai Kudai*, which she says can either mean "the God of Altai" or "Altai the God". In effect, the Altai nation has a celestial character that arose after the collapse of the Soviet system.

ALTAI NATIONALISM

The first autonomous region for the Altaians was created by the Bolsheviks in 1922, then called the Oirot Autonomous Region. Later, in 1948, it was renamed the Gorno-Altai Autonomous Oblast before it evolved into the Gorno-Altai Autonomous Soviet Socialist Republic in 1991 and one year later became the Altai Republic.

The Altai became part of the Hun Empire around 200 BCE, when the Huns created the first tribal state on the Eurasian steppe, and over ensuing centuries the Altai's fortunes were usually influenced by the Mongolian lands to the south. It was inhabited by an ancient group of people of the Pazyryk Culture from about 1000 BCE, whose burial mounds or tumuli are found throughout the Altai. From about the sixth or fifth century BCE a temporary military union among the Huns in Central Asia caused groups with a Mongol physical cast to migrate northwards, probably moving through Tuva and north-west Mongolia into the Altai via the Transbaikal region (directly east of Lake Baikal). These mixed with the ancient inhabitants. Subsequent waves of Turkic speakers from Central Asia between the sixth and tenth centuries reinforced the Turkic language of the Altai, and from about the seventh century the Altaic tribes were beginning to form. They were again influenced by Mongol domination from the late twelfth century.

From the mid-fifteenth century hegemony was established over the region by Oirats from Mongolia, which ended in 1756 when the Altai became a Russian protectorate. Until the mid-nineteenth century, most Russians living on the Altai lands descended from Old Believers, who had been exiled to Siberia to work the land, or in some cases the mines around Kolyvan. Many Russian peasants followed and some joined the communities. Christianity, however, never really took hold among Altaian tribes, who continued to adhere to shaman practices and were only to a limited extent affected by Buddhism even as late as the turn of the twentieth century.

In 1904, however, an event took place that changed beliefs and gave rise to both a new religion and a nationalist movement. Known as Burkhanism, the political and spiritual impetus developed when the adopted daughter of an Altai herdsman by the name of Chet Chalpanov reported to her stepfather that she had met a messenger who announced the return of a mythical Altai ruler, Oirat Khan. The political message of Chet Chalpanov was anti-tsarist and advocated the overthrow of Russian authority. Its religious message was of the "white faith", which rejected "black faith" shaman practices, even if in time it adopted some of these rituals. In Mongolia itself, where Buddhism was adopted earlier, a similar shaman influence lingered. Burkhanism spread across the region, and Chet and his followers were brought to trial after a conflict that began when a Russian militia member attacked the group. Chet and his people were acquitted and, unlike in Tuva, where relations between Russians and the local Tuvans culminated in clashes in the early 1990s and the departure of many skilled Russians, relations in the Altai are relatively free of conflict.

The Altai is renowned for its beauty, and its mountains have been visited by Nikolay Rerikh and others seeking the mythical kingdom of Shambhala, a heavenly domain said to exist beyond the Himalayas. In some parts it is spectacular, in others picturesque. Forested hills and rolling meadows with grazing maral deer or livestock in the north-west give way to a landscape in the west where rivers meander lazily through broad, grassed valleys framed by carved ridges. East of Gorno-Altaysk, Lake Teletskoe (Teletskoe Ozero, or in the Altai language Altyn Köl or Golden Lake) forms the largest lake in the Altai Republic. Its cool waters—in summer it rarely warms to more than 17°C—reach depths of a thousand feet, placing it among the deeper lakes in the world. Its resemblance to Lake Baikal is hard to ignore—pure, clear waters, and the fact that 71 rivers flow into it, the largest being the Chulyshman—and like Lake Baikal, it is drained by only one. In the case of Lake Teletskoe, this is the Biya river, which winds north in the Biya Valley to Biysk and joins the most important river in the Altai, the Katun, which in turn flows into the Ob. Also like Lake Baikal, Teletskoe is a long and relatively narrow stretch of water (about fifty miles long and three miles wide) surrounded by spectacular mountains rising up from its shores.

Thomas Witlam Atkinson visited part of the lake and sketched sections. He walked a circuit in the mountains above the shore and later travelled by canoe along it:

> While contemplating the scene beneath, I could not refrain from speculating upon the geological secrets that lay undivulged in the mighty abyss almost at my feet, and which it would disclose were it not for the crystal fluid that, from this elevation, looked solid and black as ink... After making the circuit, we found that, excepting the small plot on which we first encamped, there was not on any other part of the lake a single acre of flat land. Our party consisted of sixteen persons, eleven being Kalmucks to row the canoes. For the first ten versts along this shore [from the source of the Biya river] the mountains do not rise very abruptly; they slope down to the north, and are covered with a dense forest of cedars to their summits, while the banks on the opposite side of the lake, facing the south, have scarcely a tree upon them. After passing a small headland the lake expands, and a splendid view burst upon us. To our right were frowning precipices of great elevation, upon which dark cedars were growing. At the foot of these cliffs a huge mass of rock rose out of the water about five hundred feet, and from the inclination of the strata I was induced to think part of the mountain had

fallen into the lake... Beyond this, each few versts presented a new and beautiful scene; the lake stretched into a fine sheet of water, with picturesque mountains rising upon each shore.

The mountains of the Altai are among the highest in Siberia, rising to 10,000-13,000 feet in parts and at Mount Belukha to over 14,700 feet. Not surprisingly, the Altai has about 1,400 glaciers, and numerous sacred springs, including one named Arzhan-suu located some four miles from the small village of Manzherok, where a statue also stands to the Vyacheslav Shishkov (1873-45), the engineer behind the building of the 600-mile Chuysky Trakt, the M-52 road from Novosibirsk that runs through the Altai Republic to Kosh-Agach and the town of Tashanta, situated in the south near the Mongolian border.

The statue of Shishkov, a bust backed by a large slab, was erected on the centenary of the engineer's birth (in the Tver Region of European Russia). Shishkov led expeditions into the Altai between 1909 and 1913 to explore the rivers and lakes, and in May 1913 began work on the Chuysky Trakt, which largely follows an ancient trading route once used by merchants travelling up from Mongolia.

Construction of the road was interrupted by the First World War and it was only completed in the early 1930s. A large number of those who worked on the road in that period were men and women from prison camps, situated every ten to fifteen miles along the Trakt, each holding about 300 to 400 inmates. One of these camps held female prisoners. In all, up to 12,000 prisoners worked on construction, often in freezing conditions, and some of them are said to have been buried under the road.

THE KATUN RIVER AND MOUNT BELUKHA

The Katun river is the most important river in the Altai, and this is apparent from its name, which in Altaic is said to mean "Mistress of the House". It flows for almost 450 miles from its source at Gebler Glacier, at about 6,500 feet on the southern slope of Mount Belukha. At the foot of this constellation of mountains near where Kazakhstan, China, Mongolia and Russia converge is Tyungur, a small, remote and ramshackle settlement with a wooden suspension bridge spanning a shallow stretch of the Katun where it pours across the stony river bed, framed by mountains. It is a picturesque and unusual location that attracts an even more unusual

The Katun river

type of visitor, as the settlement is a base for adventure treks to Belukha, the nearby Lake Kucherla, and Lake Akkem.

Together, the Katun and Belukha form a powerful duet that inspires adventurers to test their outdoor mettle and prompts writers to put down their pens in awe. Valentin Rasputin, one of Siberia's best contemporary writers, falls into the latter category. Rasputin, who was close to the fledgling "Village Prose" movement that grew out of the Brezhnev era, dedicates a chapter of his book *Siberia, Siberia* to the Altai and condemns a proposal to dam the Katun. Proposals to dam the river are still on the agenda, and Rasputin's book remains one of the finest and most insightful on Siberia. He writes:

> When I saw Belukha for the first time in all its freedom, power and strict sculpture, I experienced confusion, nothing more. I saw everything— this was one of those rare strokes of luck when Belukha revealed the outcrop from which it earns its name ["Three Peaks"]—but I was unable to give a name to what I saw. Neither words, feelings, nor the stirring of the soul were sufficient. Everything grew crazed and froze, losing its voice, in front of this sovereign illumination, which rose with such strength and wholeness that it would have been impossible to scrape off

a single stone or flash of light to describe with words. It must have been a similar confusion, experienced many times over, that formed the superstition among Altaians never to look at Belukha.

This is one part of the Altai where experienced guides are invaluable, and some of them nowadays lead the more adventurous with packhorses to Belukha, Lake Kucherla and Lake Akkem on fourteen-day expeditions. Detailed travel descriptions of the region around Belukha were penned by Thomas Witlam Atkinson in the mid-nineteenth century. He wrote:

> ... we descended to the little river, or rather torrent, running among rocks, and often under ice and snow, that have formed natural bridges, beneath which the water rushes in many a fall. We reached the foot of a glacier [Gebler Glacier] in a deep ravine, that extends very far up the mountain; from under two small arches in this mass of ice the Katounaia [Katun] gushes forth in two streams, and is soon lost again under a bed of snow for a space of several hundred yards. This is the veritable source of the river.

He climbed to the base of its peaks—conditions prevented him from going higher—to describe the view.

> To the west the vast steppes of the Kirghis [Kazakhstan] stretched till lost in hazy distance. To the south were some high peaks, and many ridges descending toward the steppes on the east of Nor-Zaisan, and to the Desert of Gobi. Several lakes were visible in the mountains and on the distant steppes. Innumerable rivers were winding their courses in the deep valleys like a network of silver threads.

Extreme or adventure tourism is no new phenomena in the Altai. During Soviet times tourists travelled to the region to hike or climb among the mountains and kayak on the rivers, and during the social and political stagnation of the Brezhnev era groups would set off into the Altai and other landscapes to combat the drudgery of everyday life and share adventure. The popular form of narrative "bard" or "author songs" (*avtorskaya pesnya*—best typified by Vladimir Vysotsky, 1938-80) underpinned the movement with its own special genre of "tourist songs", which provided the musical accompaniment for roaming the Soviet wilds. One of the most popular was called "Manzherok", taking its title from the small town just south of Gorno-Altaysk. It begins: "Tell me my friend, what is Manzherok, maybe an island, maybe a town? Friendship, this is Manzherok. Faithfulness, this is Manzherok. This is where we're meeting—Manzherok. And friends are led here, a hundred roads and a hundred trails, where smiles and laugher await, a song for one and all."

More recently, a phenomenon known as "energy tourism" (*energetichesky turizm*) brings Russians (and an increasing number of foreigners) to the Altai to fill up on spiritual energy. The popularity of the Altai is unlikely to wane. The "Golden Mountains of Altai", including the Katun and Lake Teletskoe, are today part of the Unesco World Heritage list of sites.

Yet the Altai is facing another challenge, and this has little to do with mystics flocking into its mountains seeking Shambhala, tourists tearing up their handkerchiefs at significant sites or post-Soviet "energy tourists" wallowing beside wild rivers in bright shorts. Experts are concerned that climate warming is causing frozen earth to melt, threatening the intactness of the region's burial mounds. The Altai is renowned for its Pazyryk burial mounds—burial complexes (*kurgany*) dating from the period of the Scyth pastoral nomad horse riders in 1000-200 BCE. This is the only place in the world where frozen tombs have been found. The first of the kurgany were discovered in 1865. Well over 1,000 sites have since been documented, but very many more await discovery. Most date from the period of about 300 BCE. The best-researched sites are those of Pazyryk, Bashdar, Tuyekta, Shibin, Ulandryk and Ukok. In 1990-93, while conducting work on the Ukok Plateau, the grasslands region south of the Argut river where China, Kazakhstan and Russia meet, Altai researchers from the Siberian branch of the Russian Academy of Sciences discovered a mound with the frozen remains of a 2,400-year-old woman, the so-called "Ice Princess" or "Altai Princess". The intricately tattooed woman wore some of the oldest clothing found among nomad sites, including a silk blouse that provided evidence that the Pazyryks traded with India.

The Ice Princess has long been held in Novosibirsk—for safe-keeping it is said, as no suitable facility was available in Gorno-Altaysk. Much ill feeling accompanied her removal to Novosibirsk, and many Altaians linked this event to earthquakes that occurred afterwards in the republic—two or three Ice Princess-induced quakes a week at one point, lamented one local official in 2004. Recently, however, a new annex to the national museum was nearing completion in Gorno-Altayask, an $11-million sloping construction resembling a burial mound, with a state-of-the-art glass case to preserve the Ice Princess.

Chapter Ten

THE YENISEY RIVER:
FROM STEPPES TO THE FROZEN
TUNDRA

Kyzyl, the capital of Tuva, claims to be the centre of the Asian continent. Indeed, if you cross the Sayan Mountains into Tuva, you find yourself on the cusp of a vast, dusty steppe that looks convincingly like a Central Asian heartland. But whether Asia's true heart can be pinpointed in Kyzyl is open to debate. While one monument marks its location here, a different monument denoting a second geographical "centre of Asia" is situated 631 miles away as the crow flies, near the town of Ürümchi in the Xinjiang Uyghur Autonomous Region of Western China. In 2009 world attention was briefly focused on this city when clashes occurred between new Chinese settlers and the local Uyghur population. Ürümchi also happens to be the world's most inland city—located 1,500 miles from the Bay of Bengal. Two obscure, isolated places far from their national capitals claim to be right in the middle of something. It is probably no coincidence.

Kyzyl's monument, an obelisk situated where the Yenisey river is formed by its two sources (the Bolshoy Yenisey and Maly Yenisey), may not be as spectacular as its Chinese counterpart, but—notwithstanding the brief outburst of violence across the border—it has attracted more attention. A major reason is the fascination Tuva exerted on the Americans Ralph Leighton and Nobel prize-winning physicist Richard Feynman. It was Feynman who as a child collected postage stamps from the republic under its former name of Tannu-Tuva and later, making a chance remark to Leighton, triggered a book by Leighton, *Tuva or Bust!*, about their unsuccessful attempt to travel there during the Soviet era. Since then Leighton's book, along with the Friends of Tuva society he founded, has encouraged an ongoing interest in this unlikely part of Russia.

Discussion about the real centre of Asia is nothing new—thanks in particular to one man, it has been going on for about a century. In 1929 the Austrian traveller and sinologist Otto Mänchen-Helfen (1894-1969) travelled to Tuva from Moscow and in his *Reise ins Asiatische Tuwa* (Journey to Tuva) mentions a "kinky Englishman of the sort Jules Verne loved to take as heroes, who travelled the world with the one aim of erecting a monument in the centre of each continent: 'Here, in the centre of the continent, I was on this day'—and the date. Africa, North America and South America already had memorial stones," Mänchen-Helfen writes of the Englishman, "when he set out to plant a memorial in the heart of Asia."

> According to his calculations, this was on the banks of the upper Yenisey, in the Chinese region of Uriyankhai [the name for Tuva when it was ruled as part of Outer Mongolia]. Rich, a sportsman, and tough like many a fool, he did not allow himself to be deterred by hardship and achieved his aim. I saw the stone in summer 1929. It stands in Saldam [outside Toora-Khem], Tuva, as Uriyankhai is now called, in this republic of herders between Siberia, the Altai Mountains and the Gobi Desert in the most isolated region of Asia.

Misplaced or not, a memorial obelisk and globe were later planted in Kyzyl. It juts above the Yenisey and stands before a panorama of folded hills that rise on the opposite bank. Culturally, the memorial may strike the observer as banal or even inappropriate in a land traditionally inhabited by semi-nomadic pastoralists and—in the isolated north-east—reindeer herding Todzhas.

KHOOMEI: THROAT SINGING AND CULTURAL IDENTITY

Erecting monuments in the centre of continents is one way of expressing an understanding of a landscape; hiking through that landscape, drinking Tuvan fermented mare's milk (*araka*) or watching local wrestling, archery and horse-racing at the annual summer Naadym Festival are others, and today these are among the most popular cultural draws of the republic. Its most popular art form, however, is *khoomei*, Tuvan throat singing, and it is through khoomei that the Tuvans are said to create their national identity and their relationship to landscape.

The word khoomei is related to the Mongolian word for throat. The style of singing involves producing two or more different tones at the same time—a low, eerie tone that underscores a song and another that is higher-pitched, resonant and stylized. The origin of Tuvan throat singing is said to be in animism (today most Tuvans practise Buddhism influenced by shamanism) and a belief that spirits or souls inhabit natural features of a landscape. The higher tone we hear in throat singing is rich in timbre or tonal colour (the sound quality that distinguishes the sound of, say, a trumpet from a violin when both play the same note). This has its equivalent in nature, where wind blowing across steppe, for example, has a different timbre to wind whistling through trees. Steppe nomads are highly attuned to these natural sounds, and Tuvan singers are said to use their voices to replicate them: wind, birdsong, animals and so forth.

Yet the genre goes beyond simply mimicking sounds: Tuvan animism considers the sound of an object to be part of its spirituality, and reproducing a sound, therefore, acquires a spiritual character, creating oneness with a landscape.

The form survives today. One of the best known groups of throat singers is the ensemble Tyva, created under the auspices of local musicologist and folklorist Zoya Kyrgys in the 1980s at a time when Tuvan national culture was experiencing a revival. The ensemble has performed widely in Russia and abroad, and today is based in Kyzyl's Khoomei Centre at ulitsa Shchetkina 46. Throat singing by these and other performers such as Huun-Huur-Tu are also regular events in the Musical Drama Theatre. The latter, an internationally successful ensemble whose members live in rural yurts when not touring Europe, claim: "We... not only try to be with nature, we are still a part of nature."

Significantly, the experience of living in yurts is crucial for their art form:

Huun-Huur-Tu

Yurts are made from natural materials which are no borders to natural sounds. You hear nature and its creatures all the time when living in yurts—sheep, cows, yaks, who all talk around you, and you also can easily listen to the stories of the old people with their tales of animals and their sounds—this is quite important to Tuvan people, still listening to the stories and to the natural sounds of animals and to the spirits of nature.

Khoomei is traditionally a male domain, but in 1998 the all-woman ensemble Tyva Kyzy (Daughters of Tuva) began performing. According to some traditions, they claim, a woman singing khoomei was thought to deprive men of their vitality and cause childbirth problems for the woman in question. Another tradition, however, contends that women were, in fact, the earliest khoomei singers. The ensemble points to female throat singers such as Choldak-Kara Oyun, whose private singing led her son, Soruktu Kyrgys, to become Tuva's most famous throat singer in the early twentieth century, and the pioneering Valentina Chuldum, who toured internationally and died in 2002 at the age of 42.

As well as these, various fusion styles of throat singing have grown up in recent years—even a country & western and trance-style offshoot by the group Ug-Shig.

Traditional Khoomei, on the one hand, is a spiritual relationship to the landscape through song, and on the other at the heart of Tuvan identity. Shamanism, in its conflux with Buddhism, forms the religious foundation, and one form of throat singing in particular, the whistling *sygyt* style, brings together these two elements and plays an important role in shaman rituals. In their interesting book *Where Rivers and Mountains Sing*, Theodore Levin and Valentina Süzükei describe a visit in 2000 to the "Nestor of Tuvan neoshamanism", Mongush Kenin-Lopsan. He was ensconced in the back of the old national museum building, then a wooden house on ulitsa Lenina. There Levin asked Kenin-Lopsan—an archaeologist, poet, author, one-time practising shaman and (Levin says) "the chief architect of its [shamanism's] revival and transformation into a contemporary clinical practice in Tuva"—about the role played by sounds and music in summoning animal spirits. Kenin-Lopsan told the authors that in Tuva only shamans whistle and that before each séance this whistling is performed to call the shaman's helpers—meaning the spirits that assist the shaman in his ritual. Over time, Kenin-Lopsan said, this whistle evolved into a Tuvan form of throat singing known as sygyt.

One place to explore Tuvan culture and shamanism in more detail is inside the National Museum of the Tuva Republic (Natsionalny Muzey Respubliky Tyva) in its new building at ulitsa Titova 30. In the early 1930s about half of Tuva's seven hundred or more shamans were female. Sections of the museum deal with pre-revolutionary Tuva (including exhibits of shaman utensils), the history of the republic and the history of Soviet society. The Scythe Room, a new section created in late 2008, has a permanent collection of objects from the Arzhan-2 archaeological site numbering about 1,200 in all, and another 45 finds from the earlier Arzhan-1 site. The pieces were returned to the museum by the Hermitage Museum of St. Petersburg after touring abroad.

Another point of national identification in Tuvan culture is the epic poem (the Altai has its own form). These long oral works run to 10,000 lines or more and were traditionally told by men and women alike. Itinerant story-tellers would travel the pastures to visit nomads and recount the

Shaman site

epic over a series of days, beginning each evening after the meal. Some-times listeners interjected with a phrase to encourage the storyteller, and occasionally the epic was accompanied by music played on the *igil* (called *ikil* in Mongolia; a two-stringed fiddle with a carved horse's head and played with a bow) or comparable instrument. The longest known epics were told by Kirghiz. These could take six years to recount and might amount to 400,000 lines.

The Tuvans and their Burial Complexes

As in the Altai, Tuva's ethnic background is comprised of a complex tap-estry of cultures. Settlement of the region is said to have taken place about 100,000 to 40,000 years ago, and in the south and central parts of the re-public objects have been found that date from the late Palaeolithic era—ending about 12,000 years ago—when Europoids, Mongoloids and an ethnic blend of these lived in the region.

The most sensational early finds, however, date from the Scythian period beginning from about the late ninth century and early eighth century BCE. The so-called Arzhan burial complexes, situated about eighty miles north-west of Kyzyl in the southern foothills of the Western Sayan Range, date from this era. The region today is called the Valley of the Kings or the Valley of the Tsars (Dolina Tsarey), and is an ancient necropolis with hundreds of mound graves (*kurgany*) constructed of spruce with cir-cular chambers. The 300-foot diameter Arzhan-1 complex was opened in the early 1970s by the Russian archaeologist M. P. Gryaznov. Research began at a second site in the valley from 1997, later supported by teams from the German Archaeological Institute, and from 1998 work concen-trated on a 250-foot diameter royal grave, Arzhan-2. Surprisingly, this was spared destruction by grave robbers and survived completely intact. The tumulus (barrow) measures about six feet in height and is encircled by about two hundred chambers connected to the main tumulus. These were created as places where offerings could be made, which included burned wood and bone and a smaller number of sheet gold and bronze items. In 2001 work got underway in earnest on the main tumulus containing the royal grave. In one of these archaeologists discovered equestrian objects intended to symbolize the interment of a horse: the remains of a wooden saddle, gold decorative items and a conical sheet of gold with the head of a bird of prey, which researchers from the German Archaeological Institute say has representations similar to ones found in tumuli in the Altai Republic.

Inside the royal grave itself teams found the bodies of an interred 40- to 45-year-old man and a 30- to 35-year old woman. They say the slightly crouched bodies had been placed on their left side, the left arm laid out parallel to the torso and the right bent to rest on the pelvis. The preserved bodies were surrounded by precious objects, many of which had originally been placed on the walls. These included daggers, arrowheads and numerous ornaments such as a gold torque with animal friezes, including those of ibex, panther and camels. Excluding beads, researchers from the Institute say, about 9,300 objects have so far been found in the royal grave, and 5,700 of these are of gold. A total of 26 burials—men and women— were discovered in the entire necropolis, most dating back to the Scythe period. Part of the complex also contained fourteen horses with legs folded under their stomachs and facing west. The complex was meticulously laid out, and "nothing in layout and structure of the site was accidental", according to the German Archaeological Institute.

The arrival of the Huns from about 200 BCE brought a new layer to the ethnic make-up of the region and although Tuvans are Turkic-speaking created the basis for the Mongol physical features of many of today's Tuvans. With the Turkic Khaganate from about the mid-sixth and seventh centuries, Tuva developed into a feudal society based on farming, nomadic pastoralism and metal working. Stone tablets survive from this period with inscriptions in ancient Turkic.

For almost a hundred years from the mid-eighth century the region was part of a Central Asian Uyghur Khanate. Uyghur rulers set about fortifying their territory by creating a complex of fifteen fortresses with connected walls. The most famous of these known today is the island fortress of Por-Bazhyn, situated near the Russian-Mongolian border at Lake Tereh-Khol in south-east Tuva. It forms a rectangular labyrinth that was destroyed by fire and possibly served as a palace or temple; this island complex is today being turned into a tourist attraction.

Ethnically and culturally, the Yenisey Kirghiz, who expelled the Uyghurs in 840 and may have been responsible for the torching of Por-Bazhyn, had an enormous influence on the region, and it is Yenisey Kirghiz, Turkic and Mongolic-speaking predecessors, as well as tribes or clans of Kets and Samoyeds, who form the complex ethnic composition of

Tuvans today. One group standing out from others are some 5,000 Todzha (some but not all are still reindeer herders) in the north-east who scarcely had contact with Russians until the 1940s. Closely related reindeer people, an estimated 700 Tofolars, live across the border in Irkutsk Region.

From the period beginning in the early thirteenth century until the mid-eighteenth century Tuva was back in the hands of rulers from Mongolia. The first of these was the Mongol Empire of Ghengis Khan and his successors, who in 1238 won an important battle against Grand Duke Vladimir, 125 miles from Moscow. With the collapse of the Mongol Empire Tuva was ruled from the late sixteenth century by a small Altyn Khanate based around a princely family in northern Mongolia. Later, from the early seventeenth century, the Oirat Khans incorporated it into their state of Dzungaria.

Oirat rule, which ended in 1755 when Manchuria subjugated Dzungaria, was accompanied by a period of intense migration. But the advent of Manchu-Chinese rule over Mongol lands also drove a wedge into the Altai-Sayan region: Tuva was ruled from China, whereas the Altai was incorporated into Russia.

In 1727 treaties with China created a similar wedge between the Tofolars (who fell into the Russian border and today live in Irkutsk Region) and the Todzha, who were on the Mongolian/Manchurian side and today are Tuvan. It was also during this period of Manchu-Chinese rule that Tibetan Buddhism took hold in Tuva.

The treaties of Kiakhta and Bura in 1727, and a border protocol signed between China and Russia in 1869, formally set the boundaries between Manchu-ruled China (Outer Mongolia) and Russia at the Sayan Mountains, but the Chinese built their border posts south of the actual border, in the Tannu-Ola Range, which runs along the present-day southern Tuva border with Mongolia. The result was that Tannu-Uriankhai (Tuva) turned into a no-man's land between the two powers. Oddly, the French are said to have stolen the Chinese map of Tannu-Uriankhai during the Second Opium War of 1860 and sold it to the Russians, which only generated even greater confusion and suspicion between Russia and China.

With the Chinese Revolution of 1911 Russia saw its chance to encourage separatism among the feudal landowning chiefs, who—possibly under duress—petitioned for Tannu-Uriankhai to become a Russian protectorate. In April 1914 it was duly annexed and the capital was created and given the Russian name Belotsarsk (White Tsar), although strictly speaking Tannu-Uriankhai still belonged to now independent Mongolia.

One of those leaders who petitioned Russia to make Tannu-Uriankhai a protectorate was Buyan Badyrgy, who was later to swing his weight behind Mongolian rule. He was also among those who helped make Tuva independent from August 1921 until 1944, the year it was integrated into the Soviet Union. Buyan Badyrgy was an adopted son of one of the district heads and was fluent in Russian, Chinese and Tibetan. He was murdered in the purges of the 1930s and it was only in 2007 that he was finally rehabilitated. All this means that today he is viewed as the official founding father of the Tuvan state. His life is the subject of a book by Mongush Kenin-Lopsan and an opera based on the book.

Russian peasants, prospectors and traders had begun moving into Tuva in the early nineteenth century, but a new wave arrived after Russian annexation in 1914. Tuva's fortunes, however, were still tied to Mongolia, and once the Russian Revolution broke out, China occupied independent Mongolia in 1918-19 and employed troops to protect its interests in Tuva. By the same token, civil war in Russia led to the creation of a nominally pro-Bolshevik Outer Mongolian provisional government in 1921, and in the same year the Bolsheviks bolstered their position by creating an independent Tannu-Tuva.

This was the Tannu-Tuva that issued postage stamps and led to Feynman's interest in Tuva, Leighton's book and the off-beat "Friends of Tuva" cult.

The rulers of Tannu-Tuva, including Buyan Badyrgy, were far from Bolshevik lackeys, advocating union with Mongolia and a strengthening of Buddhism. Such attitudes set the republic on a divergent course from the Bolsheviks, especially from 1928 when Tannu-Tuva passed laws making Buddhism the state religion. Cells of young, Moscow-trained Bolsheviks moved in to oppose the pro-Mongolia faction; a pro-Soviet government was eventually installed and measures were taken to shift Tuva's cultural centre of gravity from Mongolia back to Russia.

The Soviet Union did this by abolishing Mongolian as the official language (written in Tibetan-Mongolian script) and replacing it with a Tuvan vernacular based on the Roman alphabet. Later it was changed to Cyrillic and in 1944 the last vestiges of real autonomy were removed when the republic was incorporated fully into the USSR as an "autonomous republic".

Yet with the exception of the Baltic States, Tuva was the only Soviet republic that enjoyed a semblance of independence in the twentieth century. This historical anomaly is sometimes used to explain the rise of tensions in the late 1980s and in 1990, when the Popular Front of Tuva took shape and later advocated independence. It was a difficult period for everyone. Travelling to remote regions of Tuva was often avoided by ordinary Russians in the 1980s, due to fears for their own safety (Tuvans still have a reputation for becoming violent when drunk), and reports suggested that by late 1989 parties of Tuvans on horseback were attacking Russian villages. Over the years such attacks cost the lives of hundreds of Russians, and soon the region had a full-scale revolt on its hands, which could only be quelled with reinforcements from outside. By the mid-1990s a large number of Russians had already packed their bags and left. At that time, Kyzyl was a city that improvised. Its post office sold stamps but also kept a useful selection of syringes for sale in various sizes at the counter. Presumably, the local hospital did not have adequate supplies.

Things have quietened and improved since then, but Tuva remains an exception in the Russian Federation. It has an abysmally low male average life expectancy of around fifty, and is Russia's least developed region. Nevertheless, it seems set to receive a minor industrial and tourist boost through a new 285-mile stretch of railway connecting Kyzyl with Kurigino in Krasnoyarsk Region. This will belatedly bring Tuva onto the Russian railways network and link the coal-mining regions north of Kyzyl in the Yenisey Basin with the Trans-Siberian and BAM networks. It is a difficult stretch to build, running below the peaks of the Sayan Mountains with one planned tunnel of at least two miles. Once completed, the Khakas capital of Abakan will be reached by rail in twelve hours and Krasnoyarsk in about eighteen. Currently, travelling between Abakan and Kyzyl is an arduous and sometimes hazardous road trip of at least five hours by bus or private taxi. In the winter of 2008-09 an avalanche completely cut off Tuva by land travel from the rest of the country and even the arrival of its Christmas tree—a feature of celebrations in the main squares of Russian towns—was held up.

THE YENISEY RIVER NORTH

For Tuvans, the confluence of the Kaa-Khem (Maly Yensiey) and the Bii-Khem (Bolshoy Yensiey) has shaman significance. This is where the Yenisey river (Ulug-Khem) begins.

The Yenisey, flowing 2,166 miles to the Arctic Ocean, is arguably Siberia's most important river. From Kyzyl it snakes westwards, collects the Khemchik river and veers north into the Sayan-Shushensk Reservoir (Sayano-Shushenskoe Vodokhranilishche), situated in a pretty gorge in the Western Sayan Mountains. This forms the first of two large hydroelectric dams on the river and is Russia's largest hydroelectric source.

The small town of Shushenskoe, situated about fifty miles south of Abakan on the banks of the Yenisey, is the setting for an international ethnic folk festival, the Sayan Ring Festival (Sayanskoe Koltso), held in summer over several days. Historically, however, Shushenskoe is better known as the place where Lenin spent his years in exile between 1897 and 1900—a period that by some accounts amounted to an involuntary respite for Russia's hardworking revolutionary.

Conditions for the exiled Lenin were certainly tolerable. In Shushenskoe he bathed in the Yenisey, hunted snipe and duck and gradually grew bored until the monotony of village life was relieved by the arrival of his wife-to-be, the fellow revolutionary Nadezhda Krupskaya (1869-1939), who was accompanied by her mother. Lenin had written to Krupskaya in St. Petersburg requesting her hand in marriage and thereafter Krupskaya's path led across Siberia to Lenin and her own exile in Shushenskoe. A *Time* article from 1964 describes her as "a thin, hot-eyed girl with carroty hair and many of the strong-minded qualities of the young women in the pages of Chekhov and Turgenev."

When the house they shared grew too small for the newly-weds and mother-in-law, the three moved into a larger cottage and added to the family a thirteen-year-old housekeeper, a cat and a pet dog. Henceforth, Lenin dedicated himself with gusto to his Siberian passion: hunting in the local *taiga*. He also spent his time reading, corresponded with fellow revolutionaries, wrote and translated and made frequent trips down the road to Minusinsk. In February 1900, having served his time, in the company of Krupskaya and mother-in-law, Lenin set off along the Yenisey. The group is said to have travelled two hundred miles on horseback and then by horse and carriage to Achinsk, from where they took the train west. Krupskaya was still officially in exile, and therefore had to remain in the Urals town of Ufa; meanwhile, Lenin, for whom revolution triumphed over true love, moved to Pskov in Russia's north-west, having been denied permission to live in the capital.

Today, much of this period is captured in Shushenskoe's Historical-Ethnographic Museum Reserve (Istoriko-Etnografichesky Muzey Zapovyednik), a large and popular open-air "historic" Siberian village recreated in 1970 to commemorate the centenary of Lenin's birth (work on the Sayan-Shushensk Reservoir began in 1980 to commemorate his 110th jubilee). To create the village, authorities moved the few remaining villagers into apartment blocks and hired actors in period costume to take their place and offer historical flourish. A Lenin museum has been located here since the 1930s; today the village attracts about 200,000 visitors each year.

About fifteen miles east of Abakan is the town of Minusinsk, founded in 1739 where the Minus river flows into the Yenisey. The city gradually developed into an agricultural and hide-processing centre, bolstered by early copper smelting and iron industries. Later, the discovery of gold in the region turned it into a substantial magnet for culture and trade—and of course gold processing. In 1882, in a case of poor timing, authorities decided to set up a weather station, coinciding with a bitterly cold winter that apparently ruined once and for all Minusinsk's tongue-in-cheek reputation for being a Siberian Italy. It would be wrong to view its 160 exiles—out of a population of 800 inhabitants in the early nineteenth century—as a group of embryonic Tuscan tourists, but there were colder and less hospitable regions of Siberia. By the end of the nineteenth century, the town had grown to 10,000. Today it has a population of about 80,000, with broad streets and a clutch of ramshackle wooden houses.

Its oldest building is the stone Cathedral of Our Saviour (Spassky Sobor), situated in the old town at ploshchad III Internatsionala (Square of the 3rd International), near the Regional Museum. The main body of this baroque cathedral dates from around 1800.

Minusinsk's cultural claim to fame is the Minusinsk Regional Martyanov Local Studies Museum (Minusinsky Regionalny Kraevedchesky Muzey Imena Martyanova), at ulitsa Lenina 20. The museum was founded in 1877 by the local pharmacist Martyanov and at the turn of the century won international acclaim for its natural science and archaeological collection. Today, exhibits include archaeological finds from the complex of ancient cultures that once thrived in the Minusinsk Basin, including a collection of bronze objects dating from the Karasuks (1200-700 BCE).

KHAKASSIA AND THE STEPPE CULTURES

From Minusinsk it is only a short hop to Abakan, the capital of Khakassia. The cultural and historical roots of Khakassia are close to those of the Tuvans and Altais. Together, as part of a more general Altai-Sayan region, they have been shaped by similar—and often the same—forces. In fact, with the rise of Burkhanism in the Altai in the early 1900s, some nationalists even dreamed of a new state encompassing the whole Altai-Sayan.

The closest relative of the Khakas people are the Kirghiz, mixed with various Turkic, Samoyed and Ket groups, but the concept of a single Khakas people is Soviet, as before the revolution only clan names were used. In the nineteenth century these clans were pieced together like a jigsaw puzzle into territorial groups to suit Russian administrative needs. The broad designations tsarist Russia used were Kachins, Kyzyls, Sagays, Beltirs and Koybals, but these included scores of clans and smaller ethnic clusters. The differences were considerable. According to their own legends, the Turkic-speaking Kyzyls used to live on the Tobol and Ishim rivers west of the Baraba Steppe and some descended from the son of Kuchum Khan (the khan defeated by Yermak). Well into the nineteenth century the women wore headdress similar to the Tobolsk Tartars. Koya-

Khakassia burial ground

bals, on the other hand, spoke Samoyedic and Ket languages and were only Turkicized in the seventeenth century.

The Khakas Republic Local Studies Museum (Khakasky Republikansky Kraevedchesky Muzey) was founded in 1931 and is the republic's flagship museum. Its collection of over 110,000 objects contains mostly archaeological and ethnological finds, offering an insight into early Siberian steppe culture.

The Minusinsk Basin and Sayan mountain region was inhabited by Palaeolithic and Neolithic hunters and gatherers who used fire and fashioned their clothes and tools from stone, bone and animal hide. Relics from the Afanasevo cultural period (about 5,500 years ago) indicate the breeding of domestic animals such as oxen, horses and sheep, but the Afanasevo were settled rather than nomadic. They were Europoids and therefore only very distantly related to the ethnic groups found in Khakassia today.

Around 1700 BC, a new culture, the Andronovo Culture, spread throughout the region and brought a stronger focus on pastoralism, apparent from the large number of bone and woollen objects found in the graves of the period. Around this time, too, ancient mining developed and tools were cast in metals. Pastoralism grew more specialized with the advent of the Karasuk Culture in the Minusinsk Basin between 1300 and 700 BCE, when sheep were bred for mutton, cows for milk and horses as draught animals, which were also ridden without saddles. With the arrival of a Tagar Culture (700-200 BCE), the Minusinsk Steppe to the west of the Yenisey became more densely settled and, significantly, some groups engaged in semi-nomadic pastoralism, which took hold here for the first time.

The Tagars are seen as being part of the Scythian cultural group. The Chinese called these Europoid people Dinlins, and it is believed that Dinlins are distant relatives of the Huns and paid tribute to them. The most celebrated of the finds from this period were from the Great Salbyk Burial Mound, situated about forty miles from Abakan.

We know from Chinese sources that an ancient Kirghiz (Kyagas) population also lived in the region from around 200 BCE and mixed with the Dinlins. The Kirghiz would later rise to power and create their own state in southern Siberia, but these ancient Kirghiz were part of what is generally called the Tashtyk culture. Like the Dinlins, they were dominated by the Huns. A number of funereal masks have survived from the period in the Oglakhty burial ground (where there are numerous petroglyphs) north of Abakan on the left bank of the Yenisey below its confluence with the Tuba.

All things come to pass on the south Siberian steppe, and Hun domination was no exception. Two successor cultures (Hsiang-pi, second-fourth centuries; and the Ju-jang, until the sixth century) established themselves here until the Turkic-speaking tribes of the Altai created a Turkic Khanate and brought the Sayan-Altai region under their control. The people they ruled over were a rich ethnic mix that had come together over the centuries, and it was during this period that a strong Turkicization of many of the smaller indigenous tribes such as the Samoyeds and Kets took place. This was reinforced by Turkic-speaking Uyghurs, who controlled the Selenga Valley and Upper Yenisey (including Tuva) from the mid-eighth century. The Uyghurs triggered the demise of the Turkic Khanate. Then around 950, the Kirghiz, who had long been locked in a struggle with them, gained the upper hand and created their own feudal state.

The Kirghiz, whose traditional heartland was the region just north of today's Khakassia, shifted their centre east into the Selenga Valley (south of Lake Baikal) and built an empire extending from the steppes of Kazakhstan to Tibet. The highly effective iron weapons they had once used to pay tribute to the Turkic khans were now being exported to China, along with musk and animal hide, which they exchanged for Arab cloth and other goods. Ordinary Kirghiz lived from open pastoralism, driving their animals year round to new pastures and carrying with them felt *kibitkas*—portable yurts or tents mounted on runners that could be towed across the steppe.

These Kirghiz, described by the Chinese as having a fair complexion, red hair and blue or green eyes, also ploughed, irrigated and cultivated the soil. The remnants of several of their irrigation systems, some built by tribute paying indigenes captured and worked as slaves, still survive today. Along with metal forging techniques, skills in reading and writing—like Uyghric, using a runic script—were highly developed. In 1207, during the rule of Ghengis Khan, Kirghiz leaders collected tribute from their own people and gave this to the Mongol rulers, but it was under Mongol rule that their agricultural and metal working skills also became lost. Many of the Kirghiz moved south during Mongol rule, establishing the ethnic foundations for present-day Kirghizstan.

Like the Tuvans, the Kirghiz fell into the dominions of the Oirats of western Mongolia and the Altyn Khanate, but the region was rife with fighting, which meant some groups had to pay tribute to several feudal rulers at once, easing the conquest by the *yasak*-seeking Russians, who arrived in the early seventeenth century. Fortresses, like Krasnoyarsk, founded in 1628, were constantly under attack from the Kirghiz and the Oirats (often called Kalmuks in descriptions), who rode north in large, plundering bands.

The Eastern Sayan Mountains extend for about 625 miles from the Yenisey to Lake Baikal and historically formed a physical barrier for many of the steppe cultures. The wildest and most difficult section of the range is around the Azas Plateau in Tuva, where mountains climb to 10,000 feet close to the border with Mongolia. But it is the taiga, not the mountains, which makes the region so inaccessible, and most of the conquering bands chose to ride west around them and enter southern Siberia from the steppe.

The explorer and naturalist Douglas Carruthers (1882-1962) mapped the region in 1910-11. In *Unknown Mongolia*, he describes an "impenetrable and hostile forest zone, which, even more than the mountain ranges, is effective in preserving intact the mysteries of this region." Confronted with the taiga, Carruthers' adventurous spirit waned somewhat; it depressed him, in fact, and induced something akin to a Victorian physical repulsion. He writes:

> The scenery was a study in opposites, giving a wealth of beauty in detail, but a lack of beauty as a whole. Nothing could be more monotonous than the endless expanses of unbroken forest, nothing more beautiful than the flower-spangled meadows, and nothing more striking than the upheavals of bare, jagged peaks that rise suddenly out of the forest. Overlooking the forests, the dreary monotony of the landscape brings a feeling of repulsion, as ridge after ridge of endless, sodden jungle opens up before one, and uninspiring vistas of forest stretch to the far horizon. A hundred miles of desolate sand-waste is not so repulsive. In a desert-land even, the scenery does not affect the traveller with a feeling of such hopeless uniformity. There, the eyes strain their gaze with searching;

they are fascinated by and intoxicated with the sense of light, colour, and distance; the very mystery of the desert is inviting, and its air invigorating. But a view of the taiga—the swamp-forest of the northland—chokes all such feelings. The whole impression given by the banks of pines, with their sorrowful downward-drooping lines, and the falling outlines of the scenery is one of depression.

The Upper Yenisey Basin became part of independent Mongolia in 1911. Before this, and briefly again after the Russian Revolution of 1917, China controlled it. Although Russia continued to stake its claim to the Altai from 1756, it stopped making any serious attempts to control the land across the Eastern Sayan Mountains after 1663, the year Tuvans completely wiped out a Russian yasak gang.

In 1703, in order to avoid confrontation with both the Russians and the Manchurians, the Oirat Khan Tseven Rabdan resettled the Kirghiz into western Mongolia (Dzungaria). This move placated Peter the Great and allowed Russia's tsar to establish the string of forts in the Altai Region and in Khakassia. Abakan was founded in March 1707. Twenty years later, a treaty with China opened the way for complete integration into the Russian Empire, bringing waves of Russian settlers and the gradual conversion of the Khakas people to Christianity. Today, eighty per cent of the population of the Republic of Khakassia is European Russian and only twelve per cent ethnic Khakas.

KRASNOYARSK

Perhaps one day an association of psychologists will hold its annual conference in Krasnoyarsk. This will be an international event, with visitors from New York, London, Paris, Buenos Aires, Beijing, from places important in the world. After all, Krasnsyarsk—despite being nestled deep in the Siberian taiga and once being completely closed to foreigners—is growing fast and catching up on Novosibirsk as "capital of Siberia". Late one blazing summer evening, while the sun transforms the surrounding hills into a picturesque shade of red (giving the town its Turkic name of "Red Ore") and the two-mile long row of *shashlik* and grilled chicken marquees along the Yenisey overflow with customers, the conference goers will decide to take a stroll through the town centre.

They will see a playful cascade facing the river with figures representing the important rivers of the region. They will also see a stone pavilion with a dandy Pushkin. They might stop for coffee somewhere and, asked whether they want an English or Russian drinks menu and replying, "Is there a difference?" they will be told with disarming honesty: "Yes, the English one is more expensive—but just a little." They will see several wooden houses that survived fire—the blight of all Siberian towns. And then one of the visitors—probably British—will look up towards the clock on the city town hall building, towering above the street as an imposing grey tower, and remark to his companion, "That's Big Ben, isn't it?" Walking on, the group will see another version of Big Ben, this one smaller than the mayor's big Big Ben, then another, until all clocks in Krasnoyarsk begin to resemble Big Ben. I counted—inconclusively, because more are bound to sprout out of the pavements—no fewer than three Big Bens in Krasnoyarsk. What all this means is anyone's guess.

Krasnoyarsk is situated at a crossroads. One of these "roads" is the Trans-Siberian Railway, while the other is the magnificent Yenisey, which widens to about a mile and a half and is punctuated with long islands as it swirls through the city. Together, the railway and the river provide the impetus for Krasnoyarsk's growth into a city today of almost one million inhabitants. At the one end of the railway is Vladivostok, at the other is Moscow or St. Petersburg. Between these two geometric points Siberia's trains roll through a landscape that changes between steppe, taiga, lush pastures, picturesque ranges and undulating countryside. In winter this landscape is white, in summer it is green. It is pockmarked with swamp (on the Baraba Steppe) whose waters freeze in winter and are poisonous any time of year. It is dotted with little rectangular villages mourning their own demise, with small towns consisting of one factory and rows of housing blocks, and with large cities splitting at the girth with strategic industrial complexes.

The river of this crossroads—the Yenisey—has an entirely different character. At one end, Tuva's steppe shimmers and has witnessed centuries of nomadic pastoralism. At the top end, tundra is washed by Arctic waters. Its link is Krasnoyarsk, unfolding psychologically (but not geographically) in the middle, a smoking industrial centre fringed with impressive escarpments.

In terms of its significance for Siberia, only the Amur is a serious challenger to the Yenisey. It took the eccentric Joseph Wiggins—the same trade-hungry Wiggins who sailed across the northern coast in 1893 as part of Helen Peel's flotilla and lost most of his rails in the river—numerous attempts, but he did finally hammer home his point about "Father Yenisey's" potential as a trade route. The Norwegian Fridtjof Nansen captured the mood well a couple of decades later when one of his voyages took him up the Yenisey in 1913 and he entitled his book about the journey, *Through Siberia: The Land of the Future.*

Today, we know that Krasnoyarsk Territory has the second-largest deposits of gold in Russia. Almost one-tenth of Russia's timber resources are located here, and after Tyumen Region, it has Russia's largest oil and gas deposits. It is also rich in other minerals. About sixty per cent of its foreign investment is to be found in mining, oil and manufacturing, and about half of total foreign investment comes from Britain.

In 1914, one year after Nansen's visit, British bird-watcher Maud Haviland described Krasnoyarsk as having the "mixed appearance of crude rawness and rising prosperity that is characteristic of Siberian towns. Some of the houses are of stone, but more are built of timber, with broad streets and squares of unkempt ground between them." The description still captures the flavour of many Siberian towns, even if timber houses and vacant lots are fewer in the largest cities today.

After Novosibirsk and Omsk, Krasnoyarsk is the third-largest Siberian city and was founded in 1628 as an *ostrog* (wooden stockade) named Krasny Yar in order to fend off Oirats and Kirghiz. The location of the new fort, envisaged as an outpost to protect Yeniseysk, Tomsk and Kuznetsk, was chosen by the Cossack Andrey Dubensky. Strategically, the site was a clever choice, but it also happened to be fortuitously attractive, situated on the right bank of the Yenisey and flanked by cliffs.

Chekhov, in 1890 on his way to Sakhalin Island, wrote:

> Not to offend you jealous admirers of the Volga, but I have never in my life seen a river more splendid than the Yenisey. Let the Volga be a well-dressed, modest and sad beauty, the Yenisey is the powerful, furious hero who does not know what to do with its strength and youth. On the Volga, man began with boldness but ended with a canto-like groan. Bright, golden hopes changed to impotence, which conventionally is called Russian pessimism. The Yenisey, however, began life with a groan and ended with a boldness we could never dream of. That, at least, is

what I thought while standing on the shore on the broad Yenisey and looking with greed into its waters, which with terrible rapidity and force gushed to the Arctic Ocean.

Chekhov also described Krasnoyarsk as "the best and most beautiful of all Siberian cities, with smoke-coloured and dreamy mountains that reminded me of the Caucasus."

The blind traveller Holman could not see any such Caucasus rising out of the taiga, but he felt it was "inconsiderable" and "possessing in itself little to interest the traveller" in the early 1820s, "consisting of only one good street, built on a low sandy spot, near the river Yenesai." He was writing one year after Krasnoyarsk became the provincial capital of the Yeniseysk Province, having trumped older and commercially more important Yeniseysk town.

Krasnoyarsk was a logical choice of capital. The focus of Siberia was shifting to the south, and the city was well situated, with transport links upriver to Abakan, downriver to the ocean, west to the cities on the Western Siberian Plain, and south-east to Irkutsk. Once Yeniseysk's fortunes began to wane, a stopover in Krasnoyarsk became *de rigueur* for the traveller. Although today it is something of a Cinderella city in Siberia, its star shines brighter than most. According to one survey, it ranks in the top twenty cities that interest Russian travellers (Yekaterinburg ranks 17th, Irkutsk seventh). Industrially, it is a Russian heavyweight. Perhaps all its clocks (and gushing fountains) are less Freudian than suggestions that its time has now come.

The biggest of the Big Bens is situated on the eastern flank of Teatral-naya ploshchad (350-Year Anniversary Square). Here the Hotel Krasno-yarsk broods on the northern side and the west is closed off by the Theatre of Opera and Ballet (Teatr Opery i Baleta). The square is the heart of Kras-noyarsk and possibly its most boisterous area during the short, intense summers.

The south side of the square is adorned with a fountain—an elaborate cascade known as "Siberian Rivers" that was completed in 2008 when the last sculpture, a ten-foot high, 1,700-lb Neptune-like figure (Yenisey Batyushka, or Father Yenisey) was added to symbolize the river. Along the length of the cascade is a series of sculptures of women in various states of classical pose and undress, representing the main tributaries of the Yenisey.

One of Krasnoyarsk's many clocks

Their number includes a rather undernourished Angara, seemingly sledding with an erect hairdo. The cascade is the work of sculptor Konstantin Zinich and three of his pupils and took four years to complete. Father Yenisey sits on a pedestal with depictions of deer and other animals found in the Krasnoyarsk Region and holds a boat alluding to the historic importance of the Yenisey as a water route.

From here it is a short walk across the pedestrian bridge and south to the Local Studies Museum (Kraevedchesky Muzey) at ulitsa Dubrovinskovo 84. The building dates from 1913-14 and is orientalist and neoclassical in style, with pseudo-Egyptian motifs. As you enter the museum, you see a copy of a 1701 map of Krasnoyarsk by Siberia's first cartographer Semyon Remezov, depicting the rectangular fortress in the centre. Left of the map is a small bronze of Dubensky, Krasnoyarsk's founder.

The main exhibition starts from the right, with the usual stuffed zoological specimens, but in the centre of this section is a room containing a full-size replica of a Russian *kocha* (sailing boat). The design of the original, flat-bottomed kochas comes from north-east European Russia, but Yeniseysk became an important boat-building centre in Siberia during the seventeenth century. This vessel is about as big as any from the early days of exploration, holding 35-40 people. The explorer Semyon Dezhnev—the first Russian to sail through the Bering Strait—probably used one roughly similar to this. Upstairs, a section includes religious art, and another covers the imperial epoch.

The basement section is devoted to indigenes and early settlement, including exhibits on the Tagar Culture and the Yenisey Kirghiz. You find here a chum (a tipi-like tradional dwelling) —in this case, used by the Evenks (Tungus), who have their own Evenk District within the Region. Some of the most interesting accounts of the Nenets, who inhabit the east bank of the Yenisey, and the Selkups (Yenisey Samoyeds) living mainly on the west bank, are from Nansen, or from the Polish ethnologist Marya Antonina Czaplicka (she travelled partly with Maud Haviland), whose *My Siberian Year* is a classic of ethnological travel description.

The Regional Museum includes the Literature Museum (Literaturny Muzey), housed in a wooden building from 1913, west of the cathedral at ulitsa Lenina 66. This contains a folklore section upstairs with bric-a-brac, a signed copy of Alexander Solzhenitsyn's *The Gulag Archipelago* and a signed letter from former US president Bill Clinton thanking Krasnoyarsk for an inscribed copy of the book *Commander Rezanov*, along with other Rezanov knick-knacks in a case.

Nikolay Petrovich Rezanov (1764-1807) was one of the key figures behind the early expansion of Russia into Alaska and California. He was the son-in-law of Grigory Shelikov, who co-founded an early trading company—the Shelikhov-Golikov Company—to exploit opportunities across the Bering Strait. When Shelikhov died, Shelikhov's wife Natalya ran the company, which grew and merged, thanks to Rezanov's connections, into the Russian America Company. This company enjoyed a monopoly on trade with Russian America, which included Alaska, the Aleutians and territory extending as far south in the Pacific to 51 degrees, and the company also established forts on Hawaii and at Fort Ross north of San Francisco, California.

Rezanov was a highly gifted man who played a role in the first Russian circumnavigation of the world, and it was partly thanks to his skills and connections that Alaska was a Russian possession until 1867. In 1806 Rezanov sailed to the Spanish colony of California, dropping anchor in San Francisco in the hope of securing supplies for his starving colony at

Sitka in Alaska and to negotiate a deal that would allow him to trade with the Spanish colonies of North America. The Spanish wined him, dined him and rebuffed his trade approaches, but while in San Francisco he fell in love with the fifteen-year-old daughter of the governor, María Concepción Argüello (1791-1857), known as the Juliet of California. Thereafter events became complicated for Rezanov. A marriage needed the approval of Tsar Alexander I, the Spanish king and the pope, so he sailed back to Siberia, promising to return within two years with the tsar's permission. Ill and exhausted from his exploits, Rezanov was travelling from Irkutsk to Krasnoyarsk when he fell from a horse. In March 1807 he died in Krasnoyarsk. Two years passed before rumours of Rezanov's death reached María, but it was 36 years after his demise before she received final confirmation of his fate.

Also part of the Regional Museum is the Steamship Museum St. Nicholas (Parakhod-Muzey Svyatoy Nikolay), situated on the Yenisey at the eastern end of ulitsa Dubrovinskovo. The steamship, once belonging to the industrialist I. M. Sibiryakov, dates from 1887 and was the fastest on the Yenisey in its day. In 1891 Tsar Nicholas II graced its decks on a short excursion, and in 1897 Lenin and fellow prisoners were transported on it into exile in Minusinsk. One section of the Steamship Museum is also dedicated to Rezanov.

From the Regional Museum, the Yenisey's shore lends itself to strolling (and paddle-boating in summer in a backwater). If you walk eastwards (downstream) you soon reach the river station at the head of ulitsa Parizhkoy Kommuny. Follow this away from the river (ulitsa Uritskovo, first on the left, is known for a couple of good restaurants) and you reach the main building of the arts museum.

The V. I. Surikov Krasnoyarsk Art Museum (Krasnoyarsky Khudozhestvenny Muzey V.I. Surikova), situated in three separate buildings, is the city's most important museum for fine arts. The Hall of Russian Art from the eighteenth to the early twentieth centuries (Zal Russkovo Iskusstva XVIII-nachala XX Veka) is located at ulitsa Parizhkoy Kommuny 20 and includes paintings and graphics by Ilya Repin (1844-1930) and Vasily Surikov (1848-1916). The Hall of twentieth and twenty-first-century art (Zal Iskusstva XX-XXI Veka), at prospekt Mira 12, has graphics and paintings by Kandinsky and other Russian avant-garde artists, works by artists from the former Soviet republics and visual arts by modern and contemporary regional artists. The Artist's Gallery (Khudozhestvennaya Galereya) on the right bank of the Yenisey at Krasnoyarsky Rabochy 68 contains decorative arts.

Vasily Surikov, after whom the museum is named, was born in Krasnoyarsk; he received his earliest art training here before being "discovered" by the gold mining industrialist and former mayor of Krasnoyarsk, Pyotr Kuznetsov (1818-78), who from 1870 sponsored Surikov's years of study in St. Petersburg. Having graduated—highly appropriately with a gold medal—Surikov moved to Moscow and in 1875 began working on the frescoes of the Cathedral of Christ the Saviour (Khram Khrista Spasitelya). This early period proved formative for Russia's most famous painter of historical themes. Moscow's Tretyakov Gallery began acquiring his works, and today his most famous pictures are found in the Tretyakov and in the Russian Museum. The latter contains his iconic "Yermak's Conquest of Siberia" (1895), which has been much-copied over the years and more than any other work of art has created the visual historical accompaniment to Yermak's campaigns.

Perhaps because of his choice of historical motifs, Surikov's place in Russian culture goes far beyond the works he created. His painting, "Boyarynya Morozova" (from 1887) was used by film director Sergey Eisenstein to illustrate theories of montage and movement. (Fyeodosiya Morozova was an Old Believer who supported Avvakum—who led the break-away of Old Believers—and starved in an underground cell in Borovsk, south of Moscow.) Surikov was also a founding member of the so-called Peredvizhniki (Itinerants or Wanderers) from about 1870, which included Ilya Repin (1833-82).

From the mid-eighteenth century Russian artistic life was dominated by the St. Petersburg Academy of Arts, which promoted European neo-classicism at the expense of Russian movements. This culminated in dissatisfaction among Russian artists from the 1850s. In the following decade a group of middle-class liberal students rebelled, forming a commune around the artist Ivan Kramskoy (1837-87), and this commune later developed into the Society of Itinerant Art Exhibitions.

The Itinerants sought to shift the cultural focus in visual arts back onto the Russian people. They did this not as conservative nationalists but as the descendants of a middle class that developed out of Peter the Great's outward-looking drive for modernization. According to Elena Duzs in

Russia and Western Civilisation, it was the same democratic tendency to be found in the best works of Tolstoy and Dostoevsky. The Itinerants told stories with their pictures, explored Russian historical themes and Slavic mythology, sought a broad audience and were anticlerical.

North of the main building of the Art Museum is the baroque Cathedral of the Intercession of the Holy Virgin (Svyato-Pokrovsky Kafedralny Sobor) at ulitsa Surikova 26, Krasnoyarsk's oldest building and dating from 1785-95.

On the corner of prospekt Mira and ultisa Kirova is ploshchad Pushkina and a popular pagoda with statues of Pushkin and his wife, Natalya Goncharova, whom the poet married in 1831. Natalya sits pertly to one side while Pushkin is captured in a pontificating pose. In front of them is a small fountain—Krasnoyarsk not only likes Big Ben imitations, it has over 150 fountains—and the engraved words from one of Pushkin's poems: "I remember the wonderful moment..."

Pushkin did not write the lyric to his wife but to a secret love, Anna Petrovna Kern, in 1825. After the unveiling in mid-2008, this prompted the *Novaya Gazeta* newspaper amusingly to question Pushkin's connection with Krasnoyarsk and to ask: "Why is he throwing the poems into the water, like the poet's just confused the two women? And what's Pushkin doing here in Krasnoyarsk anyway? Where are the memorials to Alexander Makedonsky, to Cleopatra and Prometheus, or for that matter, to Naomi Campbell?"

One block north and west along ulitsa Lenina at no. 98 is the Museum Estate of V. I. Surikov (Muzey Usadba V. I. Surikova), one of several picturesque retreats from the white noise of traffic and city PA systems. This was Surikov's birth house and today has two sections: one an exhibition space with his paintings, the other his downstairs living quarters. The wooden buildings date from the 1830s.

North of the town centre on Karaulnaya Gora (Karaulnaya Mountain) is the architectural symbol of Krasnoyarsk, the Paraskeva Pyatnitsa Chapel (Chasovya). The site was reputedly once the location of a Tartar temple, but with the founding of Krasnoyarsk, a watchtower was placed here to warn of impending attacks by the Kirghiz and Oirats. In 1703, to commemorate those who had died in attacks, a wooden cross was placed on the site of the watchtower. Twice each year, in May and September, in remembrance of sieges, religious processions reached the top of the hill, lending a religious-historical character to the site. Later, in 1805, a wooden chapel was erected, prompting a couple of local legends as to why. One was that a local merchant had it built as thanks for being saved one day from the swirling rapids of the Yenisey. According to another, it was a memorial to the townsfolk who survived the Kirghiz and Oirat assaults. In any case, by 1855 this chapel was falling apart and a stone version was built in its place, financed by Pyotr Kuznetsov, Surikov's sponsor; today the chapel features on Russia's most-used currency unit—the ten-rouble note.

Karaulnaya Gora offers a view over the valleys of the Yenisey and Kacha rivers and beyond to the cliffs. Surikov reportedly worked on some of his paintings from the mountain and today it is popular for wedding photographs.

The third in a triumvirate of picturesque retreats is the Stolby Reserve (Zapovednik Stolby), about one hour south-west of town by taxi and another hour and a half from the settlement—and Yenisey tourist base (*turbaza*)—Lalentino.

The *stolby* or natural pillars are situated on the south-west spur of the Eastern Sayan Mountains and form part of a natural reserve containing about 750 different species of plants and a 260 species of moss growing in fir taiga fairly typical of the region. Almost 300 species of vertebrates ranging from forest voles and sable through musk deer and polecats inhabit the park. The list of scientific notables who in past centuries have passed through here to gather, examine and classify in their quest to understand Siberia is long. Daniel Gottlieb Messerschmidt visited in the 1720s while travelling through Siberia. Peter Simon Pallas (1741-1811), Johann Georg Gmelin (1709-55) and Stepan Krasheninnikov (1711-55)—all important names in research into Siberia—have combed the rocks.

Oddly, the region gave birth to a special style of rock climbing known as "Stolby" or Siberian free soloing—extreme climbing that can draw masses to the rock-faces, some climbing head-first without ropes down vertical cracks in the pillars. Alcohol and infectious ticks are said to be the biggest dangers for climbers.

NORTH TO THE ARCTIC

The years 1913-14 were busy ones for the Yenisey. In 1913 Nansen sailed across the Kara Sea on board the *Correct*, a chartered steamer carrying an expedition team led by the Norwegian explorer and businessman Jonas

Lied. Lied, who founded the Siberia Company in 1912, was a Norwegian Wiggins—just as self-willed, but better organized and better informed about navigation of the river. Like Wiggins, he was convinced of the potential of the northern sea route as a way of exploiting Siberia's resources. In 1919, during the civil war, he is even said to have arranged a meeting with Admiral Kolchak in Omsk to discuss a trade deal that would have seen him bringing goods into the war-torn interior of Siberia (and carrying out butter and other goods he could sell). Indeed, the *Correct* was carrying a cargo of cement on Nansen's forward journey; when she sailed homewards down the Yenisey her cargo included two live camels sent from Mongolia.

After sailing up the Yenisey, Nansen struck out alone across Siberia and held public addresses, being received like a celebrity wherever he went. Paradoxically, while Europe and much of the world was perched on the brink of catastrophic war, Siberia was a place of seemingly endless optimism. "The future possibilities of Siberia may almost be called unlimited; but their development is attended with difficulties," wrote Nansen, "which is mainly due to the great distances." The cost of transporting Siberia's goods by rail —mainly grain and timber at that time—were prohibitive, usually exceeding the actual value of the goods. Nansen pointed out in his book that the Yenisey and its tributaries provided cost effective river transport to the Arctic Ocean from Mongolia and from the Baikal region in the east.

In the summer of 1914, just before the First World War broke out, another colourful group, this time comprising British and Americans, travelled overland to the Yenisey and sailed downriver to its delta. The party consisted of Polish-British anthropologist Maria Antoinette Czaplicka (1886-1921), ornithologist Maud Haviland (1889-1941), the painter Dora Curtis and Henry Usher Hall from Pennsylvania University Museum (mentioned playfully by Czaplicka as the "only 'mere man' of the party"). Czaplicka and Hall spent a year altogether in the Yenisey region, including a winter on the lower Yenisey.

Polish-born Czaplicka begins her book *My Siberian Year* (1916), an insightful ethnological travel description, with the words:

> When, as a child, I heard the word "Siberia", it meant but one thing to
> me: dire peril to the bodies, sore torture for the souls, of the bravest,

cleverest, and most independently-minded of our people... It was only as I grew older that I came to know of another aspect which more recently Siberia has assumed for the Poles, as a place in which to seek opportunities for the development of their abilities—opportunities denied them at home.

Siberia maintained its relative order in the run up to the war. As her train pulled out of London's Charing Cross station, Czaplicka became nostalgic about leaving the "happy, peaceful life of ordered work and play, for the rough, inhospitable wilds" to which, she says, she had condemned herself. "In one respect I was mistaken: Siberia, however rough, was not at all inhospitable; but my sadness—was it not prophetic. I was to return to a very different England", she writes, "no longer placid and calm and secure in its sea-girt remoteness from the cruelties and wrongs of turbulent powers".

The amateur ornithologist Haviland, whom the Russians called "the man" because of her rather hazardous predilection for wielding a loaded pistol to protect herself wherever she went, poignantly captures the historical and contemporary feel of the Yenisey in her *A Summer on the Yenisei* from 1915. The gun-toting ornithologist writes that the first allusion to the Yenisey she could find was from the time of Willem Barentsz in 1595, when the Dutch navigator came across some Muscovy hunters in a fleet of ten kochas and was told about a river to the east. Barentsz knew that the river "flowed into the northern ocean from the land of Cathay, where the sands were golden, where spices grew on all the bushes, and where silks and furs might be had for the asking." Later, she adds that "the banks of the Yenisei still hold something of the romance of an ornithological land of Cathay."

While Helen Peel in *Polar Gleams* depicts the Arctic yachtsman Francis Leybourne-Popham as a walrus-hunting buccaneer, he pops up in Maud Haviland's book as one of her role models of Siberian ornithology. Her other role model was British ornithologist Henry Seebohm, who published a book called *Birds of Siberia: To the Petchora Valley* in 1901.

In early June the travelling party boarded the *Oryol*, formerly a British registered paddle steamer that plied the Clyde, and set off north from Krasnoyarsk. The previous travel season, Fridtjof Nansen had completed the voyage with Jonas Lied in the other direction. They passed the confluence with the Angara, which at the village of Strelka spills into the Yenisey, 1,105 miles from its source at Lake Baikal. Beyond this point the Yenisey widens and flows through Yeniseysk, which Haviland describes as "a large town with schools, churches, museum, and a picture palace in the middle of the wilderness." One year earlier, Nansen was astounded that Yeniseysk did not even have its own sawmill and that all wood was being sawn by hand. Haviland missed visiting the Regional Museum in Krasnoyarsk, but she did manage the one in Yeniseysk, even if she found its natural history section "in a state of great confusion".

YENISEYSK: CHURCHES AND FAIRS

Yeniseysk is historically the most important town in Krasnoyarsk Territory. In the winter of 1718-20 John Bell described it as "a large and populous place, fenced with a ditch, palisades, and wooden towers. Here is a good market for furs of all sorts..." The town's development is connected with the early seventeenth-century push by Russians into eastern Siberia, having been founded in 1619 as a wooden stockade about five miles from the confluence of the Kem river. It owes its significance today to a handful of related historical factors. One of these is its geographical location on the Yenisey, which helped turn it into an industrial town. The discovery of gold in the region gave it a further boost, and before long Yeniseysk boasted large metal processing, shipbuilding and salt industries. The fur market mentioned by John Bell was another factor. This was Siberia's largest and explains why the sable featured on the city's coat of arms from 1635.

The dates of the Siberian trade fairs were pencilled into calendars of merchants everywhere in Russia and Central Asia. Beginning from late-February in the Urals town of Irbit, convoys of caravans and boats plied the roads and rivers of Siberia to exchange wares. Traders arrived from the large cities of European Russia and Siberia, as well as from Bukhara, Persia, China and Armenia. After Irbit, they travelled to Tobolsk, then to the Turukhansk Fair, downriver from Yeniseysk. Finally they reached Yeniseysk for its August fair.

The highpoint of Yeniseysk's growth from a stockade to a powerful trade and production centre was reached in the late eighteenth century. Early on it benefited greatly from its river connections. Starting from the Tobol river in western Siberia, it was possible to follow the Irtysh, Ob,

Ket, Kem and Yenisey rivers to the Angara. From there one could reach Lake Baikal if the canyons were negotiated. Yeniseysk's decline loomed, however, when the Sibirsky Trakt was moved south, the towns of eastern Siberia began to lose importance and—in a fatal blow—the Trans-Siberian Railway by-passed it altogether. Today the past of this town of 20,000 inhabitants is of more importance than its present. Because of its historic architecture, it is a Unesco World Heritage site.

The exhibits in the Regional Museum mentioned by Maud Haviland, located at ulitsa Lenina 106, include a portrait of Avvakum, an ethnological collection that apparently impressed Nansen and a series of photographs illustrating the town's history.

As in Tobolsk, some of Yeniseysk's architectural pearls are in disrepair. Also like Tobolsk, Yeniseysk has acquired religious importance. Avvakum, the founder of the Old Believers, spent a winter here in the mid-seventeenth century during one of his Siberian exiles before being transferred with his brutal tormentor, Afanasy Pashkov, to the Baikal region.

Church building in the former administrative region of Yeniseysk dates back to the early seventeenth century. The earliest wooden churches had strict, horizontal lines and sparse decorative elements composed in a square *kletsky* or "cell" design. None of these survives due to fires, which struck Yeniseysk in 1703, in the 1730s and again in 1869.

From the early eighteenth century, a wave of baroque church building in stone began, resulting in five stone churches in the course of the century. One of these was the Epiphany Cathedral (Bogoyavlensky Sobor, 1738-64), from 2008 earmarked for restoration. Another is the Church of the Resurrection (Voskrosenskaya Tserkov, 1737-47). The style of these earliest stone churches in the province was based on Urals baroque churches such as in Verkhoturye and those in Tyumen and Tobolsk, and a feature of many was a large square base, creating the foundations for a belfry. This fashion is typified by the base beneath the belfry of the Cathedral of the Epiphany in Yeniseysk. From the late seventeen century Yeniseysk also became a centre of Siberian icon painting.

Several other architectural highlights are the Assumption Cathedral (Uspensky Sobor, 1793-1818), situated on ulitsa Raboche-Krestyanskaya; Yeniseysk Transfiguration of our Saviour Monstery (Spaso-Preobrazhensky Monastyr, 1642), at ulitsa Raboche-Krestyanskaya 101; the Holy Iberian Convent (Svyato-Iversky Zhensky Monastyr, 1623), ulitsa Bolshaya 100; and the Trinity Church (Troiskaya Tserkov, 1772-76).

The early eighteenth century—the period of the Enlightenment—was one when empires began to take an inventory of their possessions. They wanted to know what was there and they employed science to reaffirm that it belonged to them. From the reign of Peter the Great (tsar in 1682-1725, ruling alone from 1696), this propelled a series of scientific expeditions into Siberia. Georg Gmelin, from the St. Petersburg Academy of Sciences and member of the Second Kamchatka Expedition, arrived in Yeniseysk in the autumn of 1734—almost fifteen years after John Bell. With him were the French astronomer Louis De l'Isle de la Croyère (1690-1741), who would later die on the expedition and be buried on Kamchatka, and the Siberian historian Gerhard Friedrich Müller. In Yeniseysk the mercury in l'Isle de la Croyère's thermometer solidified from cold. It was the first time anyone had observed this phenomenon—about 38° below zero is sufficient—and Yeniseysk thereby sealed Siberia's reputation in world scientific circles as a gigantic icebox. Birds, the Royal Society of London recounted in one article to readers, were falling out of the air in Yeniseysk as if dead and immediately froze on the ground unless taken into a warm room.

As well as describing plummeting birds, Gmelin captured the appearance and mood of Yeniseysk as it neared its heyday:

> In terms of public buildings it has the main church, the house of the *voyevod* [military commander], the old and new chancellery, an armoury and several small huts. These buildings stand inside the *ostrog* [stockade] remaining from the very first days of the place but which is mostly falling apart. In the other parts of town, containing 704 private houses, are the other public buildings—three parish churches, a seminary for the monks and a convent for the nuns, a powder magazine and a storehouse, the latter two surrounded by special stockades. A small brook flows almost through the middle of town, named after the watermill that stands there and was formerly known as Mühlbach (Mjelnitschnaja rietschka) [Melnichnaya Rechka]. Immediately above town is a seminary courtyard (Dworez) of the Mangaseischen Troitzkoi-Seminary. The vice of drinking and idleness is just as common here as in the other cities I have described. Syphilis rages here, too, to a high degree. Among the established Siberians, the people of Yeniseysk are considered clever and

Siberian village

deceitful, which explains why they have earned the moniker Skvosniki, which means they are people who know how to see through things.

North of Yeniseysk the landscape along the river assumes a physical relief it retains for the most part until the very lower reaches. The left bank (west), leading into the Western Siberian Plain, is flat and at times marshy, while the eastern bank rises up to the Central Siberian plateau.

For Maud Haviland, Yeniseysk was the invisible border beyond which the party "left some of the formalities of life behind." "All the villages of the Yenisei are built after the same plan", she wrote. "Each consists of a manure heap with a few wooden huts on top. Sometimes it is a small manure heap with one or two huts, and such a place smells only a little. Nasimorokoe [Nazimovo] was a large manure heap with about fifty huts, and it smelt a great deal."

Although in Haviland's day the original houses of Nazimovo, 365 miles north of Krasnoyarsk, were about to sink into oblivion, its historical pedigree is impeccable, having been founded by explorer Yerofey Khabarov (1603 to at least 1671), who explored the northern Siberian river routes from west to east.

TURUKHANSK: SAINTS AND EXILES

Beyond Nazimovo is Turukhansk, situated almost 940 miles north of Krasnoyarsk. Turukhansk, now a settlement of about 5,000, was founded in 1607 as a winter stockade (*zimovye*) near the site where the Lower Tunguska river flows into the Yenisey. At the time, Mangazeya on the Taz river was the major town in the region, but after a fire destroyed much of Mangazeya in 1619 it began its steep decline. Another event of 1619 sealed the fate of Old Mangazeya once and for all. In that year the tsar issued a decree forbidding use of the sea route across the Arctic, fearing penetration by the British and Dutch. Anyone found violating the decree was executed. The growth of Turukhansk into a town hence reflected the decline of Old Mangazeya, which was struck by two more fires that century, leading to it being abandoned altogether and all its inhabitants moving to Turukhansk, which received the status of a town and became known as New Mangazeya. Turukhansk's chief attraction, the annual fair, began in late June and ran for two weeks.

Today Turukhansk has a Museum of Political Exile (Muzey "Politicheskaya Ssylka"), inside a 1910 building at ulitsa Sverdlova 26 that was built by a criminal exile who, after serving his term, sold it to the weather observatory of Irkutsk. This was where the revolutionary Yakov Sverdlov spent his time in exile in 1913-16, partly with Joseph Stalin, who had been dispatched to the village of Kureyka, 105 miles south of Igarka. As in the case of Lenin in Minusinsk, life for the revolutionaries was something of an enforced vacation far from the madding crowd. Whenever Stalin visited, they prepared their meals together and plotted the overthrow of the man who sent them into the taiga. Sverdlov, in the company of his wife, read Marx, hunted and fished, tended his cow and generally lived without hardship. While there, he also organised a workers' cooperative and taught local children.

The museum was opened in the building in 1941, where among other things Stalin's bed took pride of place—Stalin was allowed to come here twice a month to collect his post. In 1991 the museum was revamped and now its small collection focuses more generally on political repression.

Turukhansk's other cultural attraction is its partially-restored monastery at ulitsa Partizanskaya 15. The Holy Trinity Monastery (Svyato-Troytsky Muzhskoy Monastyr) was founded in 1657 and a stone church erected here in 1779-87. The history of the monastery is closely connected to St. Basil of Mangazeya, one of Siberia's two local saints.

Basil of Mangazeya was born in 1587 in Yaroslavl on the Volga. He came from a well-heeled merchant family and at the age of nineteen was apprenticed to a merchant in Old Mangazeya on the Taz. Siberia was a rough place for young Basil, whose employer continually harassed the boy for sexual favours, trying flattery, money and then brutal punishment. Basil is believed to have repulsed all approaches, however, and remained pure. Possibly because of this, the boy was accused of theft, tortured to obtain a confession and finally killed in an act of rage when his employer struck him on the head with the keys to the storehouse. Basil was buried in an unmarked grave without Christian rites, but in 1652 strange things began to happen in Old Mangazeya: visions and dreams of revelation, spontaneous acts of healing and other miracles. In that year Basil's coffin mysteriously rose out of a swamp, was opened and the body inside was found completely intact. Although Siberian permafrost lends itself to a physical explanation, Basil's physical (and moral) intactness stood him in good stead for sainthood. A secular version of the story explains that one of the town fires caused the ground to melt and exposed the coffin. A chapel was built at the location.

No one could know at the time that Mangazeya would be abandoned, as around Basil's time it was the most dynamic of Siberian towns. It was fortuitous, therefore, that after leaving Yeniseysk and founding his own monastery in Turukhansk, the renegade monk Tikhon had a revelation that prompted him to carry the remains of Basil to Turukhansk. Tikhon trekked through frozen taiga, experiencing various miracles along the way, and brought the body, icons and a large number of books to the monastery. Basil's remains were revered over the centuries. If we can believe one version, even Evenks converted during campaigns of Christianization prayed to the saint.

Thereafter things become murky. Basil's remains are thought to have been housed in the monastery until 1923, when most of the precious items vanished without trace. The monastery was abandoned during the Soviet era and slowly fell apart until the early 1990s, when it was returned to the Krasnoyarsk diocese.

The Yenisey spills into the Kara Sea at Dikson. Describing the landscape from north to south as he moved upstream from the tundra country into forest, Nansen wrote:

What endless, monotonous, slightly undulating plains with shallow valleys along the rivers and watercourses. At first they are glimpsed entirely bare, with only moss and a little grass, up in the far north—the desolate tundra; then a few ossier beds here and there; then willow and alder and a few birches scattered far and wide. But then the first forest begins, thin at first; then thicker and higher; but the country remains as monotonous as before. And yet—and yet it has its own strange attraction. One's thoughts are drawn to this wide horizon; one longs to follow the nomad in his free, unfettered life over these boundless plains.

Meanwhile, east of Krasnoyarsk the railway closely follows the old Sibirsky Trakt towards Irkutsk and Lake Baikal. For many travellers, including Anton Chekhov, this part of Siberia was the true taiga country. Chekhov, discontented until the power of the Yenisey lifted him to better spirits, wrote:

Just beyond the Yenisey, the famous taiga begins. Much has already been said and written about the taiga, but it doesn't give you what you expect. At first you feel something like disappointment. On both sides of the road extend the usual forests of pine, larch and birch... I was told the taiga was soundless and its vegetation without scent. That's what I expected, but as I continued through the taiga it filled with birds, insects hummed, the needles, warmed by the sun, saturated the air with the heavy smell of resin, the clearings and edges of the road were covered with flowers of tender blue, pink and yellow and caressed not just the eyes. Obviously those who have written about the taiga observed it not in spring but in summer, when as elsewhere in Russia the forest is silent and doesn't give off a smell.

The power of the taiga and our fascination is not due to gigantic trees or a sepulchral silence, but because perhaps only some migratory birds know where it ends. During the first day you don't pay any attention to it, on the second and third it surprises you, and on the fourth and fifth a mood sets in as if you will never be plucked out of this green monster. You climb one high hill covered in forest, glance ahead to the east in the direction of the road, and below you see forest, another hill curled with forest, behind this another hill also bushy with forest, behind this a third, without end. In a day, again you look from a hill up ahead, and again it is the same picture. But you nevertheless know the Angara and Irkutsk are there in front of you; even the coachmen and peasants born in the taiga don't know how many hundreds of versts to the north and south the forest alongside the road extends. Their fantasy is more daring than ours, but they simply decide not to define its size, and reply: "It's endless." All they know is that in winter people arrive from the far north on reindeers to buy some bread, but not even the old men know what sort of people they are or where they come from.

Chapter Eleven
IRKUTSK: THE "PARIS OF SIBERIA"

"The few descriptions of Irkutsk had spoken of it as the Paris of Siberia.
The only points of likeness that a casual survey gives are that Irkutsk
has the sins, the false hair, and the perfume, for which Paris is noted."
Mrs John Clarence Lee, *Across Siberia Alone, An American Woman's
Adventures*, 1914

Irkutsk dates back to the early 1650s, when a winter stockade was established on the banks of the Angara river at the mouth of the Irkut. Almost
one decade later, in 1660, a Yeniseysk-born son of the aristocracy by the
name of Yakov Pokhabov received instructions to travel to the Irkut in
order to build a permanent fortified settlement on the location, collect
yasak and "protect" the local indigenes from harassment by the Cossacks
of Krasnoyarsk. In 1661, without waiting for the formal order to arrive,
Pokhabov set off with his men and established the permanent fort, which
was to have its own garrison and be administered from Yeniseysk. He gave
it the name Yandashky after a local ruler, Yandash Doroga, but it almost
immediately became known as Irkutsk.

Crossing the Angara in Irkutsk (1886) by N. Dobrovalsky

In the early seventeenth century, says James Forsyth in his *A History of the Peoples of Siberia*, the Russians set about colonizing eastern Siberia from two towns. One of these was Old Mangazeya, which was thriving but about to slide into decline, and the second was Yeniseysk. Generally, the men from Mangazeya were behind the initial drive eastwards into Yakutia to the Lower Lena, while the Upper Lena (the Pribaikal) was explored by Cossacks and hunters based in Yeniseysk. The Yeniseysk Cossacks then followed the Mangazeya Cossacks into Yakut territory; taking a very different route: sailing north along the Lena river from its upper reaches west of Lake Baikal. One of the most important expeditions was conducted by the Cossack Pyotr Beketov (ca. 1600-61), who in 1632 founded the fort that grew into present-day Yakutsk. Later, from 1652, Beketov launched another expedition into the Transbaikal region that led to the foundation of Chita, and he also led yasak gangs into the Tunka Valley west of Irkutsk and to the Eastern Sayan Mountains.

The period from the late 1620s until the founding of Irkutsk was one in which the Russians sought to establish a series of forts in the Pribaikal (west of Lake Baikal) and the Transbaikal (east of Lake Baikal in Buryatia), moving from territory dominated by Tungus (Evenks) into regions where Buryats also lived. This stage of colonization was relatively slow. Over forty years elapsed between the founding of Yeniseysk in 1619 and the Irkutsk fort in 1661. The region Chekhov described as dense *taiga*—and the region between Krasnoyarsk and Lake Baikal traversed today by train in about 24 hours— was dangerous for seventeenth century Russians, who faced ambushes in the wild Angara river valley from Buryat and Tungus indigenes. The campaign to control the region is usually called the Buryat wars.

According to Forsyth's excellent history, European Russians didn't know about the Buryats until 1609, when they tried to exact yasak from Kets and Samoyeds in the river basins east of the Yenisey and extending south into Tuva. They were promptly informed that tribute was already being paid to Buryats. Buryats who lived in the regions around Lake Baikal were causing Tungus (Evenks) to migrate further north and west, and those moving into the middle Yenisey found themselves in conflict with Kets. The Kets were exploited by the Russians to subdue the Tungus, while Tungus were used by the Russians as guides on their expeditions to push into territory they partly shared with the Buryats.

The Russians thus found themselves in a complex region of cultures where systems of tribute already existed. South of Yeniseysk in the taiga around Krasnoyarsk the Yenisey-Kyrgyz were collecting tribute from Kets and Samoyeds. Closer to Lake Baikal, the Buryats were running their own yasak collection among Tungus, Kets and Samoyeds. Deep in the upper Yenisey, some groups were paying yasak to Mongol khans.

The major hindrance to reaching Lake Baikal along the Angara river was the rugged terrain. Today an enormous reservoir has tamed the region, but in the early seventeenth century the valley of the Angara was a wild and impenetrable region dominated by violent cataracts and perilous outcrops that made travel by boat hazardous. Through this Siberian "heart of darkness" the Russians pressed towards Lake Baikal, establishing forts in Bratsk (1631), Balagansk (1654), and eventually Yakov Pokhabov established one in Irkutsk. In doing so he founded a city with one of the world's most fortuitous natural assets on its doorstep: Lake Baikal.

After two decades of being administered as an outpost from Yeniseysk, in 1682 Irkutsk was large enough to become an independent settlement with its own military governor, who oversaw a whole region. The 1680s were generally a crucial period in the town's development, and this had much to do with its location on the frontier of Mongolia and the rise of Manchu rule in China. The Manchus controlled most of inner Mongolia in the 1630s and were gradually extending their power into (outer) Mongolia proper. Meanwhile, thanks to expeditions by the explorer Vasily Poyarkov and later by Yerofey Khabarov, Russia had been moving into the Amur river region from the 1640s and so was coming into direct conflict with Manchu China. A collision of interests was inevitable. As James Forsyth aptly puts it: "The arrogance of the 'Great Lord, Tsar and Grand Duke of All Russia' who called upon each Siberian people in turn to submit and come under his 'high hand' was more than matched by the arrogance of the 'son of Heaven', the Celestial Emperor of the Middle Kingdom."

In 1646, before he founded Irkutsk, Yakov Pokhabov travelled to the western shore of Lake Baikal and in the winter of 1647 across the ice with 84 Cossacks to the southern shores and Selenga Valley. Here he encountered the Buryats of the Transbaikal and, with an eye for the gold and silver deposits the Russians had heard about, allowed himself to be taken to the Mongol Tsetsen Khan. The Buryats had told Pokhabov that it was from him they bought their silver. The journey made Pokhabov the first Russian emissary into the eastern Mongolian lands, and as a result the khan sent an envoy to Moscow the following year. Pokhabov's role in building the fort of Irkutsk was therefore something of a reward for his services in the Transbaikal. But both the Pribaikal and the Transbaikal were difficult to bring into the imperial fold, and numerous bloody battles took place between the Russians and Buryats.

Because at this time no towns of significance existed on Russian soil in the Far East, Irkutsk, as a growing fortified enclave close to the Mongolian border, was vital to the Russian presence, and in 1686 the diplomat Fyodor Golovin (1650-1706) was sent into the region by Peter the Great to negotiate borders with the Chinese after they laid siege to the Russian Cossack village of Albazino. This had been founded in 1651 by Yerofey Khabarov as the first Russian settlement on the Amur. The result of negotiations was the Treaty of Nerchinsk in 1689, which saw Russia temporarily abandon claims to land along the Amur and accept a border with China north of the Amur at the Stanovoy Ridge and the Argun river.

At around that time Irkutsk also rose to prominence as a trading town for caravans travelling between China and Russia, and even today, while moving from west to east between Krasnoyarsk and Irkutsk, one perceives a shift in the cultural centre of gravity towards Asia.

From the 1720s Irkutsk developed into a religious centre. St. Innocent (Innokent; birth unknown-1731), born as John Kulchitsky, was refused entry to China, settled here for a decade from 1721, became Irkutsk's first archbishop and later doubled Siberia's pantheon of local saints from one (St. Basil of Mangazeya) to two.

With the ideas of the Enlightenment finding their way into Russia and the foundation of the St. Petersburg Academy of Sciences, Irkutsk saw groups of learned men roaming its streets and defining the cultural, historical, political and geographic lines of the tsar's empire. The two Kamchatka Expeditions (1725-30 and 1733-43) brought most members of the Siberian overland parties (others were plying the seas) into Irkutsk, where many spent all or part of the winters.

The dominant view of Siberia at this time was of as an exotic land full of curiosities, and the job of the learned men (many of them Germans, some Swedish prisoners of war) was to collect the strange wonders that Siberia—still also an "uncivilized" and "wild" place—could offer European Russia. At the same time, as Russia was gradually making itself more European under Peter the Great, it was seeking to make Siberia more Russian.

In those days, the Lena provided a convenient water highway between the Irkutsk region and Yakutia (Sakha). Traffic between Irkutsk and Yakutsk, some 1,250 miles north as the crow flies, grew heavy during the peak seasons. Late winter or summer were the best times, when the capital of Yakutia could be reached on the frozen Lena, or boats could sail from Ust-Kut. From Yakutsk the great expeditions set out east for the Sea of Okhotsk and, beyond that, for Kamchatka.

Foreign Visitors

Irkutsk is also the place where two very different but unusual travellers happened to be arrested. One of those detained was the first American to travel Siberia (and he was therefore the first American to be arrested here). The other was the British blind traveller James Holman.

The American John Ledyard was born in Groton, Connecticut, in 1751 and entered Dartmouth College to train as a missionary among Native Americans. He brought an end to this noble calling by jumping into a dugout canoe and escaping his missionary fate by floating down the Connecticut river. In mid-1776 he enlisted in the British navy and in 1776-80 participated in the third voyage of Commander James Cook to the Pacific, sailing to Kamchatka and the island of Unalaska, where he encountered a group of Russian hunters in what is usually described as the first meeting of Americans and Russians in the Pacific.

He was with Cook when the commander died, and he depicted the unfortunate Cook's demise in tragic detail, describing in his journal how after Cook was stabbed on Hawaii a native rowed out in a canoe holding part of Cook's thigh wrapped in cloth, and how over the next few days the crew of the *Resolution* haggled for the rest of their commander, managing to get hold of the upper part of Cook's head and his scored and salted hands. Most of the rest, they were told, had already been eaten.

In late 1785 Ledyard began planning a journey overland from Europe through Siberia, across the Pacific to Alaska, and across the United States to Virginia. His contacts were good but his purse was meagre. Joseph Banks (who knew Ledyard from the Cook voyage) and Thomas Jefferson were among those who vouched for him. In 1786 he left London, rode across Siberia mostly on a *kibitka* and in August 1787 arrived in Irkutsk, where he spent ten days before heading north to Yakutsk by boat, describing this as "a very fatiguing voyage on the Lena of 22 days".

In November 1787 while Ledyard was in Yakutsk, a group of men around the explorer Captain Joseph Billings gathered in town to obtain supplies before embarking on the third large expedition of the century: voyages in 1785-94 to chart the north-east coast and Alaska. Two explorers with Billings were the British secretary to the expedition, Martin Sauer, and the Russian Gavril Sarychev, whose responsibility it was to supervise the building of ships in Okhotsk.

Bored, lonely and unable to continue his trek eastwards to Okhotsk that year due to the onset of winter, Ledyard followed the explorers back to Irkutsk. He had good reason to: at this time, Yakutsk was a desolate town of 362 houses, five churches and a cathedral, according to Martin Sauer. It was situated on an arm of the Lena that dried up by mid-July; the inhabitants had to walk two miles for fresh water. "Never was there a town in a worse situation than this," he says.

Billings took his former shipmate under his wing, but Ledyard was viewed almost universally as a stubborn eccentric with preposterous ideas. Sarychev grew irritated and bewildered by the American, and he vented his frustration with Ledyard in his *Account of a Voyage of Discovery to the Northeast of Siberia*. Ignoring the fact that the US had already been independent for a decade, he writes:

> There was at this time in Jakutsk, an English traveller of the name of Ledyard, whose eccentric conduct excited considerable attention. He was known to Mr. Billings, from having been with him in the capacity of a corporal in Captain Cook's last voyage; after which he is said to have been a colonel in the army of the United States during the war. He had formed the design of going round the world in the literal sense of the word, and for that purpose went to Petersburg, in order to begin with Russia; and on reaching the eastern boundary of Asia, to wait for some vessel in which he might pass over to the English settlements. The absurdity of this enterprise is sufficiently manifest, from the circumstance of his intending to travel through a civilized country, without money or letters of recommendation; and afterwards to cross those boundless tracks on foot, thinly clad in winter, through which we had laboured with in-

finite difficulty on horseback, and in the warmest clothing... He was relieved from the necessity of walking as far as Jakutsk, by the civility of the Russian travellers, whom he met on the road, who carried him from place to place without recompence. Here he met with still greater kindness, being admitted to the house and table of the commander... and yet the only return which Mr. Ledyard made for this extraordinary hospitality, was to calminate [calumniate] and abuse every one...

Catherine the Great, hearing about the American, questioning his motives and with her patience running out, thought Ledyard might be a French spy and ordered his arrest. Snatched one evening in February 1788, much to the satisfaction of Sauer and Sarychev, Ledyard was marched back across the subcontinent much the way he had come (albeit in greater comfort) and eventually released into Poland. He died in Cairo in 1789 while waiting to depart on an African expedition. Having flown into a rage over delays, he swallowed a self-concocted remedy of sulphuric acid and tartar emetic to treat stomach problems, was overcome by severe bouts of vomiting from getting the dose wrong and died of apoplexy.

The road across Siberia passed with a relative lack of incident for James Holman until he reached Irkutsk. Again, it was a case of a traveller being misunderstood by a monarch. On this occasion Tsar Alexander I could not grasp why a blind man would want to cross Siberia alone and ordered his arrest; like Ledyard, Holman was deported for being a spy. In fact, rumours of spying had been clinging to Holman for some time. His technique of writing must in itself have aroused suspicion. Holman wrote on a so-called Noctograph, a device that involved using carbonated paper, a stylus and wires to guide the hand.

Inside Russia Holman was hence known not as "the blind traveller" but as "the blind spy": "rather a whimsical and paradoxical appellation," writes James Wilson in his *Biography of the Blind* from 1838, "for a person totally deprived of the use of his visual organs."

Holman wrote like a man who could see and he sadly therefore missed an opportunity to be the only Siberian traveller to describe the subcontinent from the perspective of its smells, sound, taste and touch. He did, however, leave us a few heartfelt lines of verse about how he felt as his sledge crossed the frozen Angara to the Moskovsky Trakt, the road taking him back to European Russia:

> The stranger is gone—Oh, he will not forget,
> When at home he shall talk of the toil he has known,
> To tell with a sigh what endearments he met,
> As he stray'd on the banks of the Angara alone.

He never quite tells us what endearments he met on the Angara, so we can only guess.

The late eighteenth century brought the rise of a new merchant class in Irkutsk eager to exploit the fur resources of Alaska. When the Russian-America Company (based on earlier companies) was founded in 1799, Irkutsk was chosen as its headquarters and the furs of Alaska were transported here for sorting and selling. About a decade after Holman was deported, Irkutsk became a gold processing centre for eastern Siberia. Thus, by the mid-nineteenth century, Irkutsk had more advantages than most other towns: it was situated on the trade route between Asia and Europe, the wealth earned from Alaska was being pumped into its architecture, it was a centre of government and it had grown into an intellectual hub thanks to the arrival of Decembrists from the 1830s, a Siberian branch of the Russian Geographical Society established in 1851 and a publishing industry that flourished during the second half of the century. In the summer of 1879 disaster struck in the form of a large fire that destroyed almost the entire centre, and the historic architecture visible today dates largely from the period of rebuilding directly after this fire.

The man responsible for giving Irkutsk its unlikely "Paris" moniker was the nineteenth-century publicist Nikolay Shelgunov, who wrote, "As England created London and France created Paris, so too Siberia created Irkutsk. She is proud of Irkutsk, and not to see Irkutsk is not to see Siberia." To a certain extent, if one includes Lake Baikal, this boast still contains some truth.

As well as having a reputation for being a Siberian Paris, Irkutsk enjoyed notoriety in the early twentieth century for its murder rate. Most foreign travellers of the day noted it, and two in 1910, US reporters Bassett Digby and Richardson Wright, describe one remarkable event:

> One fine day in May, a year or two back, there were twenty-two assorted murders and attempted murders within a short distance of the city. These included a disastrous picnic on an island in the lower Angarar, to

which an enterprising Irkutskian invited a dozen persons he disliked. He saw that they were all busy unpacking lunch and then put off in a boat and managed to shoot down half a dozen before one of the guests hit him.

While today other cities have overtaken Irkutsk in terms of economic stature, it remains one of Siberia's most attractive. Its townsfolk have an unusually robust and direct way of dealing with each other, and it is also one the most relaxed cities in Siberia. Thanks to Baikal, it is probably also Siberia's most-visited, with a pleasant centre that can be easily covered on foot.

Central Irkutsk: Monuments, Museums and Monasteries

A convenient place to begin such a walk is from the foot of ulitsa Karla Marksa in the south-west, alongside the Angara at ulitsa Gagarina. Apart from the Angara itself, the first major feature here is the Monument to Emperor Alexander III (Pamyatnik Imperatoru Aleksandru III). The monument dates from 1908 and in its original form was the work of the St. Petersburg sculptor R. R. Bakh (1859-1933) to commemorate ten years of the Trans-Siberian Railway having reached Irkutsk.

The monument features bas-reliefs on four sides of its pedestal. The side directly facing the Angara depicts the governor of Eastern Siberia in 1848-61, Count Muraev-Amursky, from whom the Amur region takes its

Monument to Alexander III

name. Another depicts Yermak; the northern side depicts the governor-general of Siberia and later of Eastern Siberia, M. M. Speransky, and on the side looking upstream is the double-headed eagle holding in its talons a bronze copy of the tsarist decree for the building of the Trans-Siberian Railway. Following the Russian Revolution of 1917, the tsar was removed and the pedestal stood empty until 1964, when a column was erected in his place; in 2003 Alexander III was re-instated. This stretch of riverfront is, along with another section near Skver Kirova (Kirov Square) in the administrative centre, Irkutsk's popular promenade.

Across the road at bulvar Gagarina 24 (diagonally, to the left) is a house once belonging to the Sibiryakov family of merchants (Bely Dom; White House) and built in 1804 in the style of Russian neoclassicism. After the fortunes of the family declined in the 1830s, the house fell into the hands of the governor general of the day for Eastern Siberia, and later still was used by his successor, Count Muraev-Amursky, who worked and lived here while in office. Today the scientific library of the Irkutsk State University is housed inside the building, where some rare *inculabuli* (single, printed sheets produced before the advent of book printing in Europe) and rare books are stored. The most valuable of these are from the library brought to Irkutsk by St. Innocent.

Diagonally on the right from the monument is the History Section of the Irkutsk Region Local Studies Museum (Otdel Istory Irkutskovo Oblastnovo Kraevedcheskovo Muzeya), located at no. 2. The building dates from 1883-91 and once housed the Russian Geographical Society of Eastern Siberia. Its architect was Heinrich Rosen, who took his inspiration from a turreted fortress. Various stone plaques were later added to the exterior of the building, bearing the names of the scholars who passed through Irkutsk or worked here over the years, including the German natural historians Alexander von Humboldt (1769-1859) and Peter Simon Pallas (1741-1811), the "Father of Siberian History", Gerhard Friedrich Müller (1705-83); and Kamchatka explorer and scientist Stepan Petrovich Krasheninnikov (1711-55).

Several collections on the ground floor are dedicated to the aboriginal peoples of the region. The most numerous of these were the Tungus (or Evenks), who inhabited parts of a vast region between the Ob and the Pacific Ocean. The reindeer Evenks—some lived on the steppe and cultivated crops—supplemented reindeer breeding with hunting and spent winter months in conical tents called *chums* made of bark and hide—usually from reindeer.

The Buryats, whose culture figures prominently in the museum, inhabit two regions. One of these is the Pribaikal west of Lake Baikal (where about 50,000 Buryats today live in the Irkutsk region around the Ust-Ordinsky Autonomous District). The other is the Transbaikal east of Lake Baikal (in what is Buryatia today). The Transbaikal Buryats began adopting Buddhism from the seventeenth century, and Buddhism established itself more strongly among them after the arrival of 150 Tibetan lamas in 1712 and the founding of the Tsongol *datsan* (monastery) in Buryatia about forty years later near Kiakhta.

Out of the museum, ulitsa Karla Marksa leads north towards most of the major historic attractions. The street once formed the boundary of the old town and was where a palisade of logs and a rudimentary moat ran along one side of the fortress. This palisade was built in the 1720s and then about fifty years later was turned into a road when the town outgrew its edges. The fire of 1879 destroyed virtually all its wooden houses, however, giving town planners the idea of creating a wide boulevard through the centre, which they blandly named ulitsa Bolshaya (Large Street), today ulitsa Karla Marksa.

At no. 1 is the Irkutsk State University (Irkutsky Gosudarstvenny Universitet), the main administrative building of the university, dating from the 1930s. Further along at no. 14 is the Irkutsk Academic Drama Theatre (Irkutskiy Akademichesky Dramatichesky Teatr). The city lacked a professional theatre until 1851 when, under the auspices of Governor Muraev-Amursky, a troupe was assembled and began performing in numerous buildings around town, until the present building was erected in 1894-97.

In the park alongside the theatre is a memorial to the Irkutsk playwright Alexander Vampilov (1937-72). A short way along and across the street at ulitsa Karla Marksa 7 are the monumental administrative offices of the Eastern Siberian Railways, dating from the 1950s, and on the corner of ulitsa Karla Marksa and ulitsa Lenina a statue of Lenin. Across the road, at ulitsa Lenina 38, stands the turreted Irkutsk Branch of the Russian-Asian Bank (1910-12). After the Russian Revolution the building was home to the Governing Committee for War and Revolution; today it is a hospital. Directly opposite at ulitsa Lenina 11 is the building that was formerly the city school, dating from 1883.

The long building directly opposite the school, at ulitsa Lenina 13, is the present location of a youth theatre established in 1928. The building itself dates from 1860 and was erected for a local merchant. Vampilov worked here, and so too has Siberia's best-known writer, Valentin Rasputin.

For many years one part of the building was a hotel, and during the civil war the White government of Admiral Kolchak was housed here. A plaque on the building commemorates Yaroslav Hašek, the Czech writer famous for his play *The Good Soldier Schweik* (1912). Hašek was taken prisoner during the First World War, joined the Czech Legion while in prison, later switched to the Red Army and worked out of this building after the Fifth Red Army defeated Admiral Kolchak.

Turning right at ulitsa Lenina, the walker reaches the Church of the Exultation of the Cross (Krestovozdvizhenskaya Tserkov), situated several blocks south where ulitsa Lenina meets ultisa Sedova. An early wooden church stood here from 1717-19 and was consecrated by Tobolsk's archbishop Filofey Leshchinsky; construction of the baroque stone church followed in 1747-60, financed by a local merchant. Although in the early years of Soviet rule the cathedral was listed as a historic monument, during the 1930s it was turned into an anti-religious museum before being restored to a church in the mid-1940s.

Back on ulitsa Karla Marksa, another building that stands out is that of the nature section of the Regional Museum, at no. 13. This eclectic, red-brick pseudo-Gothic extravagance with towers dates from 1903 and once housed a typesetting office and bookshop. In 1920 the founder of the Mongolian People's Party, Damdin Sukhe-Bator (1893-1923), visited here to arrange the printing of his pro-independence newspaper. He later returned to Mongolia and established a pro-Soviet provisional government that ended Chinese rule of Mongolia and, with the help of the Fifth Red Army, also defeated the uncontrollable band of Cossacks that had crossed into Mongolia under Baron Roman Nikolay von Ungern-Sternberg (1886-1921).

Further along ulitsa Karla Marksa, where it intersects with ulitsa Litvinova (at ulitsa Litvinova 1), is the former Grand Hotel, with decaying brickwork and a rusting heap of cupolas; it was designed by architect A. I. Kuznetzov, completed in 1903, and in its day was the best hotel in town.

Backtracking to ulitsa Sukhe-Batora and turning right, you reach a quiet section of the street that leads onto one of the most attractive quarters of town, Skver Kirova (Kirov Square). Alternatively, returning to ulitsa Lenina and turning right (or left along ulitsa Lenina if approaching from Skver Kirova), you come across the V. P Sukachev Regional Art Museum (Oblastnoy Khudozhestvenny Muzey imena V.P. Sukacheva) at ulitsa Lenina 5.

The museum was founded with works in the collection of the nineteenth-century Irkutsk notable V. P. Sukachev (1849-1920) and today has about 16,000 paintings, graphics, sculptures and works of decorative and applied arts. Its icon collection includes fine examples of the Moscow and Novgorod schools dating from the fifteenth century, others dating from the sixteenth and seventeenth centuries from the northern parts of European Russia, and Siberian icons from the seventeenth and eighteenth centuries.

The leafy (in summer) Skver Kirova stands out for the disproportionate buildings on its fringes and attractive gardens in the centre. Beginning life as something of a marshy wasteland, small stores sprang up over the years, the square grew in size and eventually a merchant's yard (Gostiny Dvor) was located here from the 1770s. One of the several monumental buildings on its fringe is the House of Soviets (Dom Sovetov), the city administrative building on the northern (river) side. Next door, a small chapel marks the location of Irkutsk's late nineteenth-century Kazan Cathedral (Kazansky Kafedralny Sobor), badly damaged in the civil war and demolished in 1938 to make way for the House of Soviets.

Across the street from the House of Soviets, at Sukhe-Batora 1, is the Roman Catholic Church (Rimsko-Katolichesky Kostel), a Gothic revivalist structure built in 1885 for Poles exiled to Siberia after the Polish January Uprising of 1863-4. The Poles here were responsible for one of Siberia's most daring exile revolts.

The roots of this revolt can be traced back to the mines of Irkutsk, which were in decline in the 1860s and over-filled with exiles. As a result a group of 720 Poles were sent to work on the road around the southern shore of Lake Baikal. The Poles claimed they were being starved and worked to death, while the Russians believed the Poles merely wanted to escape Siberia—in any case, the Poles staged the so-called Baikal Insurrection, which took large-scale mobilization of troops to repress it. Although the revolt failed to spread, the authorities believed at the time that they had a full-scale Siberian insurrection on their hands. The revolt lasted several days, and once caught, the leaders were sentenced to death and promptly shot.

If you walk behind Dom Sovetov along Sukhe-Batora, you reach the Church of Our Saviour (Spasskaya Tserkov) at Sukhe-Batora 2. The building dates back to 1713 and is said to be the oldest surviving stone structure in eastern Siberia. It is also the only building to survive from the original fortress complex. In the imperial era it was a cathedral and the city's most important place of worship. During the Soviet era it was used as a workshop for repairing cinematic equipment, and later as an exhibition space by the Regional Museum.

Further along Sukhe-Batora at number 1a is the Epiphany Cathedral (Bogoyavlensky Sobor), which stands on the site of wooden church destroyed by fire in 1716. Two years later, work began on a new cathedral of stone in the style of Siberian baroque, with hints of the cathedral's wooden predecessor. Once it was completed it became the main place of worship in Irkutsk until the Kazan Cathedral was built in 1894.

Alongside the Church of Our Saviour is an eternal flame and memorial to the fallen soldiers of the Second World War, and beyond that the path leads down to the river and offers some splendid views across the Angara to the Irkut river.

One block north of here along the river bank is ulitsa Dekabristykh Sobity, where once the three-storey triumphal arch, the Moscow Gate, stood in front of a ferry landing where passengers and wagons could cross the Angara to the Moscow Post Road (Sibirsky Trakt, or Moskovsky Trakt). This was where Holman would have left town and concocted the poetic epitaph to his visit to Irkutsk. The arch was built in 1813 and indeed did call forth images of Paris' Arc de Triomphe. In 1912 earth tremors damaged the foundations so badly that in 1928 it had to be completely demolished.

In his book *Oriental and Western Siberia*, published in 1860, Thomas Witlam Atkinson describes entering Irkutsk along the Angara. He approached the city from the north before passing through the Moscow Gate. This was not the same route as Holman's as Atkinson appears to have crossed the Angara further downstream before taking a ferry across the rivulet, Ushakovka, just north of Skver Kirova. But it is an interesting description. He writes:

My first approach to Irkoutsk [Irkutsk] was by the post road from Russia: it enters the valley of the Angara... about seventy miles to the north-west of Irkoutsk; hence it runs along at a short distance from the river. On the west side of the valley densely wooded hills arise, and on the east side are seen cliffs at the foot where the Angara is rolling on its rapid stream. Along the bank and on the other parts of the plain fine clumps of trees are growing, between which sparkling water is seen, and then lost behind thick foliage, till, by a bend in the river, it bursts forth into a wide expanse. Several views on this route made a strong impression on my mind; they were really beautiful: indeed, many charming subjects for the pencil may be found here.

At last, at a turn in the valley, I caught sight of a dome and several tall spires rising over the tops of the forest of birches and pines. This was the monastery of Saint Irkout, which stands in a very picturesque position on the bank of the Angara. I was surprised to find an architectural edifice possessing so much taste, in these far-off regions. Having passed the monastery, Irkoutsk was before me at about two miles distant. This was a Sunday afternoon—a beautiful day, and a sky without a cloud; the Angara was seen in its full width, stretching up to the walls of the town, where it made a great bend to the westward and appeared like a lake. The gateway [Moscow Gate] formed a striking object: it was massive and imposing. As these objects were scattered over a considerable space, it gave the place the appearance of a large city. I shortly afterwards reached the river, the Yemtchik (Ushakovka), drove onto the ferry boat, and I passed through the gate.

The monastery Atkinson mentions is probably the Ascension Monastery (Voznesensky Monastyr), where Siberia's second saint-to-be, Innocent, settled in 1721, immediately embarking on missionary work to convert Buryats and Tungus. In 1727, after many attempts to enter China, he resigned himself to staying and was appointed head of the Irkutsk diocese. It was from here that Innocent created an administrative framework which later led to new dioceses in Yakutia, Kamchatka, the Far East and across the Bering Strait in Russian Alaska (the latter was subordinate to the Irkutsk diocese from 1790 and became an independent Alaskan diocese in the 1840s). This Innocent is not to be confused with St. Innocent of Alaska (1797-1879), who was born in Irkutsk Region and canonized in 1977 by the Russian Orthodox Church.

St. Innocent of Irkutsk died in 1731 and his relics were kept in a wooden church in the monastery. When fire destroyed this church in 1766, his body was said to have been found intact. A spate of miracles followed over the next few decades and in 1804 he was canonized. Two decades later, James Holman visited the grave of the saint. He wrote:

> I trust my readers will not accuse me of being tinctured with superstition; when I relate the following circumstances. A lady with whom I had the pleasure of being intimately acquainted, was pleased to take a particular interest in the state of my eyes, and was convinced that my vision might be restored, if I would place myself under the care of her favourite saint, Inakenti, (or Innocent) who, although he had been defunct for nearly a century, was, in her estimation, the best medical man and oculist in the world. Partly to oblige her, and partly to gratify my own curiosity, which was ever alive to the peculiarities of the people with whom I might associate, I consented to make trial of his miraculous powers; and, in consequence, one morning accompanied the lady and her husband to the monastery, where the saint reposes in a magnificent shrine. As soon as the appointed service of the day had concluded, I was conducted to the hallowed tomb, where, after many prayers and sprinklings of holy water, the priest directed me to approach the coffin, and kiss the withered hand of the saint. This being complied with, the priest began to apply considerable friction on my eyes with a piece of silk, that appeared to have been immersed in oil. I acknowledge that he made them smart much; but, alas! after the operation was finished I could not see an inch farther.

In 1921 the relics were apparently shifted to the Soviet Museum of Anti-religion, and after this Innocent ended up in a museum in Yaroslavl before being returned to Irkutsk in 1990. Because the Ascension Monastery had been razed in the meantime, it was decided to house the relics in a gold sarcophagus inside today's Monastery of the Holy Sign (Znamensky Monastery), located across Ushakovka Creek at Angara 14.

The Monastery of the Holy Sign was founded in 1693 as a convent and played an important role during the reign of Peter the Great in the drive to Christianize Siberia. Construction of the Znamenskaya Tserkov

(Church of the Holy Sign), the monastery's centrepiece, was financed by the merchant Ivan Bichevin and began in 1757, with three side-chapels: the Preobrazhensky, Nikolsky and Kazansky. In 1935 it was closed down and used as part of the river transport facilities but returned to the nuns in 1945. As well as being famous now for housing the relics of Innocent, the monastery grounds contain the grave of merchant-explorer Grigory Shelikov, and the graves of Ekaterina Trubetskaya (1800-54) and her children. Trubetskaya, the daughter of French immigrants, followed her husband, Decembrist Sergey Trubetskoy (1790-1860), into exile in 1826. Other Decembrists' grave can also be found here.

Outside the monastery is a large (and controversial) memorial to Admiral Kolchak, erected in 2004 as the first Kolchak memorial in Russia. It is located where Kolchak was executed in February 1920.

Remembering the Decembrists
The Decembrist museums are situated near the bus station and focus on two Decembrists and their families. The Museum Estate of the Decembrist S. P. Trubetskovo (Usadba Dekabrista S.P. Trubetskovo) is in a yard at ulitsa Dzerzhinskovo 64 and in 2008 was closed for restoration. By 2013 this

Nineteenth-century building, Irkutsk

area of wooden houses, the so-called Decembrists' Quarter, should be restored to reflect its original condition in the early nineteenth century.

The second museum already has several years of restoration behind it: the Museum Estate of the Decembrist S. V. Volkonskovo (Usadba Dekabrista S.V. Volkonskovo), which is set in an attractive garden. The house dates from 1838 and was the centre of intellectual and cultural life in Irkutsk from 1846 after the Volkonskys began living here. The museum contains various personal items belonging to the family, as well as letters and notes from notable Russians, including Leo Tolstoy, who was a second cousin of Volkonsky.

The museum dates back to 1925, when material was assembled to celebrate the hundredth anniversary of the day in December 1825 when the uprising took place on St. Petersburg's Senate Square (Senatskaya ploshchad, now Decembrists' Square) in support of a liberal constitution. Following the uprising, Sergey Volkonsky (1788-1965) was arrested and after being condemned to death by decapitation was reprieved and the sentence commuted to twenty years of penal servitude in Siberia, later reduced to nine years. Although the Decembrists of Tobolsk generally experienced tolerable conditions that allowed many to actively participate in town life, for others such as Volkonsky Siberia was a much harsher place. He served in a distillery first, and then in mines and factories in the Transbaikal before he was allowed to return to live in Irkutsk from 1845.

Maria Volkonskaya (1805-63) followed her husband into exile in 1827 as one of the first Decembrist wives to do so. Her pedigree was as good as her husband's, being the daughter of General Raevsky, one of Russia's outstanding commanders during the war of 1812 (Napoleon's invasion of Russia). Her great-great grandfather was the Russian scientist Mikhail Lomonosov (1711-65). She knew nothing about the activities of her husband when he became involved in the uprising, but along with Ekaterina Trubetskaya she petitioned for better conditions for the Decembrists and was at the centre of Irkutsk's cultural life from the late 1820s. Pushkin was one of her admirers and wrote a poem about her, and she inspired the famous poem by Nikolay Nekrasov (1821-78), "Russian Women". She is popularly idealized as "The Siberian Princess".

Chapter Twelve
LAKE BAIKAL: SIBERIA'S SACRED SEA

When the Russians began moving into the mountain and steppe of the Pribaikal and Transbaikal in the early seventeenth century, they could not have known that a magnificent body of water would await them. The earliest route into the Baikal region was in the 1620s along the Lena river, known by local Tungus as the Elyuene, towards the Pribaikal. The Russians followed the Lena to Ust-Kut, where in 1628 they built a winter stockade (*zimovye*). This was later turned into a fortress (*ostrog*) by the Cossack Ivan Galkin. In the 1630s it grew to become the site of salt works founded by the explorer and merchant Yerofey Khabarov.

Meanwhile, east of Lake Baikal, Cossacks were pressing due south from the Lena into the Transbaikal (Zabaikal) region. Here, too, they encountered Tungus. The Cossack ataman Maksim Perfilev was one of the earliest Russians to travel to the Transbaikal, reaching the region in 1638 by sailing south up the Lena with a contingent of 36 Cossacks, following the Vitim river to the mouth of the Ust-Muya, north-east of Lake Baikal, and then taking hostages in order to collect *yasak* from the Tungus. They told him about sable, silver and ores in the Transbaikal and further east on the Shilka river, a tributary of the Amur in the Transbaikal.

The first Russian known to have reached Lake Baikal, however, was the explorer Kurbat Ivanov, who in 1643 set out for this remarkable body of water which the Tungus called Lama. He and his group of 74 men, led by Tungus, arrived on the western shore of Lake Baikal across from the island of Olkhon. They sailed to Olkhon where they encountered Buryats, whose name for the lake was similar to today's "Baikal". As Valentin Rasputin writes in his collection of essays, *Sibir Sibir* (Siberia, Siberia), the origin of the name is unclear. There are resemblances to Buryat and Sakha (Yakutsk) words, and it most likely comes from the Sakha word for "sea".

Once at Lake Baikal, the contingent split up in order to explore it. A group of 36 men under the command of the Cossack Semyon Skorokhod built a boat and sailed along the west coast of the lake using a local Tungus as a guide, reaching the northern extremity of Lake Baikal near where the Upper Angara (Verkhnaya Angara, not to be confused with the Angara) flows into Baikal. They founded a winter stockade there (near today's Nizhneangarsk) and began collecting yasak from the Tungus. Then, in late 1643, the men travelled south on the ice of Lake Baikal but on reaching Chivyrkuysky Bay (Chivyrkuysky Zaliv), the northern bay formed by the Svyatoy Nos peninsula, the men fell into a Buryat ambush.

Fourteen men survived the assault. Twelve of these headed north, reaching Verkhnolensk fortress (on the Lena), but another two continued along Lake Baikal, travelled up the Angara and eventually reached Yeniseysk. In the meantime, Kurbat Ivanov had returned to the Verkhnolensk fortress and began compiling a narrative and drawings based on his own observations and information he had received from the Tungus and Buryats. This was the earliest attempt to map and describe Lake Baikal and its rivers, and when Siberia's first cartographer, Semyon Remezov compiled his atlas of Siberia in 1701, he relied partly on the rough drawings and descriptions by Ivanov.

THE WORLD'S LARGEST FRESHWATER LAKE

According to Valentin Rasputin, Lake Baikal did not make a particularly strong impression on the Russians who first explored it. Either they had other matters on their mind or, he believes, they lacked the powerful language or literary tradition to describe it.

This was about to change. In 1662, after moving from Yeniseysk into Dauria (a historic name for the Transbaikal and a small part of Mongolia), the archpriest Avvakum reached Baikal, which he depicts in *The Life of Avvakum by Himself* as a region of abundance verging on a spiritual paradise. He describes fearfully high mountains of the like he has never seen before, their summits with turrets and containing halls, gates, stone walls, pillars and courtyards—all, he says, the work of God. The onions, he wrote, are larger and sweeter than elsewhere, the flowers colourful and full of scent, the skies are full of birds and the waters of the lake abundantly rich with fish. When Avvakum comes upon a group of hunters and fishermen on the shores of the lake, the men give him a hundred sturgeons. He blesses the food and all begin to weep.

Avvakum was not alone in imagining this as a paradise. Dauria at this time had a reputation for being a land of milk and honey right across Siberia, and when Cossacks at Ilimsk fortress rose up against their corrupt military governor in 1665, they rode into Dauria and settled in Albazino, a town that had been abandoned since being founded in 1651 and briefly served the Cossacks as a convenient refuge where (notwithstanding attacks by Chinese who saw this as a threat to their own territory) the men could control their own destinies.

In 1675 the Russian envoy Nicolay Spafary (1636-1708) became the first Russian to provide a detailed geographical outline of Lake Baikal, describing major rivers that empty into it (some 336 large ones) and the single river that flows out: the Angara. Baikal's length, he said, could be covered in about ten or twelve days, and it could be sailed across in a little more than 24 hours. When he tried to measure its depth, however, he could not find the bottom.

Today we know more about this magnificent "sea". It contains over one-fifth of the world's supply of fresh water, drawing its water from a basin slightly less than the size of France. If its 336 rivers were shut down, it would take 400 years before Lake Baikal was empty, as the water that flows into it stays there for several centuries. It is the world's largest and most ancient freshwater lake, and scientists liken it to a huge natural laboratory because 84 per cent of its species are found nowhere else on earth, and some plants and animals date back to prehistoric times. It is sometimes compared to Lake Tanganyika in Central Africa, which is the third-largest and second-deepest freshwater lake in the world, has a similar shape and, like Baikal, was created out of tectonic earth movements. In summer the presence of Baikal can be felt in the cooler air, especially as one approaches the shore, while in winter Baikal makes for a more moderate climate until it freezes over.

Avvakum noted the unique fresh-water seals that inhabit this sacred sea, and fish so rich in fat that if fried they disappeared in the pan. He was not exaggerating. The *golomyanka* (*Comephorus dybowskii*), unique to Lake Baikal, is about 44 per cent fat and virtually transparent. Another of its more unusual aspects is that Lake Baikal, situated in a continental rift region, is gradually growing in size, adding another twenty million cubic metres of water annually to the already massive supply. At its deepest point, Lake Baikal is about 5,370 feet deep, and 4,215 feet below sea level.

In 25 million years of existence Lake Baikal and the region have been subject to earthquakes of various dimensions. The most severe of these in recent history occurred in 1862 in the northern section of the Selenga Delta, where land subsided over thirty feet, formed a bay (Zaliv Proval) and led to a settlement once situated there being submerged. The deepest sections of the lake are off the west coast. Some 27 islands dot Baikal, and the most important of the 336 rivers flowing into it is the Selenga, con-tributing about half the annual inflow. The Selenga also forms the lake's largest wetland delta, a significant region for flora and fauna and also for filtering out pollutants.

Human settlement in the region dates back about 30,000 years, and over the years the ethnic make-up of its inhabitants has changed signifi-cantly—the latest development, of course, being the arrival of Russians from Europe. Ghengis Khan considered Lake Baikal to be a forbidden region.

One of the biggest questions surrounding Baikal these days is the impact of human activity. Since becoming a Unesco World Heritage site in 1996, tourism around the lake has grown significantly. Those visiting tend to be Russians, and what foreign tourism does take place is focused around Listvyanka, a few tourist bases on the west coast, Severobaikalsk and the spectacular Olkhon Island. Each summer, about half a million people are said to visit or pass through Listvyanka. One project focusing on low-impact tourism is the Great Baikal Trail, a long-running scheme to develop a walking trail around the entire lake. Work on the trail is continuing, some of it with the help of foreign and Russian volunteers.

In his *Siberia, Siberia*, Valentin Rasputin devotes one chapter to Lake Baikal and environmental issues. Much of what he writes dates from 1986 but many of the issues are still current today. Those fighting to preserve the environment have mostly focused on the large Baikalsk Pulp and Paper Combine, built on the lake's southern shores in the 1960s and still controversial. Another environmental concern has been the routing of an oil pipeline near Lake Baikal. In 2006 the planned route was changed and moved further away from Baikal, as the risk of contamination was considered too great.

Much has been written about Lake Baikal, and one of the best-known literary works is a ballad by the Russian poet Dmitry Davydov (1811-88), whose "Glorious Sea, Sacred Baikal" derives from a longer text he wrote called "Ballad of a Fugitive on Baikal", dedicated to those exiles who fled hard labour in the mines (such as the notorious mines of Nerchinsk). Asked why he wrote a ballad about them, he reportedly said:

> Fugitives from factories and settlements are generally known as "passers-by". With incredible courage they overcome natural obstacles on the road. They cross mountain ridges and swamps, swim great rivers on any fragments of debris they find, and there were cases where they risked floating across Baikal in barrels they sometimes found on the shores.

The opening lines of his ballad read:

Glorious Baikal—free-wheeling Baikal
Magnificent vessel—Omul barrel
Hey, Barguzin [one of the strong Baikal winds]—Roll the waves
Not far for a young lad to swim.

As a result of a dam built on the Angara in the 1950s, the Baikal we know today is about three feet higher than in Davydov's day. As Rasputin suggests in his essay, it is almost as if human beings feel a destructive impulse to put their own mark on its magnificence. He cites the absurd vision of a Soviet engineer who wanted to sink the waters below their natural level by detonating 30,000 tonnes of ammonite explosive at the source of the Angara. When scientists pondered the effect of a tsunami rolling down the Angara, this fanciful idea of subjugating nature to the forces of Soviet five-year plans was abandoned.

IRKUTSK TO LISTVYANKA

The inhabitants of Listvyanka are no doubt immensely relieved that no one blew up the Angara, but the town did change once the dam was built, as one half of it—a row of houses directly on the bank of Lake Baikal—was demolished to allow for rising water levels, giving Listvyanka the slightly unfinished, lop-sided appearance it has today. Once a small fishing village, it is now a bustling tourist and convention resort, largely due to its proximity to Irkutsk, some forty miles down the road.

At kilometre 47 and just off the main road from Irkutsk to Listvyanka is one of the region's most interesting museums, the Taltsy Museum (Muzey Taltsy), whose architectural collection contains Russian dwellings spanning the seventeenth to the twentieth centuries. It opened in the 1980s as a showplace for eastern Siberian architectural history and includes some forty or so houses offering an insight into generations of domestic life in the Baikal region. Two of the most valued structures preserved in the complex are the Spasskaya Bashnya (Saviour's Tower) and Kazansky Chasovnya (Kazan Chapel) from the Ilimsk fort, both dating from the mid-seventeenth century.

Farther along the Baikal Trakt, about 25 miles from Irkutsk, is the 1930s forestry settlement of Bolshaya Rechka, which is now something of an artists' colony and an entry point for the Pribaikal National Park (Pribaykalsky Zapovednik).

The best-known among the artists living and working here is Yury Panov, who spent a decade in one of Stalin's gulags as a result of cartoons he drew in letters to friends while serving in the army. This was enough to land him in prison for defamation. Physically weakened, he was transferred to a second camp, where conditions were less harsh and he was employed in a workshop. This, he says, saved his life, as most of those in the first gulag died of overwork in wretched conditions. His drawing skills spared him the worst excesses when he was put to work doing party slogan posters and theatre backdrops for his captors. His main medium, however, is wood, and near his house at Angara 11 are his wooden monuments, many on the theme of oppression.

In the mid-1950s the government decided to go ahead with damming the Angara to create a reservoir and hydroelectric system to provide power for the region. As a result, the water level of the Angara rose over one hundred feet behind the dam from its original level. This flooded a river shoreline of spectacular cliffs and woodland, evoked by the British clergyman and traveller Henry Lansdell (1841-1919) in his *Through Siberia* of 1882:

> Shortly after leaving Irkutsk the road enters a wooded part of the Angara Valley, and as the road winds along it, many points are passed presenting magnificent views. In some parts the enormous sandstone cliffs rise out of the water, crowned with dark pines and cedars; in others the thick forest descends to the river's brink, and the broad sheet of water is seen rushing madly onwards. Afterwards the valley becomes more rugged, with deep ravines running up into the mountains.

Lansdell describes precarious roads that are cut into cliffs above the river:

> ... and about five miles before reaching the Baikal, a scene is presented that may well cause the traveller to stop. The valley becomes wider, and the mountains rise abruptly to a much greater elevation. The Angara is here more than a mile in width, and this great body of water is seen rolling down a steep incline, forming a rapid nearly four miles in length. At the head of this, and in the centre of the stream, a great mass of rock rises, called Shaman Kamen, or "Priest", or "spirit's stone", held sacred by the followers of Shamanism, and not to be passed by them without an act of devotion.

Beyond, he says, is the broad expanse of Baikal.

Picturesque, albeit tamer than in its untouched state, the river has lost none of its legendary beauty and symbolism. This is especially true once the Angara's opening is reached, which prior to the building of the dam made for an extremely hazardous crossing for those travelling to or from Mongolia. The precariousness of this passage was captured vividly by John Bell, who was on his way to Peking (Beijing) as the personal physician of the Russian ambassador to China in 1719-20. He begins his description just below the village of Nikola, which is part of Listvyanka but situated on the Angara proper at the source.

> Here we found our boats waiting for us below the falls of the Angara. From hence you can see the lake, bursting out betwixt two high rocks, and tumbling down over huge stones, that lie quite cross the river, which I reckon to be about an English mile broad. The whole channel of the river is covered with these rocks, from the mouth of the lake down to the Chapel of St Nicolas, about the distance of an English mile. There is no passage for the smallest boats, except along the east shore, thro' a narrow strait, between the rocks and the land. In the most shallow places, there is about five or six feet of water, and breadth all the way for any single vessel. But if, by stress of weather, or any other accident, a boat should have the misfortune to miss this opening, and be thrown upon the rocks, she must immediately be dashed to pieces, and the whole crew inevitably perish. The waters, dashing upon the stones, make a noise like the roaring of the sea, so that people near them can scarce hear one another speak. I cannot express the awfulness with which one is struck, at the sight of such astonishing scenes of nature as appear round this place, and which, I believe, are not to be equalled in the known world. The pilots and sailors who navigate the lake speak of it with such reverence, calling it the Holy Sea, and the mountains about it the Holy Mountains and are highly displeased with any person who speaks of it with disrespect, or calls it a lake. They tell a story of a certain pilot who always gave it that appellation, but was severely punished for his contempt. Being on a voyage in autumn, he and his crew were tossed from side to side of the lake, till they were nearly half starved, and in great danger of perishing. Necessity, at last, forced this hardy mariner to comply with the prevailing custom, and pray to the Holy Sea and Mountains to have compassion on him in such distress. His prayers were effectual, and he arrived safe to land; but was observed, ever after, to speak of the sea with greatest respect.

Everything Bell says about the "sacred" nature of Baikal and its surrounding mountains remains true today for Siberians, even if "worship" at the altar of Lake Baikal all-too-often takes the banal form of cold plunges and alcohol-fuelled picnics.

Bell's lasting impression of the road between Irkutsk and Nikola-Listvyanka in 1720 was of pleasant woods and open fields. Having set out after dinner on 15 May 1720 with the protection of the local Irkutsk commander and some officers, he travelled along the north bank till midnight, then the group rested near fishermen's huts at night before pressing on to Nikola, where Bell found the Chapel of St. Nicolas.

> At noon, we arrived at a small chapel, dedicated to St Nicholas, where travellers pay their devotions, and pray for a prosperous passage over the lake. About the religious house there are a few fishermen's huts. Two monks constantly attend, to put people in mind of their duty, and receive a small gratuity from the passengers.

The chapel Bell describes is probably the predecessor of the church later built in Nikola, the Church of St. Nicholas (Svyato-Nikolskaya Tserkov). This has an odd history and today is situated in Listvyanka in one of the side valleys.

The church was built at the instigation of a local merchant by the name of Ksenofont Serebyakov, who, legend has it, was crossing Lake Baikal when his boat sank. He claimed to have been saved by St. Nicholas, and this prompted him to build a church dedicated to the patron saint of travellers. Work began in 1846, but Serebyakov died before the church could be completed, and his wife continued to supervise its construction. Once completed, it was relocated not once but twice in its history. The first time was when the building was transplanted lock, stock and barrel to Listvyanka, and from its lakeside location there the church was again moved when the Angara was dammed in the 1950s and all the houses fronting the water were demolished. Today the church stands about 500 yards back from the shore in a side valley.

Another consequence of the dam is that the Shaman Rocks mentioned by Lansdell lost three feet of height. Today, they look like buoys to the naked eye; tourists sit on them to have their photographs taken while the calm waters of the Angara swirl around them.

There is, of course, another way of seeing this landscape, and this is through the eyes of the local Buryats who have their own myth of how the Angara was created. According to one popular version of this creation myth, in ancient times Baikal was a kind and joyful father who loved his only daughter, the Angara, with all his heart. Brighter than the sky, darker than the night, everybody who passed by her admired her beauty, and it is said that even the birds that migrated in summer to the Angara would fly low and out of respect hardly ever landed on her. Although old Baikal always did his best to protect his daughter, one time he fell asleep and the Angara stole away to the Yenisey. On waking, he splashed his waves in fury and caused a fierce storm. The mountains wept, the forests tumbled, the sky darkened with sorrow. Birds flew away towards the sun, animals fled and the fish dived deep down to the bottom of the waters. The wind howled and giant waves rolled across the waters of Baikal. Old Baikal struck furiously into the grey rock and threw a piece after his daughter as she fled towards the Yenisey. This fragment of rock fell into the throat of the beautiful, blue-eyed Angara and she cried, "Father, give me water for I am dying of thirst, and forgive me!" Baikal, still furious, cried out that he could only give her his tears. For one thousand years the Angara flowed like tears into the Yenisey, while grey-haired Baikal grew gloomy.

The rock the angry father threw at the source held a special place in the rite of the Buryats, who brought sacrifices to it in order to placate Baikal. Should he grow angry, they said, he would rip away the rock, causing a flood that would extinguish the earth. This was probably a suitable warning to any Soviet hydrologist with a pack of explosives in his pocket and an eye on Baikal's pure waters.

In the summer season and certain times in winter, Listvyanka swells with tourists drawn to the shores of Lake Baikal to eat smoked *omul* (the most popular of Baikal fish and one of Russia's culinary highlights) at the local market or to bask in the sun, swim (briefly, because the waters are cold), go ice fishing or simply take in the handful of sights such as the church and limnological museum.

The Baikal Museum (Baykalsky Muzey) at ulitsa Akademicheskaya 1 near the entrance to town, grew out of a station founded in 1928 to study the lake. This later became a limnological institute, and today it also has a museum section with displays on life in and around the lake. The collection includes an aquarium with a live *nerpa*, the world's only species of freshwater seal, as well as unique Baikal fish species such as the scale-less *golomyanka*.

The Baikal nerpa (Baikal seal) is the only mammal endemic to the lake and its origins are mysterious. Scientists suspect it came from the Arctic Ocean and reached Lake Baikal by swimming up the Lena river some two million years ago. The seals live to a ripe old age of about fifty years and can dive to depths of up to 1,300 feet for periods of more than an hour. When the lake begins to freeze over, the seals create holes in the ice where they can surface and keep these holes free throughout the winter by scratching away the newly formed ice with the claws of their front flippers. They spend most of the winter offshore on the ice and use one of the holes as their main lair and several others for occasional surfacing points while hunting and swimming. The seal calves are born in February or March, and usually only one is born to a mother. The natural cycle of the seals is to mate in April, when ice still covers the lake, then emerge from the waters as the ice melts in late May or early June in order to congregate in moulting rookeries in groups of hundreds that bask in the sun. The population in Baikal is thought to be between 60,000 and 100,000, but it is said that hunting and natural causes are causing their number to fall by about 1,000 each year.

About 58 species of fish inhabit Baikal, most of these unique to the lake. Their ancestors probably inhabited waters in the region some 20-25 million years ago around the time Lake Baikal was being formed. A small and large species of golomyanka (the large one is often called bullhead) and to a lesser extent the omul are the favoured diet of the nerpa seals. Oddly, the golomyanka gives birth to live offspring, a characteristic usually associated with tropical fish. The small variety and the male bullheads appear a beautiful, transparent blue colour when they come in contact with sunlight, and it is also possible to see the blood vessels and vertebrae through their skin.

In addition to the Baikal Museum, Listvyanka has its own art gallery (the Kartinaya Galereya) at Chapaeva 76, created largely due to the efforts of the poet and architect Vladimir Plamenevsky (1946-2003). The gallery is a centre for various artists and styles, but a common thread running through the works permanently exhibited is Lake Baikal itself.

A "Nerparium" (Nerpariya) on the shore is where a couple of nerpas have been trained to break-dance, feign feeling cold and perform other tricks by following the hand and arm signals of a trainer. It is unlikely that the nerpas get much from the performances except a few fish they could otherwise have snapped up in the wild themselves, but the show is conducted with care and in a slightly educational tone, and does leave the viewer with respect for these remarkable creatures. Taking photographs or touching the nerpas is not allowed.

Wooden house, Listvyanka

Though pleasant in itself and easily accessed from Irkutsk, Listvyanka's main street on a busy day metamorphoses into a limnological Marbella. Side-streets offer a retreat, leading off into the scrubland valleys of six small streams that flow towards Baikal. On most nights once the buses depart and the last of the line taxis has set off for Irkutsk, the town sinks into darkness and silence punctuated by the lapping of Baikal's waves against the shoreline and a dull glow from the town's only nightspot of note, the inauspiciously named Berg House.

THE CIRCUMBAIKAL RAILWAY
Irkutsk's monument to Alexander III celebrates the tsar who instigated the Trans-Siberian Railway. Perhaps the most poignant reminder, however, is a spectacular stretch of historic railway track that today begins in Port Baikal, across the source of the Angara from Nikola-Listvyanka, and winds around and through the mountain slopes of Lake Baikal to a terminus some fifty miles away in Kultuk. On a subcontinent with sufficient railways to keep an enthusiast occupied for a lifetime, this is undoubtedly a highlight, and the zenith of achievement in the construction of the Trans-

Siberian line.

In 1891 Alexander III issued his decree to build a line to the Pacific Ocean, and the earliest foundations for the "camel track" were laid in Vladivostok that same year. On 16 August 1898 Irkutsk was connected to the tsar's new railway network. It soon became clear to the authorities that they quickly needed to complete the section of track around Lake Baikal. The engineers faced a landscape here that was as difficult as it was spectacular. To bridge the gap in the line until one could be built around the southern fringe of the lake (from the southern bank of the Angara), the government decided to commission a special boat which, after twelve companies tendered for the contract, was constructed in Britain—a steampowered icebreaker produced by the shipyard Armstrong Whitworth & Co. Ltd and christened the *Baikal*. The *Baikal* stayed in regular service for almost seven years until 1905, although ferries were occasionally used right up until 1917.

The *Baikal* was assembled and tested in Europe before being delivered to St. Petersburg, where it was put in pieces on a train and freighted to Krasnoyarsk and then by barge and sledge to Irkutsk, finally reaching Listvyanka on horse-drawn carts. After it went into service the *Baikal* crossed between Port Baikal and the settlement of Mysovaya, 45 miles across the water, carrying a score of wagons and the locomotive as well as freight and passengers, 200 of whom could be accommodated in cabins. She could cut through ice of up to five feet in depth and took about 4.5 hours to complete the crossing.

In 1900 the *Baikal* was joined by a second ship, the *Angara*, today the Icebreaker Museum "Angara" (Lyedokol-Muzey "Angara"), moored in Irkutsk in the suburb of Solnyechny at prospekt Zhukova.

Yet the icebreaker solution proved makeshift and inadequate for large-scale transport or during cold winters when the ice was too thick to plough through. Another event, Russia's disastrous war with Japan in 1904-5, which resulted in the first defeat of a European power by an Asian nation, also exposed the shortcomings of using ships or (as happened in an experiment during the war) placing rails on ice and using draught horses to pull the engine. This experiment failed when the locomotive plunged through the ice, tearing a fourteen-mile gap across the lake surface. After that, the method used was to transport the engines in pieces loaded onto flat cars, which the horses dragged.

The period of construction around the southern shore, which began in 1902, was a remarkable achievement but it also coincided with a period when tsarist Russia was forced to confront its own military and political shortcomings. The railway was completed ahead of schedule in 1904, but it only began regular service in 1905.

From an engineering perspective, it was the most ambitious railway project in Russia up to that time. Work involved hacking out a total of 39 tunnels sometimes at a rate of just 15-20 inches per day. Fifteen galleries were hollowed out and 29 substantial bridges were constructed in addition to over 400 small bridges required to span streams and hollows. The longest and most difficult tunnel to build was at Cape Polovinny (Mys Polovinny), where specialist stonemasons experienced in dry techniques (i.e. without using mortar) brought in from Italy and Albania reinforced a 2,552-foot burrow through the cape. The cost of building the line was about six times higher per mile than the average for the rest of the Trans-Siberian Railway.

The Circumbaikal Railway in its original form began in Irkutsk and ran along the left bank of the Angara for 158 miles to Mysovaya. When the dam was built in the 1950s, however, the tracks along the Angara were flooded and the line was re-laid inland on higher ground. Although today most passengers on the line board at Irkutsk, the interesting section of the journey begins at Port Baikal (where it is also possible to board) and runs around the lake along the mountainous section of track. Between Kultuk and Slyudyanka the line joins the modern Trans-Siberian route.

The region around the Circumbaikal Railway had a reputation for being rugged and dangerous long before engineers got to work on the line. Crossing the mountains here by foot or with horses was a hazardous venture. Flanking Lake Baikal on the southern shore is the Komarinsky Range, whose highest mountain, Chersky Peak, named after the geologist, astronomer and first curator of Irkutsk's Regional Museum, I. D. Chersky, rises 6,856 feet about sixteen miles inland. (A fairly popular walking trail leads up there from Sludyanka, but like many in the region, it is far from a Sunday stroll, sometimes involving river wading and steep climbs in a landscape marked by clefts and cliffs.) Thomas Witlam Atkinson described the path he and other travellers used at that time as a winding, treacherous "staircase" down the mountain slopes to Sludyanka.

The distances between the landmarks of the railway are usually meas-

Walkers on the Circumbaikal

ured from Irkutsk. At 44 miles from Irkutsk is Port Baikal, across the Angara from Listvyanka, where you find a reconstructed wooden station building based on a design from 1905. At 48 miles Gallery 1 is reached, the first of many galleries and tunnels. At 55 miles the train reaches Katorzhanka Valley, where stone was quarried for the building of the railway. Here the supporting walls are among the thickest along the route. At Cape Tolstoy (56 miles), the train reaches a mooring where occasional boats arrive from Listvyanka, and a 1,125-foot section of tunnel that can be covered by foot (though a torch and caution are highly advisable). At the 61 mile (99 km) mark, a tunnel plunges towards the waters of Berezovskaya Bay, where a bridge used to be located. The 1,640-foot tunnel was later constructed due to the danger of rock falls, and its portals are considered to be the most beautiful on the route. Beyond (or before, depending on your direction), the route passes Cape Shumikinsky (63 miles) and a gallery with protective walls built by Italian masons. The longest tunnel, which is dead straight for its length of 2,552 feet, is reached at Cape Polovinny (68 miles), after which at 74 miles the Marituy station is reached, with a small settlement of wooden houses dating from the early twentieth century, situated alongside the Marituy river. Impressive multitiered supports and double parallel tunnels characterize Cape Kirkerey (76 miles), followed by twin bridges across the Shabartuy river at 81 miles. At the 83-mile point a cliff offers a nesting ground for herring gulls from May to August. The viaduct across the Angasolka river is reached at 92 miles, where a trail (also for cross-country skiing) leads to the former station known as Staraya Angasolka (Old Angasolka). Finally, after a tunnel at Kirkidaysky, the Circumbaikal reaches its end at Kultuk, 94 miles (or 152 km) from Irkutsk.

OLKHON ISLAND: WHERE SPIRITS AND CULTURES MEET

Olkhon Island, known as the "Pearl of Baikal", which is reached by *raketa* fast boat services from Listvyanka or by bus or the same raketa from Irkutsk, is situated off the western shore about mid-way along Baikal. This makes it a spiritual, geographical and also an historical centre of Baikal. It also has its own microclimate, which makes it hotter than the mainland in summer, colder in winter, drier any time of year and means it is buffeted in autumn and winter by unusually strong north-west winds that tear at the topsoil and explain the rocky, exposed character of parts of the island. The Sarma is the strongest of these and can arise suddenly and violently, wreaking havoc on anyone who happens to be caught in it while out on the water.

The 45-mile long island (population almost 1,500) is essentially a continuation of the Primorsky Range along the western shore and separated from the mainland by Maloe More (Small Sea), where some of the warmest waters of Baikal are to be found. The western shore is rocky and broken, the central region of the island is forested, while the south tends to be steppe.

While Olkhon quite literally rises up prominently as a symbol of Baikal and shaman belief, less apparent in its craggy form is a cultural-spiritual wrestle that has taken place here and elsewhere in the Baikal region over past centuries. The original inhabitants of the island were the western Buryats of the Pribaikal region. While Buryats in the Transbaikal (in Buryatia) adopted Buddhism relatively early, Buryats west of Baikal were the target of Christian missionary activities from Irkutsk that long obstructed the spread of Buddhism there.

In *A Journey in Southern Siberia*, Jeremiah Curtin, is prompted by the Baikal region to view the course of history as an "endless succession of...

collisions". In the Pribaikal and the Transbaikal, the "collisions" over time resulted in two different courses, and this was partly because of the different landscapes and political borders. The western Buryats inhabited an extraordinarily wild and remote landscape and, unlike the Buryats of the Transbaikal, could not avoid conflict with the Russians when Cossacks arrived in the seventeenth century by fleeing across the border into Mongolia whenever this was convenient. The result was the Buryat wars. James Forsyth, in an interesting section of *A History of the Peoples of Siberia* explains that the eastern Buryats of the Transbaikal could uphold their traditional social systems until the nineteenth century. Ironically, groups of eastern Buryats and Tungus even served the Russian Empire as border guards in Cossack regiments to protect the southern border from the Manchu-Chinese in Mongolia. Eventually, Forsyth explains, these were integrated into the Transbaikal Cossack Host that was sent to protect the frontier with Manchu-controlled Mongolia in 1851.

In the early eighteenth century, the Buryats of the Transbaikal adopted the Gelug or so-called "yellow hat" Tibetan form of Buddhism. As in Mongolia, it is heavily infused with shamanism. Enlightened religious policies by Catherine the Great in the late eighteenth century were a further stimulus for Buddhism among Buryats, but its spread into the west to the Pribaikal was slowed by the greater influence of missionaries and because it was not a border region where pragmatic considerations of empire and frontier enjoyed greater priority. During the second half of the nineteenth century especially, the lives of western Buryats were at varying times affected by the spread of Christianity and Buddhism, while a profound shamanistic character continued to survive in Buryat culture. In an ironic twist, the survival of shaman practices even appears to have owed something to Irkutsk religious men who were suspicious of the rise of Buddhism. As late as 1909, Jeremiah Curtin writes (in language common for his time):

> With reference to preserving their religion [shamanism] the position of the western Buriats was specially favorable, and continues to be so. Their fellow tribemen, who live east of Lake Baikal, and touch on the great world of Buddhism, became Buddhists. The western Buriats are secluded considerably, and little troubled by neighbors. They prefer their own primitive religion thus far. The Russians have no objection to offer,

and would rather that they retain Shamanism than become Buddhists. If they have no wish to become Christian they may remain Pagan.

Curtin was writing precisely at a time when restrictive laws against Buddhism, James Forsyth says, were relaxed and Buddhism began to grow in popularity in the Pribaikal at the expense of Christianity and shamanism.

Buryatia, east of Baikal, has long been a region inhabited by tribes of pastoral nomads and these people saw themselves as Mongols. Ghengis Khan was born just across the border on the Onon river in Mongolia. Several tribes (including tribes known as the Bulagat, Ekherit and Khongodor people) migrated into the Angara Valley and spread out in the valleys there and into the upper reaches of the Lena river. These tribes were the basis for the western Buryats of the Pribaikal. Another tribe, however, the Khori, moved to the immediate western shore of Baikal, and it is these Khori people whose ancestors today live on and around Olkhon Island. The Khori are the most numerous of the Buryats.

Unlike the eastern Buryats who lived in felt *yurts*, the western Buryats of the steppe became more settled and lived in wooden yurt-shaped dwellings, and a couple of these, as well as eastern Buryat, Evenk (Tungus)

Shaman Rock, Olkhon Island

and other types of dwelling can be seen at Ulan-Ude's Architectural-Ethnographic Museum of the Transbaikal People (Arkhitekturno-Etnograficheesky Muzey Narodov Zabaykalya).

Shaman Rock (Shaman-Skala), in earlier days known as Shaman Temple, is one of Central Asia's most sacred sites and has become the unofficial symbol of Baikal. This rock is situated near Khuzhir (1,200 inhabitants), the main settlement on Olkhon and therefore the most heavily visited part of this unusually beautiful island that has over a dozen walking routes.

One of the island's peculiar archaeological features is the presence of yurt-shaped grave sites constructed of sandstone and arranged in circles. Stone fortifications can also be found. Both are relics of a Turkic Kurikan tribe that inhabited Olkhon, the shores of Baikal and valleys of the upper Angara and upper Lena rivers between the sixth and eleventh centuries. In the complex ethnic fabric of Siberia these Turks had an influence that would survive their own culture. When from the early thirteenth century the first Buryats arrived in the region from Mongolia, they encountered these Kurikans, and it was from remainders of these that the Buryats acquired their advanced blacksmith skills, eventually integrating the Kurikans into their own culture and creating the basis for the modern Pribaikal Buryats on and around Olkhon today.

Chapter Thirteen

THE ARCHIPELAGO OF EXILE: MAGADAN

"My friend left for Magadan... take off your hat...He left on his own...
Not in étapes... not because my friend was unlucky...just like that. 'Sure,
there are camp sites everywhere... but they're full of murderers...'. 'No
more murderers than in Moscow'... Then he packs his suitcase—for
Magadan."

Vladimir Vysotsky, "My Friend Left for Magadan", 1965

In 1885 the American explorer and journalist George Kennan (1845-1924) travelled to Siberia to write a book about the exile system. It was not Kennan's first time there. He had already spent two years on Kamchatka conducting survey work for the Russian-American Telegraph Company, and he had also travelled into the Caucasus. After returning to the United States from the Kamchatka journey he gave a series of lectures on Siberia and was criticized for taking too positive a view of the exile system. As a result, he left for Siberia again, spent two years travelling to different prisons and wrote his two-volume work *Siberia and the Exile System*, published in 1891 in London. The Russian government gave Kennan full access to the prisons, and unlike in his earlier reports, he painted a damning picture of conditions. It is a fascinating account and a fine descriptive record of the prison system in its day. At one point he describes travelling from Tomsk to Irkutsk when, noticing a horse in handcuffs, he laconically muses whether the tsar has taken to banishing horses. Handcuffing and banishing an errant nag beyond the Urals would be an unusual step but not a precedent in the bizarre history of exile. In 1591, when the regent, Boris Godunov, ordered the exile of the Uglich Bell for sounding the death of the young pretender to the throne Dmitry, he also ordered the cutting out of its "tongue" and a good flogging.

As it turned out, a peasant had lacked rope to tie his horse, decided to use a pair of handcuffs, and sometime later he lost the keys. Since then, the horse had stood around in handcuffs with nothing to do.

The history of Siberia and its exiles is as brutal and tragic as it is

Prisoners on the road to exile in Siberia, c.1800

absurd. While banishing a horse was only marginally beyond belief, many of the real events that have occurred in the use of Siberia as a prison are so horrific as to defy the imagination.

The first legal framework for using Siberia as a place of exile dates from 1648 and the reign of Tsar Alexei Mikhailovic (1645-80). In these earliest times Siberia was the finale of a punishment that began with mutilation in captivity. These two things, physical punishment and banishment, went hand-in-hand well into the nineteenth century, and even as late as 1863 prisoners were being branded before being marched across the Urals in gangs.

Writing about physical punishment in early Russia, Kennan says:

Men were impaled on sharp stakes, hanged, and beheaded by the hundred for crimes that would not now [in 1891] be regarded as capital in any civilized country in the world; while lesser offenders were flogged with the knut and bastinado, branded with hot irons, mutilated by amputation of one or more of their limbs, deprived of their tongues, and suspended in the air by hooks passed under two of their ribs until they died a lingering and miserable death.

In the late seventeenth century you could be exiled for vagrancy if you were not fit for military service, or for fortune telling, prize-fighting or even using snuff, in which case, Kennan says, the septum between your nostrils was also torn out. In the course of time, however, both the degree and use of mutilation gradually diminished. In 1785 it was abolished for the gentry, and during the rule of Alexander I in 1801-25 further changes reduced the use of physical punishment. But in this regard Russia lagged far behind the mores of western Europe, where physical abuse before transportation into exile was rapidly going out of fashion.

Throughout the eighteenth century repressive laws sent new waves of the banished into Siberia. This coincided with the founding of industrial towns like Yekaterinburg and a growing demand for labour in Siberia in places such as the Nerchinsk lead ore and silver mines. In 1762 a law allowed landowners to deliver their serfs to the authorities for banishment even for trivial reasons. The death penalty was abolished in 1753 for a brief period, however, and it was abhorred by Catherine the Great during her reign. Those who would previously have been executed were simply driven into Siberia, providing the region with a coerced labour force.

One of Catherine the Great's most famous exiles was Alexander Radishchev (1749-1802), who, inspired by the French Revolution of 1789, influenced by George Washington and enlightened by his time at Germany's Leipzig University, triggered her outrage with his *Journey from St. Petersburg to Moscow* in 1790. This openly condemned autocracy and, for the first time, serfdom. Russia's "first radical" was tried, sentenced to death and reprieved, and then sent to Siberia for ten years. He spent two months in Tobolsk, where he was joined by his family before they continued on to Ilimsk. His second wife (his first wife had died and he married her sister), who would have been free to marry again, decided to accompany him. In Tobolsk, he wrote:

You want to know: Who am I? What am I? Where am I going?
I'm the same as I was and will be for all my epoch:
Not an animal, not a tree, not a slave, but a human being!

The path is lain where no tracks are found
For the very brave in prose and poems
For those feeling hearts and the tender truth, I give myself to fear
To Ilimsk fort, that's where I'm going!

Until the late eighteenth century, Kennan says, treatment en route to Siberia was horrific and poorly organized, with prisoners being driven "like cattle, from one provincial town to another, sometimes begging their way... and sometimes starving to death on the road."

HOUSE OF THE DEAD

In the following decades something happened that had an impact on the way we see Siberia today. In 1845 the use of physical punishment was further restricted, by which time Siberia was being viewed as a form of punishment in itself. The geographical aspect of Siberia alone, therefore, had acquired a more sinister edge. Long gone, it seems, were the days when everything beyond the Urals called forth the fantastic, bizarre or the repellent. Siberia itself had become a punitive version of hell on earth, and as long as the guilty were exposed to various degrees of hell, this was punishment enough. The harsher the punishment, the farther away they were sent. Western Siberia was mild; being sent to Yakutia or the Transbaikal region were the most severe forms of punishment.

Women were among those exiled to Siberia from the earliest days. Boris Godunov is said to have exiled the whole town of Uglich to Pelym in the Urals region. Families were allowed to accompany the banished, and this was the path taken by many of the wives of those Decembrists exiled or sentenced to hard labour. Once in Siberia, though, members of the family were not allowed to return unless the banished person died or had served his or her term. The sentimental myth of the Russian woman who accompanies her husband into exile does not, however, represent quite as selfless and faithful an act as we might believe. Exile wives suffered ostracism at home, and faced the problem of having to earn a living. Often they had little choice.

Generally, even someone who was sentenced to prison in Siberia was eventually released from their cell to live in a hut just outside the prison walls. Another development was a gradual shift in focus of most penal servitude to eastern Siberia

In 1817, the *étapes* or "exile station houses" forming an untranslatable pun in Vysotsky's song, were established along the way. These were rudimentary log shelters where the exiles could sleep. Between Tomsk and Irkutsk, Kennan says, the exile station houses stood at a distance of about 25-40 miles, and the groups of 300 to 400 exiles needed about four months to cover the 1,250 miles to Irkutsk. Those in fetters who could not keep up stayed in even more rudimentary half-way houses between the major étapes. Until 1883, men, women and children were bundled together in one sorrowful marching party, but thereafter men with families were separated from the single men. This reduced the depravity experienced by women and children at the hands of the men, but according to Kennan, not altogether. Those who could not walk at all were placed onto carts.

In the late 1880s, the years Kennan witnessed, there were four main categories of exiles: *Katorzhniki*, who had been sentenced to hard labour; *Poselentsy*, ordinary penal colonists; *Ssylny*, those who had simply been banished for a period of time and could return; and the *Dobrovolny* ("volunteers") who were family members accompanying a relative. In Kennan's time the prisoners were taken from Kazan to the Urals either in barges or by rail, crossed the Urals by rail to Tyumen and stayed there for about two weeks in a forwarding station before being loaded onto barges again and freighted along the Irtysh and Ob rivers for the journey to Tomsk, from where the exiles were marched in parties to their final destinations.

Conditions in Tyumen were pitiful for the prisoners. Kennan describes the forwarding station as a small three-storey tin-roofed brick building about 75 feet long and 50 feet wide inside a yard with sentry boxes in each corner. Guards wielding Berdan rifles with bayonets made sure no one escaped. "A dozen or more girls and old women were sitting on the ground in front of the prison with baskets full of black rye-bread, cold meat, boiled eggs, milk, and fish-pies for sale to the imprisoned exiles," he observed. Of the prisoners in leg fetters, he writes: "the air was filled with a peculiar clinking of chains which suggested the continuous jingling of innumerable bunches of keys... As we entered the cell, the convicts, with a sudden jingling of chains, sprang to their feet." Apart from long wooden platforms upon which the convicts slept like sardines packed into a can— the cells were overcrowded and some prisoners had to sleep on the muddy ground—the cell contained only a large wooden tub for excrement.

The turmoil of the second half of the nineteenth century in Russia led to political crimes being considered worse than common crimes like murder or theft. Then, in 1903, the definition of a political crime was broadened, which was indicative of the unrest troubling Russia. One interesting development around Kennan's time was that the numerous intellectuals exiled for political activities played an important role in early Siberian ethnological studies. The historian Yuri Slezkine explains in his *Arctic Mirrors*, a book about the history of Russian relations with the indigenes of the north, that with southern Siberia becoming a place for the living (more European), the far east and the far north slipped into the role of being Russia's "House of the Dead"—the ideal place for a political outcast.

Three important works were written in the nineteenth century about the tsarist system of exile and banishment: Dostoevsky's *House of the Dead* (1862; also called *Buried Alive*), Chekhov's *Sakhalin* (1890) and the novel *Resurrection* (1899) by Leo Tolstoy.

Chekhov left us with a record of his travels and descriptions of the appalling conditions endured by inmates of the camps on Sakhalin Island, but he also grappled with the idea of what was worse, exile or death. He writes:

> All higher punitive measures replacing the death penalty continue to bear the same important and very real characteristic, namely a life sentence, forever. All these measures have the same purpose inherited directly from the death penalty—the removal of the criminal forever from a normal human environment; and a person who has committed a severe crime dies for the society in which he was born and grew up in, just as it was during the era of the death penalty... The deprivation of rights in almost all cases has the character etc. of lifelong. Thus, all higher punitive measures do not give the criminal eternal rest in his grave—the very thing that could reconcile me with the death penalty.

Dostoevsky wrote a haunting novel that narrates many of his own experiences through the figure of a Russian nobleman who is exiled to Siberia for murdering his wife in a rage. After serving his term, the nobleman ekes out a living as a teacher near the convict colony, and when he dies his papers (the novel) are bought by the narrator.

Like Dostoevsky himself, the nobleman arrives in Tobolsk and is given a copy of the Old Testament with money concealed inside the cover. It is an interesting detail because it portrays a paradox of Siberia as a land of cruelty, but also of human kindness in difficult circumstances. "There are, and ever will be in Siberia," the nobleman writes, "persons who have devoted their whole life to doing good to convict prisoners. They care for them as they would their own children, and try to lighten their burden in every possible way."

In another scene Dostoevsky offers us one of Russia's most evocative descriptions of a bathhouse—in this case filled with Siberian prisoners on one of the infrequent occasions they are allowed to bath. For Dostoevsky, it is a steamy underworld:

... my first thought was that I must have got into hell by mistake. Into a room not more than twelve feet long, and as many broad, a crowd of human beings had been crowded. A thick cloud of vapour hung over the bathers, nearly enveloping them, and the floor was so filthy that I did not know where to set my foot... When at last we got to the wall where the bench was, we found that every available place on the forms had already been taken... Even the spaces under the benches was occupied; the men squatted about on the floor washing themselves, while others who had been less fortunate in obtaining a place stood upright between them, the dirty water trickling down from their bodies on the cropped heads of those who sat below. The shelves were covered in convicts, who tried to screw themselves into the smallest possible space. Few, however, of the convicts really washed themselves... their idea of a bath consisting in getting up to the highest shelf, whipping themselves violently with a bundle of birch twigs, and then pouring cold water down their backs. About fifty birch rods were in constant movement on the shelves, water was being continually thrown at the hot oven to make more steam, till the heat was almost unbearable. And all this mass of human beings was swaying backwards and forwards, shouting and yelling, and clanking their chains on the floor.

Dostoevsky also describes sleeping in prisoners' dormitories where "almost all the men talked in their sleep, generally about knives or other cutting instruments. 'We have been so much beaten,' they used to say by way of explanation, 'that our bowels are loose in our bellies, and that makes us cry out in our sleep.'"

By the time of the revolution of 1917, a long line of banished souls had struggled across the Urals into Siberia. One group was of Old Believers, beginning with the tortured tribulations of Avvakum in the mid-seventeenth century (many of these Old Believers settled in the Altai mountains and Transbaikal region). An unlikely group became known as "Castrati" and believed in self-emasculation. In Siberia, most of the Castrati settled in Yakutia and some played an important role in the development of agriculture there. Another group was comprised of prisoners who had fallen into Russian hands over the centuries, beginning from the time of the Livonian War of 1558-82. On top of these were political exiles such as Decembrists and later in the nineteenth century Dostoevsky and the Petrashevsky Circle. And then there were the criminals of one shade or another. In the early years of colonization, many common criminals joined the ranks of the Cossacks.

THE GULAGS

In the course of the twentieth century the outside world would become familiar with one of those acronyms so favoured by Soviet administrators, and this acronym stood less for a land of dead souls than for a separate world cut off completely from the one we knew. It had its own barbaric rules of conduct and it cost millions of people their lives. This word was *gulag*—an ugly piece of Soviet officialese that quickly acquired connotations of horror.

Gulag stands for Glavnoe Upravlenie Ispravitelno-Trudovykh Lagerey i Kolonii (Main Administrative Correction-Labour Camp and Colonies) and has two meanings. The literal one is simply a correction camp anywhere in Russia; yet because many of these camps were located in the remote regions of Siberia, the word gulag acquired a second meaning as an unimaginably abhorrent system of forced labour and punishment in Siberia. Since the publication of *Gulag Archipelago* by Alexander Solzhenitsyn in 1973, the system has been likened to a chain of islands—as depraved as they were brutal—completely isolated from the civilized world. In his book Solzhenitsyn describes Kolyma as "the harshest and most famous island, the pole of cruelty in this surprising country Gulag, a geography torn into an archipelago but bound psychologically to the continent—almost as an invisible, intangible country inhabited by a people known as zeks." *Zek* is an abbreviation of the Russian prison term for prisoner.

He also writes: "If only it were so simple—that there are evil people somewhere, insidiously doing evil deeds and it were only necessary to distinguish them from the remainder and destroy them. But the line dividing good from evil crosses through the heart of each human being, and who would destroy a piece of his or her own heart?"

Conditions in the Kolyma region are among the harshest on this planet. They are captured ironically in one of the songs sung by prisoners: "Kolyma, Kolyma, a wonderful planet—twelve months of winter and the rest is summer." This is the permafrost zone, which means that surface water during the short but often intense summer cannot penetrate the frozen ground; instead, it coagulates in swampy pools and creates ideal conditions for mosquitoes and other insects. In winter the region is regularly struck by severe snow storms, known as *purga* in the north, and in the interior the Kolyma winter can begin as early as August and last until May. From April the waters of Nagaevo Bay at Magadan can be navigated with the help of ice-breakers; they freeze over again in December.

In late 1931 the Central Committee of the Communist Party resolved to create a state trust for building roads and industrial facilities in the upper Kolyma and called it Dalstroy. It controlled a region amounting to one-seventh of the entire territory of the Soviet Union. As the first head, the government appointed a 37-year-old Latvian Bolshevik and a commander of the troops responsible for Lenin's protection during the civil war, Eduard Berzin (1894-1938). In the spring of 1932 a group of men on an ice-breaker and two steam-powered vessels arrived in Nagaevo Bay and, led by Berzin, set about building a harbour on this remote and difficult stretch of coast. The men, some of them engineers who were prisoners, worked with rudimentary equipment and in addition to building the harbour also worked on developing a town at the site of an Evenk cultural base and opening up the region for industrial-scale gold mining.

During that first cold winter of 1932-33, the men lived in makeshift tents. A large number of them died. Probably about 12,000 men were labouring in the region by the end of the first winter.

It is said that the early years of Kolyma—the period under Berzin— were relatively tolerable as far as gulags were concerned. Berzin himself seems to have relished his new position, cruising through Magadan in a Rolls Royce that had probably earlier served as the official car of Felix Dzerzhinsky, head of the Cheka security services. Things would end badly for him, however. When Stalin's campaigns intensified throughout the 1930s, Berzin came under suspicion and himself fell victim to the purges that were supplying his mines with labour. Once the head of Dalstroy had been purged, the town of Magadan remedied a minor oversight and gave itself its first ulitsa Stalina—the street used to be called ulitsa Berzina.

In 1938 Dalstroy was incorporated into the NKVD, (Commissariat for the Interior). This had also housed the Cheka security service, which was established after the revolution and with several name changes became the KGB. Kolyma was never an easy place to be, but this period of terror made it a "white hell", as some survivors came to call it.

It took until 1937 for prisoners working under the worst possible conditions to complete a 550-mile stretch of road across the permafrost into the north. Sections between Magadan and the village of Yagodnoe and beyond are known as the "road of bones", constructed to reach the goldfields and a string of prison camps in the Kolyma. This forms a ring (the Zolotoe Koltso or Circle of Gold) to Susuman and back to Magadan. From this road the main highway leads off to Yakutsk, 1,250 miles away, where another road, a continuation of the M56 from Magadan, connects the frozen north with the border region of the Amur. Those who died while building the road were buried beneath it as ballast. Few would have given a thought to the picturesque landscape of valleys, rivers and small canyons it traverses.

During the Second World War Russia was party to the US Lend-Lease Agreement, designed to supply allies with war equipment. This saw US supplies such as bulldozers arriving into the region, and according to some accounts, they were used to dig mass graves in the frozen soil. It is also said that inmates were so desperate that they tried to eat the grease in order to survive.

In 1944 US Vice-president Henry Wallace visited Kolyma to see what Russia was doing with American equipment and to engage in diplomacy on the side. Before he arrived, over-conspicuous barbed wire was removed, several camps were made presentable and in at least one camp even the watch towers were reportedly taken down after rumours of an impending visit swept through. One of the inmates in a camp he visited is said to have thrown herself at Wallace's feet and pleaded for help, but Wallace, unable to understand Russian, was told the woman was insane.

In *The Unquiet Ghost*, Adam Hochschild writes: "Watchtowers along the Kolyma Highway outside Magadan were pulled down. The hungry, ill-clad prisoners normally at work under armed guard paving the city's streets and constructing its buildings received, probably for the first time in their terms, a three-day holiday, so they could stay in their barracks and out of sight. NKVD clerks and secretaries were rushed out to a pig farm Wallace was to visit, to play the roles of farmhands."

On his own visit, Hochschild also memorably describes unmarked and abandoned camps gradually being reclaimed by the landscape:

> We wind our way out of the valley, past the town where Wallace stayed [Seymchan, north of Magadan], between the tops of the rocky sopki [hills] back towards Omsukchan. And even though most don't appear on the maps of known Kolyma camps, on this final part of our route it seems as if every valley holds its own prison camp. We fly over more than half a dozen as the helicopter turns this way and that: collapsed remnants of barracks and watchtowers and gold-mining works, the wood blackened by decades of snow and sun and rain. The ruins lie around every bend, beyond every ridge, as if a giant hand has angrily thrown them down from the sky every few miles across the barren moonscape.

The horror of the Kolyma camps—the hideous conditions under which the inmates worked, the vicious power hierarchies, the mass rapes sinisterly known as the Kolyma Streetcar and the executions—produced a number of vivid and disturbing accounts by Russian writers, who have tried to convey the inhumane conditions to the outside world. On top of these come non-fiction accounts by non-Russians such as Robert Conquest's *Kolyma: The Arctic Death Camps*, Martin J. Bollinger's *Stalin's Slave Ships* and Anne Applebaum's *Gulag: A History*. All give an intense insight into the horrors of the camps.

One of the passengers on the *Dzhurma*, a slave ship described by Martin Bollinger that transported prisoners between Vladivostok and Magadan, was Yevgenia Ginzburg (1904-77). Her memoir, *Krutoy Marshrut* (published in English as *Journey into the Whirlwind* and *Within the Whirlwind*) was completed in 1967 and published abroad after being smuggled out of Russia. Ginzburg spent eighteen years in all in Stalin's gulags and was the first woman writer to give an account of the camps. Echoing the fine line described by Solzhenitsyn, she writes: "I am ashamed. And at the moment when I stop feeling ashamed and begin to feel responsible for all this? Indeed, I haven't been a hammer for a long time, rather an anvil. But might I really become this hammer?"

Varlam Shalamov (1907-82) published a collection of short stories called *Kolyma Tales*, and in one of these, *Cherry Brandy*, he describes the death of the poet Osip Mandelstam (1891-1938) who came to grief in the Vladivostok transit camp in December 1938.

Those who were sent to Kolyma passed either through Vladivostok, Nakhodka or Vanino (near Sovetskaya Gavan) and were freighted in the holds of ships along the coast on a journey that could take up to eleven days. The prisoners slept on cramped, wooden bunks built into the holds and used open barrels as toilets that sometimes spilt over and flooded the hold with excrement.

Elena Glinka, a survivor of the Kolyma camps from the 1950s, describes in an article entitled "Kolyma Streetcar" a mass rape that occurred at the fishing settlement of Bugurchan, a place, she says, that "dragged out an obscure existence on the shores of the Sea of Okhotsk, consisted of five or six miserable huts scattered randomly over the surface of the taiga and a squalid little log-built club-house jutting out of the ground, above which an old flag flapped in the wind." Her account is disturbing and illustrates the extent to which this and other crimes were tolerated in the camps.

After news of the arrival of the women spread, men arrived from all over the region, plied the guards with alcohol, then dragged the women into the local clubhouse. "A merry group of fish-salters and the settlement's only copper, already pretty drunk, brought out a parcel of Siberian salmon, cut the fish into chunks and threw them to the women prisoners. Exhausted by seasickness and two days without food in the hold of the ship, the women clutched greedily at the scraps as they flew by, hastily stuffing them into their mouths and swallowing them without chewing."

The rapes commonly took place "under the state flag", she says, "with the connivance of the guards and the authorities":

I offer this documentary narrative to all Stalin's loyal devotees who to this very day do not wish to believe that their idol deliberately propagated lawlessness and sadistic violence. Let them just for one moment imagine their wives, daughters and sisters in that Bugurchan penal team: it was only by chance that they were not there and we were.

They raped at the command of the "driver", who periodically waved his arms in the air and cried: "Mount up!..." At the command, "Stop the racket!" they tumbled off, reluctantly giving up their place to the next man in line, who was standing there in a state of total sexual readiness. The dead women were dragged off by the legs to the door and piled up there. The rest were splashed with water to bring them back to consciousness, and the men lined up by them again.

COMPANY TOWN

Magadan's provenance is unfortunate and unusual to say to the least, and the town therefore offers a dark window into the worst aspects of repression during the Soviet era. It was never, however, simply just a dumping ground for those being punished by the regime. The Soviet exile system was also an industry.

Magadan viewed from mountains

Magadan was founded as a company town and from its earliest days was run by two organizations. One of these was Dalstroy, on paper a harmless trust whose brief was to develop resources in the region. The other was the successor of the Cheka Soviet political security service, the OGPU. While in theory the two organizations reported to different masters, the reality was that Dalstroy's head and founding father of Magadan, Berzin, was a former Cheka man who had scaled the ranks of the OGPU to run a forced labour camp in the Urals. Although Dalstroy was independent of the Soviet political police at this time, it received its labour from Sevvostlag, created by the OGPU and part of the organization responsible for camps—Gulag. The arrangement was a convenient one because Dalstroy could present a clean public face while the Soviet security service did the dirty work behind the scenes at the camps located along the Golden Ring.

Today, a statue of Berzin stands outside Magadan's town hall. While this might seem incongruous, Berzin was in comparison to others who followed a moderate head of Dalstroy who championed the values of the Bolsheviks of 1917 and predated Stalinist brutality. People like him are said to have staffed the Soviet secret services until 1934, when the assassination of Sergey Kirov (1886-1934), another old Bolshevik, marked the beginning of the purges. The old Bolsheviks were then murdered and the Soviet Union was firmly in the hands of Stalin's men and women.

Strangely for a man who would help administer a harsh system of forced labour in Kolyma, Berzin studied fine art in Berlin before the outbreak of the First World War. He was more inclined to propaganda than pogrom, taking the path from art to an idealistic belief in surmounting nature's obstacles for the Soviet state. But Kolyma was also his step up the ladder after the Urals.

If the OGPU was behind running the labour force, Dalstroy and its employees were behind virtually everything else. The town's flagship museum, the Magadan Region Local Studies Museum (Magadansky Oblastnoy Kraevedchesky Muzey), situated at ulitsa Karla Marksa 55, is no exception. This was founded in 1931 and its original collection of about 600 exhibits was assembled by volunteers, including those who were—the museum says—"enthusiasts from Dalstroy".

The first theatre ensemble in Magadan was established in 1933 by a special culture section of Sevvostlag devoted to the arts. It was, in effect, a theatre group run under the auspices of the Soviet security service. Not sur-

Mask of sorrow

prisingly, Magadan benefited from a large number of talented artists who fell victim to the purges. The Russian stage designer Leonid Vegener (1908-91) was arrested in 1938 on charges of espionage and worked as a stage designer and producer at the Magadan Theatre of Music and Drama (Musykalny i Dramatichesky Teatr; ulitsa Karla Marksa 30) in 1942. After he finished his term he stayed here and in 1955-58 headed stage design at the theatre before returning to Moscow in 1958. Magadan's most poignant memorial is the Mask of Sorrow (Maska Skorbi), unveiled in 1996, and dedicated to the prisoners who suffered and died in the gulags of the Kolyma. It is the work of the Russian-Jewish sculptor Ernst Neizvestny, and is a fifty-foot high mask whose main feature is a cross that forms the nose and eyes.

With the death of Stalin in 1953, the camps were gradually abandoned. According to Anne Applebaum, Stalin's successor Nikita Krushchev (1894-1971) recognized they were uneconomic, but he also feared political repercussions due to their existence. Prisoners were released and either went home or settled where they had once been held captive. Only one former camp—Perm-36—has been turned into a memorial. The camp is situated just west of the Urals in European Russia. Applebaum remarks:

"Perm-36 is... unique simply because it exists; virtually all of the thousands of other camps that once made up the Soviet Gulag have disappeared. In part, this is because the camps were mostly made of wood, or at best cheap brick, and they have simply deteriorated. In part, this is because most camps were located near factories or mines, and have simply been reabsorbed into workplaces. But many camps were also deliberately destroyed. Perm-36 almost met the same fate."

But the system did not cease entirely until the 1980s, Applebaum concludes: "Instead, it evolved—and so did Perm-36. In fact, it was in 1972, at the outset of the second, later phase of political repression in the USSR, that Perm-36 attained real notoriety, when the camp was converted into a political prison for people whom the regime described as hardened political criminals. For the next 15 years, the camp, along with two others nearby—Perm-35 and Perm-37—held many of the Soviet Union's most prominent dissidents." Russia's only gulag museum on its original site represents, she says, a continuity of the Soviet prison system from the 1940s until the 1980s.

Further Reading

Although the availability of information about Siberia is gradually improving, researching a region so large and culturally rich presents challenges. I found myself resorting to a range of resources in Russian, English, German and French to gather information for this book. Some of these resources are academic works I reinterpreted (for example, using research by anthropologists to convey a feeling for a people or landscape). In such cases, the interpretations are my own, as are any errors of interpretation. Other sources were more straightforward: local Russian newspaper or magazine articles, official websites of regions, towns and organizations, or even material gleaned from reliable and knowledgeable tour operators who regularly take visitors around the sights or regions.

Mostly, however, I have relied on a range of travel descriptions in order to give an insight into Siberia's changing people, culture and landscape. Again, the choice is eclectic and subjective. Passages were chosen to give a flavour of Siberia, its people and landscape, and I hope this whets the reader's appetite to pick up one or the other original description and read more. Finally, I hope this book will foster a better understanding of Siberia—among armchair travellers and ground travellers seeking a passage into Siberia and all it offers.

The books I consulted most frequently were James Forsyth, *A History of the Peoples of Siberia: Russia's North Asian Colony 1581-1990* (Cambridge: Cambridge University Press, 1992)—an invaluable work that I often drew on for background on contact between indigenes and European Russians; Igor V. Naumov (editor David N. Collins), *The History of Siberia* (London: Routledge, 2006)—a good general source for background on Siberia; E. Akbalian, V. Golubchikova, Z. Khvtisiashvili, *Practical Dictionary of Siberia and the North* (Moscow: European Publications, 2005); *The Peoples of Siberia*, ed. M. G. Levin & L. P. Popatov (Chicago & London: The University of Chicago Press, 1964); *Between Heaven and Hell: The Myth of Siberia in Russian Culture*, eds. Galya Diment and Yuri Slezkine (New York: St. Martin's Press, 1993). Chapters by Yuri Slezkine, Galya Diment and Harriet Murav were invaluable resources. For the Altai understanding of space in the Altai chapter I am indebted to the ideas and inspiration provided by Agnieszka E. Halemba, *The Telengits of Southern Siberia: Landscape, Religion and Knowledge in Motion* (London & New York: Routledge, 2006).

SELECTED BIBLIOGRAPHY

Markus Ackeret, *In der Welt der Katorga. Die Zwangsarbeitsstrafe für politische Delinquenten im ausgehenden Zarenreich (Ostsibirien und Sachalin).* April 2007. Online publication, Osteuropa-Institut, Mitteilungen, No. 56. Online version retrieved January 15, 2009 from www.osteuropa-institut.de.

American Philosophical Society, *Proceedings.* Vol. 114, No. 3. Philadelphia: American Philosophical Society, 1970.

Anne Applebaum, *Gulag: A History.* New York: Doubleday, 2003.

Anne Applebaum. *Tales from the Gulag.* Retrieved September 29, 2009 from www.wmf.org/html/PDF/gulag.pdf.

Terrence Armstrong (ed.), *Yermak's Campaign in Siberia: A Selection of Documents,* translated by Tatiana Minorsky and David Wileman. London: The Hakluyt Society, 1975.

Terrence Armstrong. *The Northern Sea Route. Soviet Exploitation of the North East Passage.* Scott Polar Research Institute Cambridge. Cambridge, UK: Cambridge University Press, 1952.

Thomas Witlam Atkinson, *Oriental and Western Siberia: A Narrative of Seven Years' Exploration and Adventures in Siberia, Mongolia, the Kirghis Steppes, Chinese Tartary, and a Part of Central Asia.* New York: Harper & Brothers, 1858.

F. Chappe d'Auteroche, *A Journey to Siberia.* London: T. Jefferys, 1770.

Lindon Bates Jr., *The Russian Road to China.* Boston & New York: Houghton Mifflin Co., 1910.

Mark Bassin, *Asia,* in *The Cambridge Companion to Modern Russian Culture.* Nicholas Rzhevsky (ed.). Cambridge, UK: Cambridge University Press, 1998.

Mark R. Beissinger, *Nationalist Mobilization and the Collapse of the Soviet State: A Tidal Approach to the Study of Nationalism.* Cambridge, UK: Cambridge University Press, 2002.

Anastasiya Belenkova, *Vakansiya Tretevo Goroda Rossy, Marketing Territory.* Kontinent Sibir, No. 7, July 2008. (Visitor figures in this article are from www.travel.ru.)

John Bell, *Travels from St. Petersburg in Russia to Diverse Parts of Asia.* Glasgow: Robert & Andrew Foulis, 1763.

Martin J. Bollinger, *Stalin's Slave Ships: Kolyma, the Gulag fleet, and the Role of the West.* Westport, CT: Praeger, 2003.

Douglas Carruthers, *Unknown Mongolia: A Record of Travel and Exploration in*

North-West Mongolia and Dzungaria. London: Hutchinson & Co., 1914.

Anton Chekhov, *Iz Sibiri*. *Polnoe sobranie Sochineniy i Pisem v Tridtsati Tomakh. Sochinenie v Vosemnadtsati Tomakh. Toma Chetyrnadtsaty-Pyatnadtsaty.* Moscow: Nauka, 1987.

Anton Chekhov, *Letters of Anton Chekhov to his family and friends, with biographical sketch*, translated by Constance Garnett. New York: The Macmillan Company, 1920. Retrieved September 29, 2009 from Project Gutenberg: www.gutenberg.org.

Dittmar Dahlmann, *Sibirien. Vom 16. Jahrhundert bis zur Gegenwart.* *Paderborn*: Schöningh, 2009.

John Dundas Cochrane, *Narrative of a Pedestrian Journey through Russia and Siberian Tartary to the Frontiers of China, the Frozen Sea, and Kamtchatka.* Philadelphia: H.C. Carey, & I. Lea, & A. Small, 1824.

Archibald R. Colquhoun. *The "Overland" to China*. London: Harper & Bros, 1900.

Robert Conquest, *Kolyma: The Arctic Death Camps*. Oxford, UK: Oxford University Press, 1979.

Marya Antonia Czaplicka, *My Siberian Year. Collected Works of M. A. Czaplicka* (David Collins ed.). Richmond, UK: Curzon, 1999.

Marya Antonia Czaplicka. *Aboriginal Siberia, a Study in Social Anthropology.* Oxford, UK: Clarendon Press, 1914.

Daniel Defoe, *The Adventures of Robinson Crusoe: With Memoir of the Auth*or. London: Bickers & Bush, 1862.

Gerrit de Veer. *The True and Perfect Description of Three Voyages by the Ships of Holland and Zeland*. London: Pavier, 1609.

Bassett Digby and R. L. Wright. *Through Siberia: An Empire in the Making.* London: Hurst and Blackett, 1913.

Fedor Dostoyeffsky, *Buried Alive or Ten Years of Penal Servitude in Siberia*, translated by Marie von Thilo. London: Longmans, Green, and Co., 1881.

Fyodor M. Dostoevsky, *Pisma 1834 -1881: Sobranie Sochineny v 15 Tomakh.* Leningrad: Nauka, 1988-96.

Fyodor M. Dostoevsky, *Pisma 1832-1859, Polnoe Sobranie Sochineny.* Leningrad: Nauka, 1985.

Alexandre Dumas, *Impressions de Voyage: En Russie*. Paris: Michel Lévy Frères, 1866.

Elena Duzs, *Russian Art in Search of Identity*, in *Russia and Western Civilization: Cultural and Historical Encounters* (Russel Bova, ed.). Armonk, New York, & London: Sharpe, 2003.

Adolph Erman, *Travels in Siberia, Including Excursions Northwards, Down the Obi, to the Polar Circle, and, Southwards, to the Chinese Frontier*, translated by W.D. Cooley. Philadelphia: Lea & Blanchard, 1850.

Jon Foster Fraser, *The Real Siberia: Together With An Account of a Dash Through Manchuria*. London: Cassell & Co., 1905.

Joseph Frank, *Dostoevsky: The Years of Ordeal, 1850-1859*. Princeton: Princeton University Press, 1987.

D.A. Funk & L. Sillanpää, *The Small Indigenous Nations of Northern Russia: A Guide for Researchers*. Åbo Akademi University: Social Science Research Unit. Publication No. 29, 1999. Vaasa, Finnland: 1999.

Elena Glinka. *Kolyma Streetcar*. From *Women's View*, edited by Natasha Perova (*Glas New Russian Writing*). Translated by Andrew Bromfield. Moscow: Glas, 1992.

Johann Georg Gmelin, *Expedition ins Unbekannte Sibirien*. Sigmaringen, Germany: Jan Thorbeke Verlag, 1999.

G. Grebenshchikov. *Altai - Chemchuzha Sibiri*. Retrieved September 29, 2009 from http://irbis.asu.ru.

Agnieszka Halemba. *Power in places and politics in Altai*. Retrieved 10 July 2009 from www.anthrobase.com/Txt/H/Halemba_A_01.htm

Maud Haviland, *A Summer on the Yenesei*. London: E. Arnold, 1915.

S. S. Hill, *Travels in Siberia*. London: Longman, Brown, Green, & Longmans, 1854.

Adam Hochschild. *The Unquiet Ghost: Russians Remember Stalin*. New York: Viking, 1994.

James Holman, *Travels Through Russia, Siberia, Poland, Austria, Saxony, Prussia, Hanover etc. Undertaken during the Years 1822, 1823, and 1824, while Suffering from Total Blindness*. London: Whittaker, 1825.

Frederick George Jackson. *A Thousand Days in the Arctic*. New York & London: Harper & Brothers Publishers, 1899.

Henry Johnson, *The Life and Voyages of Joseph Wiggins, F.R.G.S.: Modern Discoverer of the Kara Sea Route to Siberia Based on his Journals and Letters*. Richmond, UK: Curzon, 2000.

George Kennan, *Siberia and the Exile System*. New York: Century Co., 1891.

Vladimir Korolenko, *Rasskazy 1903-1915: Publitsistika. Stati. Vospominaniya o pisatelyakh*. Leningradsky Otdel, Chudozhestvennaya Literatura. Leningrad: 1990.

Vladimir Korolenko, *Sokolinets*. In *Sibirskie Rasskazy i Ocherki*. Moscow: Khudozhestvennaya Literatura, 1980. (Retrieved September 29, 2009 from http://lib.sarbc.ru).

Constantin Krypton, *The Northern Sea Route. Its place in Russian economic history before 1917*. New York: Research Program on the U.S.S.R, 1953.

Henry Lansdell. *Through Siberia*. London: Low, 1882

John Ledyard, *John Ledyard's Journal* (James Kenneth Munford, ed., & Georg Barr Carson, consulting ed.). 1963 Oregon State Monographs, Studies in History. Corvallis, OR: Oregon State University Press, 1963.

Mrs John Clarence Lee, *Across Siberia alone: An American Woman's Adventures*. New York & London: J. Lane, 1914. Retrieved January 7, 2008 from www.archive.org.

Theodore Craig Levin (with Valentina Süzükei), *Where Rivers and Mountains Sing: Sound, Music, and Nomadism in Tuva and Beyond*. Bloomington: Indiana University Press, 2006.

Theodore C. Levin & Michael E. Edgerton, *The Throat Singers of Tuva*. Scientific American, September, 1999. Retrieved September 29, 2009 from www.sciam.com.

Bruce W. Lincoln. *The Conquest of a Continent: Siberia and the Russians*. New York: Random House, 1994.

Dmitry Mamin-Sibiryak. Privalovskie Milliony. Publisher: Pravda, Moscow. 1981. (Retrieved 29 September 2009 from http://az.lib.ru.).

Otto Mänchen-Helfen, *Reise ins Asiatische Tuwa*. Berlin: Verlag der Bücherkreis, 1931.

Robert K. Massie. *The Romanovs. The Final Chapter*. New York: Random House, 1995.

Victor L. Mote, *Siberia: Worlds Apart*. Boulder, CO: Westview Press, 1998.

Gerhard Friedrich Müller, *Nachrichten von Seereisen, und zur See gemachten Entdeckungen, die von Rußland aus längst den Küsten des Eißmeeres und auf dem Ostlichen Weltmeere gegen Japon und Amerika geschehen sind*. Sammlung Russischer Geschichte. Band 3. St. Petersburg: Kayserliche Akademie der Wissenschaften, 1758.

G. F. Müller & P. S. Pallas, *Conquest of Siberia and the History of Transactions, Wars, Commerce Carried on Between Russia and China from the Earliest Period*. Cornhill: Smith, Elder, & Co., 1842.

Fridtjof Nansen, *Through Siberia: The Land of the Future*, translated by Arthur G. Chater. New York: F. A. Stokes, 1914.

Fridtjof Nansen. *Farthest north; being the record of a voyage of exploration of the ship "Fram" 1893-96 and of a fifteen months' sleigh journey by Dr. Nansen and Lieut. Johansen*. New York: Harper & Brothers, 1897.

Nils Adolf Erik Nordenskjold, *The Voyage of the Vega round Asia and Europe: With a Historical Review of Previous Journeys along the North Coast of the Old World*. London: Macmillan & Co., 1881.

Helen Peel, *Polar Gleams: An Account of a Voyage on the Yacht 'Blencathra'*. London: Edward Arnold, 1894.

Alexander Radishchev, Puteshestvie iz Peterburga v Moskvy. Retrieved 12 January 2009 from http://az.lib.ru.

Valentin Rasputin, *Sibir, Sibir...: Ocherki, Publitsistika*. Sobranie Sochineny v Tryokh Tomakh. Moscow: Molodaya Gvardiya, 1994.

Christopher Read, *Lenin: A Revolutionary Life*. New York: Routledge Chapman & Hall, 2005.

Anna Reid, *The Shaman's Coat: A Native History of Siberia*. London: Weidenfeld & Nicolson, 2002.

John F. Richards, *The Unending Frontier: An Environmental History of the Early Modern World*. Berkeley, CA: University of California Press, 2003.

Nicholas Roerich. *Fiery Stronghold*. Boston, MA: The Stratford Company, 1933.

Ralf Roth & Marie-Noëlle Polino (eds.), *The City and the Railway in Europe*. Aldershot, UK: Ashgate Publishing, 2003.

Royal Society (Great Britain), Charles Hutton, George Shaw, Richard Pearson, *The Philosophical Transactions of the Royal Society of London*. Notices: Vol. 15, 1781-1785. London: C. & R. Baldwin, 1809.

Gawrila Sarytschew, *Account of a Voyage of Discovery to the North-East of Siberia, the Frozen Ocean, and the North-East Sea*. London: Richard Phillips, 1806.

Martin Sauer & Joseph Billings, *An Account of a Geographical and Astronomical Expedition to the Northern Parts of Russia*. London: Cadell and Davies, 1802.

Ina Schröder, 'Keeping our Traditions through the Centuries': Indigenous Ways to Cultural Revival in Khanty Mansi Autonomous District, Western Siberia. Master's Thesis, Social Sciences Faculty, Georg August University, Göttingen, Germany, 2008.

Michael Myers Shoemaker, *The Great Siberian Railway from St. Petersburg to Pekin*.
New York & London: G. P. Putnam's Sons, 1903.

Wendy Slater. *The Many Deaths of Tsar Nicholas II: Relics, Remains and the Romanovs* (Routledge Studies in the History of Russia and Eastern Europe). London: Routledge, 2007.

Yuri Slezkine, *Arctic Mirrors. Russia and the small Peoples of the North*. Ithaca and London: Cornell University Press, 1994.

Vladimir Sollogub, *The Tarantas: Travelling Impressions of Young Russia*. London: Chapman and Hall, 1850.

Jonathan D. Smele, *Civil War in Siberia: The Anti-Bolshevik Government of Admiral Kolchak, 1918-1920*. Cambridge, UK: Cambridge University Press, 1996.

Aleksandar Solzenycin. Arhipelag Gulag: 1918-1956: opit hudozhestvennogo issledovania. Paris : YMCA-press, 1973. Retrieved 29 September 2009 from http://lib.ru/PROZA/SOLZHENICYN.

Georg Wilhelm Steller, Journal of a Voyage with Bering 1741-1742 (Edited with an introduction by O. W. Frost), translated by Margritt A. Engel & O. W. Frost. Stanford: Stanford University Press, 1988.

Eva-Maria Stolberg, Sibirien – Russlands "Wilder Osten": Mythos und soziale Realität im 19. und 20. Jahrhundert. Revised version of a post-doctoral thesis from the Philosophy Faculty of the Rhine Friedrich Wilhelm University in Bonn, 2006. Retrieved 29 September 2009 from http://hss.ulb.uni-bonn.de/diss_online/phil_fak/2006/stolberg_eva-maria/0796.pdf.

Marcus Lorenzo Taft, *Strange Siberia: Along the Trans-Siberian Railway*. New York: Eaton & Mains, 1911.

George Gustav Telberg & Robert Wilton, *The Last Days of the Romanovs*. New York: George H. Doran Company, 1920.

Colin Thubron, *In Siberia*. London: Penguin Books, 2000.

Jules Verne, *Michael Strogoff: or, The Courier of the Czar*. Retrieved: Gutenberg Project.

Stephen D. Watrous (ed.), John Ledyard's Journey Through Russia and Siberia 1787-1788. The Journal and Selected Letters. Madison: University of Wisconsin Press, 1966.

James Wilson, *Biography of the Blind: Or the Lives of Such as Have Distinguished Themselves as Poets, Philosophers, Artists*. Birmingham, UK: Showell, 1838.

Harry De Windt, *The New Siberia: Being an Account of a Visit to the Penal Island of Sakhalin, and Political Prison and Mines of the Trans-Baikal District, Eastern Siberia*. London: Chapman & Hall, 1896.

ONLINE RESOURCES

In addition to these books and articles, the following selected websites were helpful in one way or another:

Baikal Wave: www.baikalwave.eu.org.

Baikal World: www.bww.irk.ru. (Excellent general resource on Lake Baikal and culture.)

Dikorossy. *Imperator Listvyanskoy Galerey*: www.dikoross.ru.

Friends of Tuva: www.fotuva.org.

German Archaeological Institute: www.dainst.org/index_596_en.html. (Very informative description of the the archaeological digs at the Arzhan sites in Tuva.)

Gulag Memorial: http://gulag.memorial.de. (Very good database on the gulags.)

Irkutsk, Ocherk ob Irkutske: www.manus.baikal.ru. Information about Irkutsk. (Used as source for quote from N. Shelgunov in Chapter 11.)

Magadan Regional Administration. Department of Culture: www.culture.goldkolyma.ru. (Excellent source of information about the Kolyma region.)

Magic Baikal: www.magicbaikal.com.

Max Planck Institute for Social Anthropology, Siberian Studies Centre: www.eth.mpg.de/people/halemba/project.html (Personal page of social anthropologist Agnieszka E. Halemba).

Ministry of Foreign Affairs of the Russian Federation, *Passport of Krasnoyarsk Krai*: www.ln.mid.ru.

Nomer Odin. *Filosof iz Bolshoy Rechki*: http://pressa.irk.ru. (Article on sculptor Yuri Panov.)

Novaya Gazeta. *Fontan "Nevolnik Cheski": Pushkin Chitaet Natale Goncharovoy Stikhi, Posvyashchennye Anne Kerne*: www.novayagazeta.ru.

Pribaikalsky Central Regional Library. *The Rebellious Daughter of the Baikal*: http://az-kozin.narod.ru/terra-eng.html.

Romanov-Memorial: www.romanov-memorial.com. (Useful resource on the Romanov family.)

Taki's Magazine. *Solzhenitsyn in America* by Jeffry Hart. Retrieved September 29, 2009 from www.takimag.com/site/article/solzhenitsyn_in_america.

The New York Times. *Big Cities Favour a Republic*, New York Times, March 27, 1917; *Her Point of View*, New York Times, August 12, 1894; *Travels in Asia. Siberia and the East as Two Women See Them*, New York Times, July 19, 1914. See www.nytimes.com.

The White Crematorium: www.gulag.eu/default.htm (information on Kolyma).

Time. *The Battle over the Tomb*: www.time.com (information on Lenin in exile).

Tourist Resources in the Tyumen Region: www.w-siberia.com. Official Tyumen Region website.

Tuva Kyzy: http://tyvakyzy.com.

Tuvaonline. *HHT Have Finally Arrived in Germany for Two Ground-Breaking Concerts* (an interview with the Tuvan performers Huun Huur Tu), and *Keeper of the Reindeer of the Great Taiga*: http://en.tuvaonline.ru.

Way to Siberia, a website from the Tyumen Research Centre of Siberian branch of Russian Academy of Science: www.ikz.ru

Index of Literary & Historical Names

Yakovlev, Vasily 44
Yavlensky Alexei 114
Yediger (Khan) 16
Yeltsin, Boris 35, 36, 46
Yermak (Timofeyevich) 14-20, 29, 49,
    54-5, 64, 86, 90, 94, 115, 118, 202,
    213, 236
Yershov, Pyotr 86, 87

Zhukovsky, Vasily 66
Zimov, Sergey 165
Zinich, Konstantin 210

❧

Index of Places & Landmarks